MW01241221

JOB #:

Author Name:

Title of Book:

ISBN: 0791469248

Publisher:

Trim Size: 6 x 9

Bulk in mm: 14

IMPERIALISM
AND
HUMAN RIGHTS

SUNY series in Human Rights

Zehra F. Kabasakal Arat, editor

IMPERIALISM
AND
HUMAN RIGHTS

Colonial Discourses of Rights and Liberties in African History

Bonny Ibhawoh

State University of New York Press

Published by
State University of New York

© 2007 State University of New York Press, Albany

For information, contact State University of New York Press, Albany, NY
www.sunypress.edu

Production by Ryan Hacker
Marketing by Anne M. Valentine

Library of Congress Cataloging-in-Publication Data

Ibhawoh, Bonny.
   Imperialism and human rights : colonial discourses of rights and liberties in
African history / Bonny Ibhawoh.
       p. cm.—(SUNY series in Human Rights)
   Includes bibliographical references and index.
   978-0-7914-6923-1 (hardcover : alk. paper)
   978-0-7914-6924-8 (paperback : alk. paper)
   1. Human rights—Africa, Sub–Saharan—History—19th century.
   2. Human rights—Africa, Sub–Saharan—History—20th century.
   3. Colonies—Africa, Sub-Saharan—Law and legislation.
I. Title. II. Series.

KQC572. I24 2007
323. 096—dc22
                                                 2005037168

10 9 8 7 6 5 4 3 2 1

For
Omoaruni

Contents

Illustrations

Foreword

The interdisciplinary field of human rights is rather new but rapidly expanding. The SUNY series in Human Rights attempts to advance scholarship on the political and social processes of human rights and disseminate research findings to a large audience in an accessible style. It intends to address vital issues related to the full spectrum of human rights recognized by the International Bill of Rights, as well as different conceptualizations that expand or contract the scope of human rights. Including volumes that examine cultural, economic, political, and international factors that contribute to the violation or improvement of human rights or analyze the consequences of human rights violations, the series aspires to promote human rights, offer policy guidelines that would help improve human rights practices, and contribute to the theory-building efforts in social sciences.

Bonny Ibhawoh's *Imperialism and Human Rights* is the first book in the series. As such it holds privileged position, and by presenting interesting data and analysis in an engaging style, it lives up to the expectations above and sets a high standard for the other books to follow. This historical analysis, which focuses on the human rights discourse in the Niger delta area under the British colonial rule, seems to be examining largely what happened before the establishment of the global human rights regime under the leadership of the United Nations. However, by introducing the complexities surrounding the use of human rights language by different groups—by the colonists to legitimize their presence and empire, by the religious humanists to advance their "civilizing" mission, and by the colonized to negotiate with the dominant groups and seek liberation—the volume alerts us to the fact that a rights-oriented discourse is not always emancipatory or empowering, yet once introduced, the meaning of the terms or their applications can be altered and subverted to support different causes. The dualism in British law and justice, as revealed by the different levels of respect for human rights in the motherland and those of the colonial subjects, established a foundation to claim for the universal application of rights. Although the colonized people and their leaders could not participate in drafting the international human rights documents, it is also noted that the Atlantic Charter, and to a lesser extent the Universal Declaration of Human Rights, resonated with the African nationalist elites who welcomed and invoked the principles and content of these documents in their struggles. Nevertheless, they too fell short of applying human rights universally. The independence constitution of Nigeria, for example, was adopted without granting equality to minorities and women.

This discourse analysis speaks to the power of rhetoric and the legitimizing function of the concept of human rights, but it also shows that the advancement of human rights is also about power. Ibhawoh is too sophisticated to appeal to the cliché that history repeats itself, but what he notes about the Nigerian colonial experience also applies to a story that has been unfolding in other parts of the world, including the Middle East today, with significant ramifications for the future.

Zehra F. Kabasakal Arat

Acknowledgments

"Those who can, do; those who can't, teach." So goes the famous saying. Yet, human rights scholarship is one of those rare fields where even those who teach can also attempt some doing. For me, this has been one of the attractions of human rights work and scholarship—the nexus between academics and activists that provides unique opportunities to connect theory and practice. Although this book explores a subject that many activists would find more academic than practical, it has benefited immensely from my frequent shuttles between the relatively secure world of academia and the "trenches" of human rights work. Along the way, I have incurred many debts among friends and colleagues of both the town and gown. My association with a number of institutions over the past few years provided me with opportunities for research and scholarly interaction that have been crucial to this project. I am grateful to the Centre for African Studies of the School of Oriental and African Studies, University of London; the Danish Institute for Human Rights (DIHR), Copenhagen; the Carnegie Council for Ethics and International Affairs, New York; and the Constitutional Rights Project for a series of collaborative work that provided opportunities for research into the more recent history of human rights in Africa.

I am indebted to many individuals and institutions that made possible my research in Canada, the United Kingdom and Nigeria. I owe a special debt to the staff of the Public Record Office, London; DIHR library; University of Ibadan library; and the Nigerian National Archives Ibadan, particularly the archivist Mike Elumadu. I must thank Jane Parpart and Philip

Zachernuck, who supervised the dissertation that provided the foundations for this project, and Omoniyi Adewoye, former Vice Chancellor of the University of Ibadan, who ignited my interest in this subject. I am also grateful to Loris Gasparotto for drawing the maps in this volume and to colleagues who have offered suggestions along the way—Tunde Odutan, Harvey Amani Whitfied, Mark Gibney, John Sainsbury, and the graduate students in my "Human Rights and Social Justice" class at Brock University.

Funding for this project came for varied sources. I am grateful to the Izaak Walton Killam Trust and Dalhousie University for a generous fellowship that provided much of the funding for the early stages of this project; the Carnegie Council for Ethics and International Affairs for a research grant and Brock University and McMasters University for institutional support.

Finally, I am grateful to my parents and my family, Omo and our boys, Ehiane, Osezua and Aivona, who endured my many absences away for research. I can only hope that this work is a fitting tribute to their love and support.

Abbreviations

Abe. Dist.	Abeokuta District Files
Abe. Prof.	Abeokuta Province Files
AG	Action Group
ANLR	All Nigeria Law Report
AS-APS	Antislavery Society and Aborigines Protection Society
Ben. Prof.	Benin Province Files
CMS	Church Missionary Society
CO	Colonial Office
Com. Col.	Commissioner for Colony Files
CSC	Council of Swaziland Churches
CSO	Colonial Secretary's Office
EUG	Egba United Government
Ijebu Prof.	Ijebu Province Files
NAI	(Nigerian) National Archives Ibadan
NCBWA	National Congress for British West Africa

NCNC	National Council for Nigeria and the Camerons
	(Later the National Council for Nigerian Citizen)
NEPU	Northern Elements Progressive Union
NNDP	Nigerian National Democratic Party
NLR	*Nigeria Law Report*
NPC	Northern People's Congress
NYM	Nigerian Youth Movement
Oyo Prof.	Oyo Province Files
PRO	Public Record Office, London
SBC	Southern Baptist Convention
SMA	Société des Missions Africaines
UDHR	Universal Declaration of Human Rights
UP	United Presbyterian Church of Scotland
War. Prof.	Warri Province Files
WMMS	Wesley Methodist Missionary Society

1

The Subject of Rights and the Rights of Subjects

The Subject of Rights

The end of the Second World War marked the dawn of a new age of rights. Since the adoption of the United Nations' Universal Declaration of Human Rights (UDHR) soon after the war in 1948, the subject of rights has become a theme of great popular and academic interest. Rights have become the dominant language for public good around the globe[1] as well as the language of choice for making and contesting entitlement claims. The language of rights has attained such importance that today it underlies almost every facet of public and private discourse, from claims within the family unit to national and global political debates. Indeed, the past five decades have spawned a global "rights revolution"—a revolution of norms and values that has redefined our understanding of ethics and justice.[2]

Academic interest in the rights discourse has centered for the most part on contemporary understanding of "human rights" in a way that tends to obscure how the language of rights has historically been deployed to further more complex and contradictory agendas. Within African studies, scholars have explored various aspects of "human rights," "civil rights," and "constitutional rights" mainly within the context of post-UDHR developments. However, the tradition of rights discourses in the continent goes much further back. In many parts of Africa, rights discourses underlined several aspects of local history—the workings of traditional social and political systems, European missionary incursion and activities, the antislavery movement, colonial conquest and control, the colonial legal system, contestations over land, press activism, and, most significantly, the nationalist movement. These aspects of the rights discourse, which predate more recent concerns with "universal human rights," have received very little attention. Yet, many would agree that a thorough historical treatment of these pre-UDHR themes is crucial to our understanding of contemporary human rights. Therefore, the primary object of this book is to produce a historically grounded study of rights discourses in an African society in a way that engages, and yet goes beyond, contemporary fixations with universal human rights. This work focuses on late colonial and immediate post-colonial Western Nigeria. This part of Africa provides a window through which I seek to explore discourses of rights in colonial African history. Much of the discussion here bears relevance to other parts of Africa, particularly British colonial Africa.

More specifically, this book aims to draw attention to the historical complexities and nuances underlying rights discourses in colonial Africa. This task is significant because contemporary human rights discourse has, for the most part, produced a rather triumphant vision of the role of rights talk in securing progressive and transformative social change. Philosopher Ronald Dworkin famously argued that rights are "trumps" against the tyranny of the majority.[3] To exercise one's rights has come to be taken as something inherently good, an index of social and political progress. What has not been sufficiently explored or emphasized in the discussion is the way in which rights talk has been deployed to further more complex and sometimes contradictory agendas—progressive and reactionary. I argue the need to move away from the linear progressivism that underlines contemporary human rights scholarship. In the African context that I examine, the rights discourse is not a simple monolithic, progressive narrative. The language of rights has been variously deployed for purposes of legitimization, opposition, and even negotiation. Rights discourses have served to insulate and legitimize power just as much they have facilitated transformative processes.

Against this background, this work seeks to explore, from a distinctly historical perspective, the complexities, changes, and continuities that have attended notions and discussions about rights and civil liberties in Nigeria from the introduction of colonial rule at the end of the nineteenth century through the early postcolonial period. It draws attention to the multi-layered discourses about rights and liberties employed by both the colonial state and its African subjects. It focuses on the complex dynamics engendered by the intersection between existing African notions of rights and the more formal regimes of rights introduced within European Christian humanism, colonial customary law, and the imported English common law systems. It seeks to examine how diverse interest groups within this African society—including colonial officials, missionaries, African elites, women's groups, and later, nationalist activists—employed the language of rights and liberty to serve varied social and political ends. Part of the objective is to connect the significance of the evolution of the rights discourse within colonial African contexts to the quest for a viable human rights regime in the continent. This object is addressed in two ways: first, examining longer-standing debates about rights to put the current human rights discourse in historical context, and second, exploring the existence of traditions of rights discourse in African societies that were different from the post-Second World War tradition that is often emphasized in contemporary human rights scholarship.

One obvious reason for undertaking a study of rights and liberties is the renewed significance that these ideas have come to assume in our world. There is the belief, though anecdotal, that a better understanding of rights traditions can ultimately improve the protection of human rights. This is particularly pertinent in Africa where there have been repeated calls for African states to develop regimes of human rights that are rooted in their own societies and relevant to the present challenges of nation building. The hope here is that by focusing on the changes and continuities that attended discourses of rights and liberties in specific African societies, we can gain new insights into African perceptions of themselves and others, as well as the social transformations engendered by their encounters with others. Discourses about rights provide unique perspectives into such historical encounters and experiences. The way in which individuals and communities defined and articulated their rights reveals a lot about their definition of themselves, their relationships with each other, and their understanding of outsiders.[4]

Discussions about rights occur in almost every facet of human life. Individuals and groups are constantly asserting what they consider to be their rights in the constructions of personhood and possession, and in daily dealings with each other. Individual and collective rights are continuously invoked, both verbally and textually, in discussions about issues as diverse as social status, political authority, and the use of private and public resources. Much of these are issues of "civil liberties," broadly understood as the freedom to think or act without being constrained by force. Others pertain to customary notions of legal and moral entitlements. Given the sheer ubiquity and diversity of the appeal to rights and liberties in daily encounters and in varied settings, any study of these themes is confronted by real problems of scope and context. What aspects of the many discussions about rights and liberties are being examined here? In what discursive contexts are the appeals to rights and liberties being examined? To address these questions, it is necessary to set out the discursive contexts in which this work is located and some of the methodological parameters that guide it.

This study is located within two intellectual traditions and discursive contexts. While one is long-standing and universal, the other is emergent and peculiar to African studies. The first context is the familiar debate about the historical development of universal human rights that has dominated contemporary human rights scholarship. In the past few decades, many scholars of area/regional studies, including Africanists, have become fully engaged in the thriving interdisciplinary discussion about the philosophical and historical antecedents of the contemporary notion of universal human rights. The central concern here can be posed in the form of simple questions:

What is the origin of human rights? Are human rights Western concepts, or are they truly universal? If they are universal, what normative contribution has Africa made (or can Africa make) to the development of the "universal human rights" movement? The engagement of Africanist scholars in these and other aspects of the human rights discourse have spawned a whole new genre of scholarship—an Africanist human rights discourse that I have described elsewhere as convoluted and largely critical of the orthodoxies of human rights scholarship. This discourse provides one framework for this study.[5]

The second discursive context for this study emerges from more recent developments in African studies. Several writers have emphasized the centrality of colonialism to the emergence of the contemporary human rights movement. It has been suggested that international human rights have an inherently colonial dimension since they involve challenges to the practice, and sometimes even sovereignty, of particular regions in the name of universal standards deriving from and largely enforced by the West. In the case of Africa, such asymmetrical moral discourse has its roots in the literal history of colonialism. The questions that need to be pursued, therefore, should involve the double relationship of human rights issues to, on one hand, colonized African societies and their own sense of the "human," and on the other, European colonizers whose agenda included more than the concern for the rights of subjected "Others" in Africa and elsewhere.[6] But there is an even stronger link between European colonialism and human rights. Although not often recognized as such, anticolonial struggles in Africa as elsewhere in the colonized world were not only nationalist movements but also veritable human rights movements. Therefore reconstructing the histories of nationalist and anticolonial movements as rights histories can help us better understand the trajectories of contemporary human rights movements in postcolonial societies.

This work brings a historical approach to human rights scholarship—a subject dominated by social scientists and legal scholars. But it is a historical work that seeks to engage rather than overlook the necessarily interdisciplinary nature of human rights scholarship. Yet, conceptual and methodological differences are bound to arise. For instance, some human rights scholars may argue that the discourse on legal rights in colonial Africa (or other colonial contexts) is not really a discourse about human rights but rather a discourse about moral and legal rights. Others may argue that it is not even possible to talk of "human rights" before the introduction of the Universal Declaration of Human Rights (UDHR) in 1948 and that such use would be anachronistic. I disagree. While I acknowledge the clear difference between customary legal/moral rights (such as generational or gendered rights) and the UDHR-inspired definition of human rights (rights that pertain to individuals simply by virtue of their humanity), the main thrust of this book is that in the colonial African context I examine, these two were inextricably connected. This study proceeds from the premise that the tendency within human rights scholarship to wall off each sphere of rights discourse from the other stands in the way of a full understanding of the subject. I find it more useful to think in terms of a concatenation of rights discourses rather than a compartmentalization of rights discourses.

Although this book focuses primarily on discourses of rights and liberties in Africa, it seeks to address broader concepts about imperialism and human rights. One of these is the development of the human rights movement and its humanist antecedents within the context of nineteenth-century European imperialism. This book is intended as a contribution toward understanding the place of European imperialism and the initiatives and responses of colonized peoples in shaping the history of the human rights movement. Although imperialism features prominently in contemporary debates about the theory and practice of human rights, it has received little detailed attention within traditional human rights scholarship. For instance, proponents of cultural pluralism have repeatedly criticized the human rights movement for being too Western-oriented and for being reminiscent of a tradition of Western imperialism and paternalism. One scholar has argued that the human rights movement falls into the historical continuum of the Eurocentric missionary-colonial project that seeks to "supplant all other traditions and casts actors into superior and subordinate positions."[7] But, in spite of such references to the history of colonialism, very little attention has been given to actually exploring the historical links between imperialism and the human rights movement at both national and international levels. This book explores some of these links. It seeks not simply to examine how the exigencies of colonial rule circumscribed rights and liberties but also to investigate how the rhetoric of rights was deployed by colonizers to legitimize empire and by the colonized to oppose it and negotiate their positions within empire.

A related object of this work is to provide a study of human rights based on empirical research of specific social and historical contexts rather than on generalized postulations. In the past two decades, human rights scholarship has produced many engaging theories and conceptual frameworks for understanding, interpreting, and promoting human rights. There have also been several insightful studies of human rights within the context of the UDHR and the post-war human rights movement. This reflects the predominantly presentist approach to human rights scholarship—a preoccupation with the here and now. What has clearly been lacking are thorough and specific historical studies of human rights that go beyond these contemporary contexts. Yet, as many scholars have acknowledged, such detailed contextual and empirical studies, rather than more generalized theoretical postulations, should be the current direction of human rights scholarship. We now need sustained empirical studies that buttress, challenge, or explicate theories of human rights. This is one of the aspirations of this project.

The Rights of Subjects

The sustained interaction between Africans and Europeans in the nineteenth century following the end of the Atlantic slave trade ushered a distinctly new phase in the notions and discussions about rights and liberties in Africa. Nineteenth-century missionary activities and the anti-slavery movement were underlined by discourses about rights within the framework of European liberal traditions and Christian humanism. Discussions about rights were also central to the institution and promotion of British colonial hegemony. Colonial social and political objectives were couched in the language of rights, freedom, and liberty. British incursion was often justified on the grounds of liberating Africans from despotic chiefs and protecting their rights as British subjects. In this regard, the language of rights, like that of "civilization" and "modernity" was an important part of the discourses deployed to legitimize empire. However, the language of rights was not only a tool for legitimizing the colonial status quo; it was also an instrument of opposition, engagement, and negotiation. Africans appropriated colonial rhetoric of rights and deployed it to challenge imperial policies and negotiate their positions within a changing society. The rhetoric of "native rights" and, later, "universal rights" that underlined colonial propaganda became an important instrument with which Africans expressed dissent and articulated nationalist aspirations. One of the central arguments of this book is that in the African context I examine, later post-war discourses of "universal human rights" were greatly influenced by earlier colonial traditions of rights talk.

In many ways, the human rights discourse only marked a new chapter in an evolving tradition of rights talk with several underlying contradictions and paradoxes. The paradox of colonial rights discourse in Africa manifests at two levels. The primary paradox is that rights talk, which was a crucial factor in the rise of empire, was also a factor in its eventual collapse. But the rights discourse was not only relevant in the tension between colonizers and colonized. African elites also used rights talk to further class, ethnic, generational, and gender interests. Indeed, human rights, or at least the discourses of rights, were "trumps." But they were not always trumps against the tyranny of the majority. They were also trumps deployed to further the dominance of the majority and maintain existing power structures. This is the secondary and more complex paradox of rights talk. Rights discourses facilitated domination at one moment, had a liberating effect at another, and, in between, were used to promote competing agendas. By examining these longstanding traditions of rights talk and the complexities that underlie them, this study seeks to put the contemporary human rights discourse in Africa in some historical context.

This book focuses mainly on discussions about rights and civil liberties rather than the objective conditions of rights and liberties in the study area. It focuses more on how people understood and used the language of rights and liberty in their oral and written discussions than on the actual conditions they encountered in their daily lives. However, I recognize that it is difficult, if not impossible, to examine discourses of rights without drawing links between what people talked and wrote about, on one hand, and the conditions they actually encountered, on the other. Thus, although the primary concern of the study is discourses about rights and civil liberties, it also seeks to examine how these discourses reflected or failed to reflect actual conditions. The approach to discourse here is along the lines of colonial and postcolonial discourse analysis.[8] Its usage goes beyond simple oral and written communication. "Discourse" here is speech or writing seen from the point of view of the beliefs and values that they embody. It constitutes the organization and representation of people's experiences and understanding of their world. Speech and writing are not taken at their face value but analyzed on the basis of the practices and rules that produced these texts and the methodical organization of thought underlying these texts.[9]

This work is based primarily on archival research and oral interviews. Although some of the data for this study comes from courts records, I am not primarily concerned with discussions about rights in strict legal contexts and usage. My focus goes beyond legal rights, although I do not preclude them. Discussions about rights in colonial Africa did not always take place in the law courts. Few people had access to the colonial legal system or even understood how it worked. Rather, most rights claims were made in petitions to colonial officials and local chiefs, in newspaper editorials and letters to editors, and at meetings of town unions, trade unions, and political groups. To retrieve the often-ignored voices of ordinary people and subaltern groups in the society, I have placed particular emphasis on petitions available in the colonial archives. Many of these petitions written by ordinary people in earnest, if sometimes Pidgin English, together with the responses they elicited from colonial officials, provide unique insights into the issues of rights that dominated this period.

Between Customary Rights and Human Rights

A central question in any discussion about rights is defining what rights are and situating that definition within a specific historical context. While many scholars trace the philosophical foundations of human rights to natural law and Western liberal traditions, others argue for a more eclectic understanding of the term, focusing on differing notions of rights within both Western and non-Western societies. Even more contentious is the debate over the meaning of "human rights" and the appropriateness of employing the concept within the context of the history of colonial societies. Some writers have argued for a precise and historically specific definition of human rights that is distinct from general notions of rights that may include customary moral/legal notions of rights. Such advocates of conceptual specificity contend that the notion of human rights is a relatively recent idea founded on post-Second World War developments and, specifically, the adoption of the Universal Declaration of Human Rights (UDHR) by the United Nations in 1948. In contrast, others argue for a more fluid and flexible definition of human rights that focuses not so much on the restricted context of postwar usage as on the continuing ideas that have historically been central to the concept of human rights and social justice in various societies. These differing conceptions are central to defining human rights.

The discourse on the origins and philosophical foundations of rights has focused mainly on natural law theory. Many writers have traced contemporary conceptions of rights and liberties from natural law and ancient Greek stoicism through the medieval period and the Enlightenment. Natural law philosophy as characterized by a belief that laws and rules of conduct are embedded and derivable from the nature of man is fundamental to the inalienable character of human rights. Since the nature of man is the same the world over, the laws derived from that nature are seen as universal and true to all men (and women), at all times and places—they are objective and eternal and are neither changeable nor alterable.[10] Some suggest this philosophy underlies the concept of rights as expressed in the sociopolitical and philosophical developments in fifteenth- and sixteenth-century Europe. The Renaissance and the decline of feudalism inaugurated a long period of transition to the liberal notions of freedom and equality, particularly in the use and ownership of property. This created an unprecedented commitment to individual expression and world experience that was subsequently reflected in diverse writings—from the teachings of Thomas Aquinas and Hugo Grotius to the Magna Carta, the Petition of Rights of 1628, and the English Bill of Rights of 1689.[11]

The European philosophers of the seventeenth and eighteenth centuries developed their theories of rights and liberties within a tradition of natural rights underscored by the notion that every human being is endowed with certain natural rights essential and fundamental to his rational existence. For these philosophers, natural law traditions and the idea of natural rights translated into political liberalism that was based on the theory of individualism and the notion of the equality of all men before the law. In the writings of Hobbes, Locke, and Rousseau, the autonomous individual in pursuit of his survival and happiness enters into a social contract to escape from his "brutish nature" to establish order (Hobbes), to install a limited government (Locke), or to constitute the general will without divesting himself of his natural rights (Rousseau).[12]

These writings reflected a new intellectual and political tradition in which the individual as a political actor was abstracted from the holistic totality of medieval society. Locke argued that certain rights self-evidently pertained to individuals as human beings and that chief among them were the rights to life, liberty (freedom from arbitrary rule), and property. Upon entering civil society, humankind surrendered to the state, in a "social contract," the right to enforce these natural rights. The state's failure to safeguard the interests of its members gives rise to a right to responsible, popular revolution.[13] Hobbes saw a "right of nature" as the liberty each man has to use his own power, as he will himself, for the preservation of his own life.[14] He defined liberty as "the absence of external impediments to motion," and having rights meant having no impediments on the individual's "natural motions."[15] These ideas of the rights of man played a key role in the late eighteenth- and nineteenth-century struggles against political absolutism in Europe. They also deeply influenced the Western world from the seventeenth to nineteenth centuries, provoking a wave of revolutionary agitation that swept across America and Europe. They inspired documents such as the English Petition of Rights, the United States Declaration of Independence, and the French Declaration of the Rights of Man and Citizen. All three documents were based on the image of the autonomous man endowed with certain inalienable rights.[16]

The defining character of contemporary notions of human rights has also been significantly shaped by the reformist impulse of the late nineteenth century. The abolition of the slave trade; the development of factory legislation; and the beginnings of mass education, trade unionism, and universal suffrage all served to broaden the dimensions of individual rights and stimulate an increasing international interest in their protection. However, perhaps the rise and fall of Nazi Germany had the most profound impact on the idea of universal human rights in the twentieth century. The world united in horror and condemnation of the state-authorized extermination of Jews and other minorities, the promulgation of laws permitting arbitrary police search and seizure, and the legalization of imprisonment, torture, and execution without public trials. Nazi atrocities, more than any previous event, brought home the realization that law and morality cannot be grounded in any purely utilitarian, idealist, or positivist doctrines.[17] Certain actions are wrong, no matter the social or political context, and certain rights are inalienable no matter the social or political exigencies. The atrocities also led to a growing acknowledgment that all human beings are entitled to a basic level of rights and that states and societies have a duty to protect and promote these rights. Postwar decolonization movements in Africa and elsewhere in the colonized world also had a significant impact on the development of the idea of universal human rights as colonized people drew on the language of rights emerging in the West in their ideological struggles against imperial powers and their demands for national self-government. This process of appropriating and deploying the language of universal rights to serve varied ends, by both Africans and Europeans in colonial Western Nigeria, is one of the primary concerns of this study.

The new postwar international consciousness of the need to protect the basic rights of all peoples by means of some universally acceptable parameters partly influenced the 1945 Charter of the United Nations, which reaffirmed a "faith in fundamental human rights, in the dignity and worth of the human person, in the equal rights of men and women and of nations large or small." It also stated the United Nations' commitment to fostering the development of friendly relations among nations, based on respect for the principle of equal rights and self-determination for all peoples and the promotion of human rights and fundamental freedoms for all without distinction as to race, sex, language or religion.[18] The commitment to the promotion of human rights expressed in the United Nations charter were followed by the UDHR in 1948 and international human rights conventions that have come to be collectively known as the International Bill of Rights.[19] These conventions, which were subsequently complemented at regional levels in Europe, the Americas, and Africa, today constitute the core indicators of contemporary international human rights standards.[20]

In spite of disagreements over the precise origins of the idea of human rights, what is evident is that the contemporary meaning of human rights has evolved over the years. The naturalist philosophies of the sixteenth century, the bourgeois revolutions of the seventeenth and eighteenth centuries, the socialist and Marxist revolutions of the twentieth century and the anticolonialist revolutions that began after the Second World War have all combined to broadly define the modern concept of human rights. Like all normative traditions, the rights tradition reflects the process of historical continuity and change that is the product of varied cumulative human experiences. The contemporary idea of human rights also stems from a universalization of rights defined through a political process by international agreements. Indeed, most contemporary studies on rights refer specifically to "human rights" and define them as those embodied in the UDHR and its subsequent conventions. However, the approach in this work goes beyond the restricted definition of human rights in the UDHR. The definition of rights here necessarily embraces broad ideas about rights and liberties that predated and shaped the UDHR.

Human Rights: Issues of Change and Continuity

This book focuses broadly on discussions around rights as popular entitlements that individuals and communities hold in relation to the rest of society, rather than on the contemporary concept of "human rights" per se. However, like most studies in "human rights," it confronts some of the methodological questions that have been raised about fitting historical actors into twentieth-century categories or analyzing their experiences with twentieth-century notions and concepts. Pieter Boele van Hensbroek has described this as "the problem of anachronism" in writing intellectual history. Historians sometimes unavoidably infuse individual orientations in the presentation of historical material. Notions about the historical process, such as the idea of modernization or of the continuity of traditions, preclude understanding historical authors and actors within their own frame and within their own historical contexts. The historian, in such cases, enters the field of inquiry with a prior substantial theory of history—having some a priori knowledge about what this period in history is really about. Therefore, Hensbroek cautions that historians must leave open the possibility that the people who are subject to historical studies may have considered themselves to be actors in a different drama. There is a chance that as historians, we may sometimes be burdening the past with the present by projecting our problem definitions upon them. For example, can one speak of "nationalism" when the actors did not have the concept of a nation? Can there be Pan-Africanists when the idea of an all-African identity had not been formulated? Can there be modernists without the notion of modernity, or traditionalists without the idea that African societies were "traditional"?[21] These questions are pertinent to this study. In this case, can we speak of rights, or specifically, "human rights" when the actors may not have employed these notions in the precise sense that we employ them today?

This question has been extensively debated in relation to the study of human rights in African and other non-Western societies. In reaction to arguments for cultural relativism in the definition of human rights, some writers—mainly legal and social science scholars—have argued that although the humanistic values that underlie the concept of human rights may be universally shared, a distinction must be made between the moral standards of human dignity, which all cultures share to some extent, and contemporary human rights that are enforceable legal or quasi-legal entitlements held by individuals in relation to the state. The concept of human rights, it is argued, is essentially a modern one founded on specific historical developments in the West—enlightenment libertarianism, the *Magna Carta,* the French and American Revolutions and, ultimately, the Universal Declaration of Human Rights of 1948.[22] It is argued, therefore, that reference to "human rights" in contexts before 1948 is anachronistic. For this reason, scholars are divided on the appropriateness of employing the concept of "human rights" within the context of the history of pre-1948 colonial societies in Africa or elsewhere.

In response to arguments for an African concept of human rights, some writers have argued that what has been described as an African concept of human rights is actually a concept of human dignity that defines the inner moral nature and worth of the human person and his or her proper relations with society. Human dignity and human rights are therefore not coterminous as dignity can be protected in a society that is not based on rights.[23] Others make the distinction between the concepts of *distributive justice* and human rights. Distributive justice involves giving a person that which he or she is entitled (his or her rights). Unless these rights are those to which the individual is entitled simply as a human being, the rights in question will not be "human rights." In much of pre-colonial Africa for instance, rights were assigned on the basis of communal membership, family, status, or achievement. These were, therefore, strictly speaking, "privileges" granted by ruling elites, not human rights.[24] The idea of human rights, properly so called, has its roots in the adoption of the UDHR by the United Nations in 1948.

These arguments for a restricted definition of human rights that exclude customary notions of legal and moral rights may be categorized as the "UDHR as epoch" school. Proponents of this school see the UDHR of 1948 as an epoch-making event that "created" the concept of human rights and should, therefore, define our understanding of it. The UDHR, it is argued, articulated for the first time in human history a regime of basic and inalienable rights to which all human beings are entitled by virtue of their humanity, regardless of race, sex, social status, or orientations.

On the other side of the fence are other scholars who see the developments of 1948 more as an episode or just another phase rather than an epoch-making event in the definition of human rights. This may be termed the "UDHR as episode" school. This school of thought leans toward a more fluid and flexible definition of human rights that focuses not so much on the restricted context of post-World War II usage but on the continuing notions and ideas that have historically underlined the concept of rights in various societies. Although the UDHR was a groundbreaking document, it was built on preexisting traditions of rights around the world. The UDHR was more a rearticulation of an old concept than the creation of an entirely new one.[25]

The problem, it seems, is largely one of ontology—of labels that we choose to designate ideas rather than the ideas that underlie the labels. Although it may be useful to distinguish between the abstract ideals of human dignity or distributive justice and the more precise legal principles of human rights, we must not overlook the close connection between these sets of concepts and the ways they reinforce each other. Indeed, one would argue that the whole debate over distinction between the concept of human rights before and after 1948 arises from a failure to put the evolution of the idea of human rights in historical context. There has been a tendency to conceptualize human rights within the narrow sense of modern legal language, the emphasis being on the strict legal definition of the term rather than the idea that underlies it. This approach is problematic because it tends to emphasize change while ignoring underlying continuities.

Admittedly, the UDHR was a groundbreaking document. The idea that underlined it—that all human beings are entitled to some basic inalienable rights by virtue of their humanity—marked a shift from earlier notions of rights, because, at least in theory, it was applicable to everyone irrespective of gender, race, and social status. However, this idea of universal inalienable rights enshrined in the UDHR did not emerge as a bolt out of the blue or develop in vacuum. Rather, it was an expansion and rearticulation of earlier traditions of rights. The idea that human beings are born free and equal did not emerge in 1948, and few would suggest it did. Its articulation as a universal principle under the auspices of a body representative of most nations of the world is what is unique about 1948.[26]

Moreover, to many people in the non-Western world who were not represented at the United Nations and still under colonial domination in the 1940s, the adoption of the UDHR did not mean very much. As I argue later in this book, many Africans were ambivalent and even skeptical about a declaration purportedly affirming the rights of all human beings, drawn up by the same imperial powers that were actively denying them of their right to self-determination. It is important, therefore, not to overstate the significance of the UDHR. A more historical approach to the study of the evolution of the contemporary concept of human rights will find no difficulty in drawing the link between earlier notions of human dignity or distributive justice and the modern idea of human rights which are, in fact, merely contextual reinterpretations of the age-long notions of defining human worth and value. The object is to understand and appreciate the distinct historical contexts in which this idea has manifested itself. But in a field long dominated by legal and social science scholars with their predilection for structural analysis, contemporary human rights scholarship tends to be driven by the quest for neat models and precise labels. The messy middle has, for the most part, been left out. While structural analyses may be useful in systematizing our study of rights, a fuller understanding can only come from going beyond these structures to explore the complexities and nuances that underlie them. This is where a historical perspective becomes particularly relevant. Even if we agree, as some have argued, that the UDHR was an epoch-making event, the historian cannot start or stop the story at such break points. It is the historian's task to look for continuities and discontinuities in such supposedly epoch-making events.

Toward a Contextual Definition of Rights

At the most basic level, rights may be defined simply as legally enforceable claims to something, or someone, or some group.[27]

"Rights" occupy the same semantic field as the sometimes nearly synonymous terms "freedom" and "liberties." However, what seems to have confused the definition of rights are the attempts by philosophers, political theorists, and practitioners to theorize, specify, and justify a special category of fundamental or essential rights that pertain to individuals simply by virtue of their humanity. This confusion poses a significant conceptual challenge for this study. Because of the many debates that have been associated with the meaning of rights, we need to clarify the use of the term in this study. The definition of rights adopted here is necessarily broad and inclusive. Rights, like laws, are viewed not as a body of immutable rules, institutions, and procedures but as dynamic historical formations that at once shape and are shaped by economic, political, and social processes.

It is the contention here that rights generally, and human rights in particular, are best defined and understood within the linguistic and social context of popular usage by the historical actors who employed the language. Today, we may all have a fairly common and definite idea of what the legal regime of universal human rights is. But beyond that, rights claims derive their meaning only within specific universes.[28] In this study, I have chosen to refer more to "rights" generally rather than "human rights" per se for two reasons. The first is to avoid the controversy and confusion often associated with the contemporary usage of the concept of human rights. The second reason is because this study focuses on rights defined broadly as popular entitlements that individuals and communities hold in relation to other individuals and groups or in relation to the community as a whole. This goes beyond the conventional definition of human rights as enforceable legal or quasi-legal entitlements that individuals hold against the state.

Since rights are articulated in language and are socially constructed, the emphasis in defining rights in this study is based primarily on how people employed the language of rights or articulated their claims to it, whether orally or in documents. The definition of rights here is guided by the ideas and notions to which people referred when they talked about those entitlements (beyond privileges) that they considered intrinsically theirs. It focuses on the specific contexts in which these rights were asserted, whether individually or collectively. The definition of rights here is also guided by the relationship of rights claims to power—whether deriving from traditional, colonial, or post-colonial hegemonies. "Power" in this context refers to more than just control over other people and their actions. It also embraces the Foucauldian conception of power as the production of knowledge.[29] The concept of rights and freedom achieves its conceptual coherence through the idea of power since rights claims are often articulated in relation to prevailing orthodoxies that are sustained by ascendant regimes of power. People consider themselves free and at liberty primarily when they are released from the power of another or unrestrained by the power of another to do what they want.[30] In this sense, rights are those entitlement claims that essentially go beyond the entitlements of power and privilege.

In a historically contextual study like this, which seeks to identify specific trends and patterns in discussions about rights, it is important to understand where people's ideas about rights and liberties come from and how they have gone about articulating and legitimizing rights claims. What references are used to legitimize rights? Were they "traditional" or "modern," indigenous or imported? Here, I recognize the need to guard against the tendency to lapse into the binary opposites of tradition and modernity. Multiple and diverse influences shaped the rights discourse in many African societies, and these cannot simply be reduced to choices between tradition and modernity. However, notions of "modernity," "civilization," and, later, "development" did at various times influence notions of rights and liberties. The extent to which individuals and groups could claim certain rights against the colonial state, particularly in the early colonial period, depended largely on the level of "civilization" and "modernity" they were considered to have attained. Another consideration is the role of exclusion in discourses about rights. It is important to understand what people claimed as rights. It is also just as important to understand what they did not. It is necessary to recognize that some rights claims did not apply to everyone and excluded particular individuals and groups. Some would argue that this very fact means that they were not really "human rights" since they did not equally apply to everyone in the same way at every time. Yet, they are important to us because they are customary rights

claims founded on law and social acceptance that have shaped
contemporary understandings of human rights.

Equally significant is the need to identify claims that are
made and understood as discretionary privileges rather than
as rights. Certain entitlements enjoyed by members of particular social groups or classes were clearly understood to be
privileges that were discretionarily given and contingent on
certain conditions. For instance, in some African societies, foreigners who settled in the community were entitled to a piece
of land, granted gratis, to enable them to farm for their liveli-
hood. Such an entitlement was clearly understood by all parties involved as a privilege. With changes in circumstances,
this privilege could be lost. In other cases, however, individual
entailments to land were understood and claimed as a matter
of right rather than privilege. "Legitimate" sons born within
wedlock were usually entitled to land as an inalienable right.
Again, some may argue that this, in fact, amounts to a privilege rather than a right since it pertains only to "legitimate
sons." This may be true when we examine this through the
lens of present-day definitions of human rights. But my concern here is not so much with how these customary notions or
rights measure against today's standards but with how the
people who deployed this language of rights construed it themselves. My concern is with the discourse of rights in a specific
context, centered on how the historical actors themselves perceived particular entitlements and the language with which
they made claims to such entitlements. In this case of farmlands, local people typically understood a land grant to a legitimate son as a right rather than a privilege. For a historical
and contextual study in discourse analysis, this needs to be a
primary consideration.

Rights Discourse in the African Context

The discussion about rights in the African context has centered on the distinction between an African concept of human
rights founded on communal values, as distinct from Western
notions of rights that were subsequently introduced into the
continent with European incursion.[31] This debate has, for the

most part, been a response to arguments for a restricted definition of human rights as typified by the "UDHR as epoch" thesis and the assumption that the philosophical foundations of the modern concept of human rights are traceable uniquely to the liberal traditions of Western Europe. This position has been interpreted as implying that the modern concept of human rights was extraneous to precolonial Africa and other non-Western societies.[32] As we have seen, some proponents of the "UDHR as epoch" thesis argue specifically that what are usually put forward as traditional African conceptions of human rights are nothing more than notions of human dignity and worth that existed in all pre-industrial societies. They argue that all human societies, including those in Africa, have gone through a stage when, because of the low level of productive forces, collective ownership of the means of production and the communal organization of society was necessary for subsistence.[33] This communal social structure allowed for the development of humanistic ideals, which are not necessarily coterminous with contemporary notions of human rights.

Another variant of this school is the argument that traditional African societies, as indeed most pre-modern societies, could not have evolved perceptions of human rights because they did not recognize the concept of a human being as a descriptive category. Instead, persons were defined by social status or group membership, and, as such, traditional societies generally did not recognize rights one held simply as a human being.[34] Therefore, the kind of social relationship between the state and the individual, which is the basis of the notion of human rights, was never created within the context of such traditional societies.[35] According to this approach, human rights were thus alien to Africa until Western modernizing incursions dislocated community and denied newly isolated individuals access to the customary ways of protecting their lives and human dignity.[36] One of the implications of this argument is that the origins of the concept of human rights in Africa must be sought beyond Africa's precolonial history.

This externalist approach to the conceptual origins of human rights in Africa has met with forceful Afrocentric rebuttals arguing that the concept and philosophy of human rights are neither alien to traditional African societies nor exclusive to

Western liberal traditions. Proponents reject the notion that the concept of human rights, having originated, developed, and been refined in the West, was thereafter "transplanted" to Africa. This view has been variously described as paternalistic, inherently ahistorical, and philosophically bankrupt.[37] As one writer puts it, it is difficult to accept that the concept of human rights is a theoretical notion created only three centuries ago by philosophers in Europe.[38] What was unique about the Enlightenment, and the writings of the French and American Revolutions, was the discussion of human rights in the context of formally articulated philosophical and political systems.

Some of those who challenge the exclusivity of Western liberalism as foundations of human rights point out that precolonial African societies knew of human rights adapted to the political and social situations existing in that period. These rights were recognized and protected, but must be looked at in the context of societies that were hierarchical and at the same time unified by mythological beliefs. Within these societies, the object of law was to maintain society in the condition in which the ancestors bequeathed it. Therefore, the concept of human rights within such social contexts was necessarily communal and humanist, fostering a mutual respect and recognition of the rights and liberties of each individual within the wider context of the community.[39]

The distinction between a Western or contemporary notion of rights, on one hand, and the African or "traditional" conception of rights, on the other, is reflected in the different philosophical worldviews of Western European and African societies, particularly with reference to the collectivist rather than individualistic nature of rights and duties. The modern Western-oriented conception of human rights, it has been argued, contains three elements that make it quite distinct from traditional African concepts of rights.[40] First, in the Western conception of rights, the fundamental unit of the society is the individual, not the family or community. Notions of rights and justice within Western law are constructed around the fetish of the abstract individual.[41] Second, the primary basis of securing human existence in society is through rights, not duties. Third, the primary method of securing these rights is through a legal process where rights are claimed as absolute entitlements and adjudicated upon, not through reconciliation, repentance, and education as in many African societies.[42] For these reasons, contemporary rights talk continues to be problematic in non-Western settings.[43]

It has also been frequently argued that in traditional Africa the concept of rights was founded not on the individual but on the community to which the individual related on the basis of obligation and duties. Rights in this context included but were not limited to the right to political representation often guaranteed by the family, age groups, and the clan. The society developed certain central social features that tended to foster the promotion of both individual and collective rights. These included deference to age, commitment to the family and the community, and solidarity with other members of the community. These ideals strengthened community ties and social cohesiveness, engendering a shared fate and a common destiny. Under these circumstances, the concept of rights did not stand in isolation. It went with duties. For every right to which a member of society was entitled, there was a corresponding communal duty. Expressed differently, "the right of one kinship member was the duty of the other and the duty of the other kinship member was the right of another."[44] Although certain rights were often gendered, and attached to the individual by virtue of birth and membership of the community, there were also corresponding communal duties and obligations. This matrix of entitlements and obligations fostered communal solidarity and sustained the kinship system that was the basis of the African conception of human rights.

The philosophy behind this customary concept of rights is based on the presumption that the full development of the individual is only possible where individuals care about how their action affects others. Thus, in contrast with the Western conception of rights, which conceives rights in terms of abstract individualism without corresponding duties, the dominant customary African conception of human rights was integrated within a system of rights and obligations, which gave the community cohesion and viability. This conception of the individual as a moral being endowed with rights but also bounded by duties proactively uniting his needs with the needs of others was the quintessence of the formulation of rights in precolonial African societies.[45] This argument for a communitarian rather than individualistic conception of human rights is not merely another case of African exceptionalism. Similar arguments have been made for "Asian values" in the conception of human rights. Some leaders and scholars of East and Southeast Asian countries have stressed Asia's incommensurable differences from the West and argue for a distinct understanding of human rights in the Asian context. It is also argued that the importance of the community in Asian culture is incompatible with the primacy of the individual upon which the Western notion of human rights rests. This relationship between individuals and communities constitutes the key difference between Asian and Western cultural values.[46] This and similar thinking provided the basis for the Bangkok Declaration, seen by many as a counter-document to the UDHR by Asian countries.[47]

Arguments for a peculiarly communal African concept of human rights are confronted with their own theoretical and empirical limitations, particularly in their relevance to contemporary African societies. First, there is the monolithic treatment of Africa that belies historical diversity and contemporary realities. Rather than the persistence of traditional cultural values in the face of modern incursions, the reality in contemporary Africa, as in the rest of the developing world, is a situation of disruptive and incomplete Westernization, cultural confusion, or even the enthusiastic embrace of what are considered "modern" practices and values. The reality is that ideals of traditional culture and its community-centered values, advanced to justify arguments for the cultural relativism of human rights in the African context, far too often no longer exist. In fact, some critics have argued that the much-vaunted communal concept of human rights never existed in traditional African communities in the ways that have been suggested. African notions of human rights do not overemphasize the community, as most African leaders and writers would have us believe. Rather, traditional African rights models primarily emphasized individual rights, and there was always a balance between individual and the community rights.[48]

Although scholars have been at the forefront of advancing arguments for the cultural relativism of human rights in the African context, the assertion of "African values" gains prominence when it is articulated in the political rhetoric of African leaders and elite. It has been suggested that in asserting these values, leaders from the continent find that they have a convenient tool to silence internal criticism and to fan anti-Western nationalist sentiments.[49] Some writers have even suggested that the picture of an idyllic, communitarian society has been presented by African rulers and elite to hide and rationalize their own unbridled violations of human rights.[50] The arguments for cultural relativism are far too often made by urban economic and political elites who have long left traditional culture behind. Their appeal to cultural practices is often a mere cloak for self-interest and arbitrary rule.[51] There is some truth to this. In many parts of the developing world, culture-based arguments are often a pretext for restricting fundamental rights. Culture has become simply a cover for elite privilege and a language of rulers.[52] There is justified suspicion of African political elites who use the constant references to culture, "communal values," and the primacy of socio-economic well-being over civil and political rights, to mask systematic violations of human rights in the interest of the ruling elite.

But persuasive as the critique against culture talk in the human rights discourse may be, it fails to address some important questions. If the accent on culture in the human rights discourse is nothing but a demagogic posture of dominant and hegemonic local interests, why does it resonate with others beyond their narrow confines? Why do subaltern players such as women and minority groups also find the language of culture appealing in articulating rights claims? Why does the National Federation of Women Lawyers in Ghana canvass the employment of traditional methods of conflict resolution in promoting human rights even at it argues for changes in culture-based legislation that no longer safeguard women?[53] Why is the dominant women's rights Non-Governmental Organization in Swaziland, the Council of Swaziland Churches (CSC), always "careful to avoid bias against traditional systems" even as it pushes for critical debate over cultural practices that no longer safeguard women?[54] The failure to address these questions has been attributed, in part, to the "selfrighteousness and intolerance of the rights movement"—its tendency to dismiss every local cultural assertion as masking a defense of privilege and inequality at the expense of the individual rights of the disadvantaged in the same society.[55] I am inclined to agree. We should not be too quick to dismiss all culture talk relating to human rights from Africa or elsewhere in the South as nothing more than opportunistic elite posturing. To do so would be to throw the baby away with the bath water. True, the language of culture has been used by elites to limit human rights, but these elites have no monopoly over this language, and we shouldn't assume that they do. Culture talk can, and also has been, effectively used to legitimize rights claims by marginalized groups within these societies.

Given the limitations of the arguments for "cultural relativism" in the human rights discourse, on one hand, and the problems of applying Western or supposedly "universal" concepts of human rights to non-Western societies, on the other, there have been suggestions for the opening up of a "third space" from which a critique of both tradition and modernity can be made.[56] If culture talk involves more than just a defense of local privilege, and rights talk too is more than just a Western assertion, how do we explore the possibilities of each discourse? To the extent that culture talk is about dignity and difference and rights talk about equality and sameness, do we not need a language that transcends (or encompasses) both rights and culture? Against this background, one writer has argued the need to go beyond the confines of "rights talk and culture talk" and embrace instead a "language of protest" that bears a relationship to the "language of power."[57] Appealing as this suggestion is, its main limitation is that it assumes that the discourses about rights can be understood simply in terms of power and protest. This is not always true. Although rights talk is often related to power, it certainly goes beyond protest. As I argue later in this volume, the language of rights in colonial Nigeria was not only a language of protest. It was also variously deployed as a language of negotiation, engagement, and even to legitimize the status quo.

In sum, we can identify three levels of argument in the Africanist discourse on human rights. At the first level is the debate as to whether or not the foundations of human rights conceptions are also to be found in the African historical experience. On this, it is difficult to escape the conclusion that the extreme Afrocentric argument for a distinctively communitarian African concept of human rights that stands in contrast with the concepts and traditions of the West or the rest of the world has its limitations. If anything, the notion of the absolute cultural relativism of human rights comes through as a misunderstanding inspired by cultural nationalism. What its proponents see as radically distinctive communitarian African traditions and conceptions also clearly possess ideals that are universal. When African leaders such as Julius Nyerere of Tanzania argued for a concept of human rights that is peculiar and relevant to Africa in the immediate post-independence years, they were clearly echoing the sentiments of cultural nationalism that was the general spirit of the era. Much of the humanistic and communitarian "non-Western" values that were exclusively ascribed to African societies also generally apply to most preindustrial societies elsewhere in the world.[58]

On the other hand, it is difficult to accept the equally extremist argument that human rights are founded solely on the liberal traditions of Western Europe or that the concept of human rights was alien to specific precapitalist traditions in precolonial Africa. Such monolithic interpretations of human rights are not convincing. They are also unhelpful. If the emerging universal culture of rights is to take roots in Africa and other non-Western societies in a sustainable way, the association of human rights with Western thought and the Western worldview in the public imagination constitutes a hindrance.[59] Discussions about rights as the heritage of all humankind and about the concept of human rights must be construed as something that has been developed, struggled for, and won by people in all societies. These struggles and victories should combine to give our contemporary understanding of human rights its essence and universal validity. There is little basis or need for the rather sweeping assertion that precolonial Africa, or indeed any "premodern" society for that matter, has made no normative contribution to the contemporary human rights corpus or the global rights discourse.

To hold this middle-of-the-road position is not to be ambivalent or contradictory. Elsewhere, I have argued that in spite of the tendency of some of its proponents to stretch it too far, an Afrocentric conception of human rights is a valid worldview.[60] Its significance to the discourse on the cultural relativism of human rights, however, demands careful consideration. Rather than being the basis for abrogating or delegitimizing human rights values that have universal appeal, it should inform the cross-fertilization of ideas between Africa and the rest of the world. It can also provide the moral and philosophical basis for the legit-imization of a universal human rights regime in the African con-text. The present challenge for Africanist human rights scholars generally is to articulate an African sense of human rights that flows from the African historical experience and that the rest of the international community can also use. The construction and definition of human rights norms is a continuous and dynamic process. As a dynamic process, the cultures and traditions of the world must make comparisons, and, hopefully, come to some agreement on what constitutes human rights and seek how these values can best find some form of cross-cultural legitimacy. This is one of the aspirations of this book.

2

Right, Liberties, and the Imperial World Order

The Dawn of Colonial Rule

Like the rest of Africa, Nigeria in the late 1800s and early 1900s was a society in transition. It was characterized by the loss of autonomy by African states and societies following years of European intervention, culminating in the imposition of colonial control. Toward the turn of the nineteenth century, many indigenous states and societies in Western Nigeria saw their control over both external and internal affairs either lost or severely curtailed by growing European influence. Politically, internal dissension within these communities threatened their stability and made them more vulnerable to external influences. This was compounded by economic changes following the abolition and collapse of the slave trade. In one of the earliest of such interventions, the British, in their campaign against the Atlantic slave trade, intervened on the coast of Lagos in the 1820s. This gave the British a major foothold in Southern Nigeria from which to pursue their interests against the overseas slave trade, promote "legitimate" trade in agricultural produce, and encourage missionary activities. These activities marked the beginning of British colonial rule over two-hundred indigenous ethnic groups of what was to become the British colony of Nigeria. The largest of these ethnic groups were the Hausa-Fulani in the north, the Yoruba in the west, and the Igbo in the East.

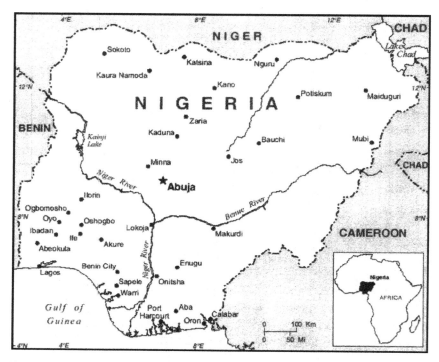

Figure 2.1. Map of Nigeria

One of the early tasks of British administration in this part of Nigeria was to suppress the slave trade, which thrived despite its abolition, and to remove all obstacles to free trade. Trade was evidently the central goal of British imperial projects in this and other parts of Africa. British officials were willing to pursue these goals even if it meant widespread intervention in the affairs of autonomous African states and societies. In Yorubaland of western Nigeria, British penetration was a combination of both coercion and diplomacy. Following the Berlin West African Conference of 1884, which effectively divided Africa among contending European powers, British consuls and later colonial administrators signed several bilateral treaties of friendship and trade in which the indigenous people "agreed" to come under British jurisdiction in return for British protection and friendship.[1] For many Yoruba communities, this was an expedient decision given the prevailing conditions of civil war insecurity and economic decline. But in some other cases, local states were not so accommodating of British intervention. African resistance inevitably brought on armed conflict with British troops. Between 1900 and 1920, no less than twenty-five military expeditions were mounted against different communities, especially east of the River Niger. It was largely through this process that much of Nigeria became conquered territory.

Even at this early stage, one central issue in the conflict between the British and indigenous communities centered on the rights of local peoples and the limits imposed on their traditional liberties by the British. For instance, British punitive expeditions against the against indigenous states like Egba in 1867, Ijebu in 1892, and Benin in 1897 were the result of their steadfastness in defending their political autonomy and economic rights. Yoruba states that opposed the British saw their

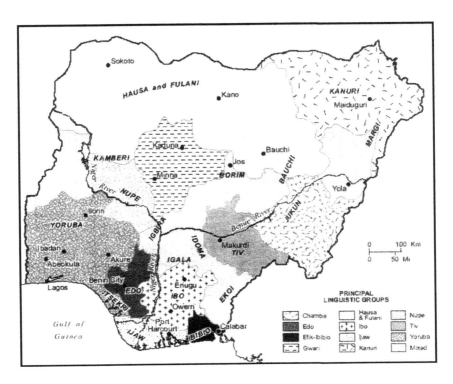

Figure 2.2. Map of Nigeria Showing Ethno-linguistic Groups

opposition primarily in terms of protecting their economic rights within the larger context of the regional political economy. Such concerns did not begin with British intervention. Similar issues of economic rights, independence, and self-determination were at the roots of the protracted civil wars that ravaged Yorubaland in the mid-nineteenth century. As far as the Ijebu were concerned, the British expedition of 1892 was only the external aspect of an otherwise internal war to safeguard their commercial, social, and political rights. For these communities, the right to trade on their own terms was central to their conflict with the British. To give up their right to trade with whomever they wished and in whatever commodities they chose was considered a diminution of their sovereignty.[2] In the end, the Egba were able to strike a diplomatic compromise with the British that allowed them to retain much of their autonomy—even when the rest of Western Nigeria fell under colonial rule—until 1914. Many other indigenous states were not so lucky. By 1900, the once powerful Kingdom of Benin, whose influence stretched across West Africa, and the Itsekiri, Urhobo, Ijaw states in the Niger Delta, had all fallen under British colonial rule.

Treaty Rights and "Rights of Intervention"

African rulers saw British intervention as a threat to their authority and resisted in order to protect their political and economic prerogatives. Local rulers who sought to limit the expansion of British jurisdiction appealed to treaties, agreements, and pledges made with British consuls. These treaties and agreements provided a basis for such rulers to demand political and economic autonomy as a matter of right rather than British concession. For instance, the treaty of "peace and friendship" between Britain and the chiefs of Ife in 1888 recognized the independence of the kingdom of Ife, which "paid tribute to no other power."[3] In a letter to the chiefs and people of Ibadan in 1893, the British colonial Governor pledged that Britain would not infringe upon their "traditional rights and liberties" of the people.[4] The "treaty of friendship and commerce" between the British authorities and the Egba in 1893 also fully recognized Egba independence. This treaty provided the basis for the formation and autonomous operation of the Egba United Government (EUG) even when the rest of the country had come completely under colonial control.

Conflicting interpretations about the scope of these treaty rights became a major source of tension between the British authorities and local rulers. On their part, local kings and chiefs interpreted African rights under these treaties quite broadly and saw growing British intervention in trade and politics as infringements on these rights. The *Record,* a leading African-run newspaper of the period, challenged the constitutional right of the colonial Legislative Council to legislate for Yoruba states on the grounds that they had never by treaty or otherwise conferred such rights upon the British Crown. The newspaper considered the British proposal to make laws for these indigenous states as "an alarming extension of power" that should be resisted.[5] The *Standard,* another local newspaper, stated that all West African people were bound to oppose British legislation because it was "in arbitrary disregard of solemn treaty obligations."[6] Similarly, in seeking to maintain their political autonomy, the chiefs of Ibadan emphasized the pledge of the colonial government based in Lagos not to interfere with the rights of indigenous Yoruba states in the interior.[7]

The appeal to treaty rights as a basis for making specific entitlement claims was not limited to African chiefs and elites. European missionaries who preceded the colonial administration also referred to treaty rights to justify their demands from the colonial government. When the Alafin (King) of Oyo expelled the Southern Baptist Convention from his domain in 1909 on the grounds that the group was stirring up discontent among his people, the head of the mission, Rev. S. G. Pinnock, petitioned the Resident Commissioner, stating: "As a British subject, in the enjoyment of Treaty Rights I urgently request that steps be taken to secure my person and property from molestation in the hands of the Alafin . . . and [his] interferences with our liberties."[8] When the Resident Commissioner declined to intervene on his behalf and advised the mission to comply with the Alafin's order "in the interest of the European population," Reverend Pinnock refused on the grounds that the Alafin's order contravened the treaty of 1891.[9] The reply from the Resident Commissioner in this case was typical. In general, the British authorities tended to be selective in their interpretation of African treaty rights and were sometime even dismissive of the language of treaty agreements. Responding to allegations of treaty rights infringement by Egba chiefs and the London-based humanitarian organization, the Aborigines Protection Society, in 1902, Governor MacGregor insisted that Egbaland was never intended under the terms of the treaty to be an independent state but a "responsible authority." Another official later stated more bluntly that the term "independent" used in the Egba treaty was "a mere phrase."[10]

Paradoxically, the British administration also saw its role partly in terms of promoting the liberties of Africans under its influence through active intervention in local politics. Punitive expeditions against uncooperative African communities and the deportation of their rulers were often justified on the grounds that they were undertaken to protect the rights and liberties of British subjects, both African and European, in such areas. For instance, in 1891 the colonial government deported and detained Asada Awopa, the King of Addo, for, among other offences, "interfering with the liberty of British subjects."[11] Such British appeals to the language of rights and liberty were also evident in the process of conquest and pacification. In a treaty signed with chiefs of Abeokuta in 1852, the British authorities insisted that the chiefs, in accordance with "British libertarian traditions," guarantee the freedom of movement throughout the country for Europeans and the African immigrants in their community.[12] Although the main object of this provision was clearly to further British goals of opening up the Yoruba interior to free trade, the language of freedom and liberty in which this treaty, like many others after it, was couched in terms that legitimized British intervention.

The view that British intervention was ultimately for the benefit of local peoples by expanding their rights and liberties was not limited to colonial officials. Some African elites, particularly the emergent Western-educated intelligentsia, shared this view. When the British annexed Ilaro and Ado in 1885, the *Record* newspaper hailed it as evidence of British determination to promote the interest and welfare of the African people of the colony. It remarked that while there would be those who would frown at the action as an infringement of the rights of African chiefs, the "majority of intelligent natives" regarded it as "an imperative step" toward the future well-being of Yorubaland.[13] Thus, although most traditional rulers and sections of the local elite opposed the expansion of British influence as a contravention of existing treaty obligations and their traditional political rights, some others, mainly among the growing class of mission-educated elites, welcomed such expansion. They saw British influence as, among other things, a better guarantee of the rights and liberties of local peoples. Such paradoxes in the multiple understandings and uses of the language of freedom and liberty by colonial officials, African chiefs and educated elites, and missionaries and humanitarians characterized the rights discourse in the early colonial period.

As Britain set about building this part of its African empire and putting in place the structures for colonial administration, indigenous African political institutions became progressively weakened. With colonial penetration, a new leadership of loyal African chiefs and educated elite emerged in some of these communities. Oftentimes, these were local chiefs and elites disposed to working with the British authorities as a means of furthering their own political and economic interests. Where chieftaincy institutions did not exist, the British created them artificially. In some cases, these "chiefs" were village headmen to whom the British ascribed new levels of authority. This class of African chiefs became political agents in the local tier of the colonial government called the Native Councils, which filled the vacuum created by the demise of traditional political institutions.

As the local tier of government, the Native Councils had perhaps the most profound impact on African societies. Through them the British authorities hoped to institute and maintain a new dispensation of law and social order based on the continued observance of traditional practices alongside new government regulations. This was the foundation of British colonial policy of "Indirect Rule" in Nigeria as in other parts of Africa. However, much in the Native Council system was artificial and unacceptable to local people. For one, the members were often chosen in a haphazard fashion without proper inquiry into the indigenous political practices and systems of authority. Consequently, many members of the councils were not even village heads. Their authority derived entirely from the "warrants" or "certificates of recognition" given to them by the government. Second, even where members of Native Councils were traditional village heads, they were accorded artificial positions that gave them control over villages in which they traditionally had no authority.[14] For these reasons, many people found the Native Council system objectionable. Even among the educated African elites, many believed that the Native Councils weakened the authority and influence of traditional African rulers because they were more responsive to the needs of the colonial administration than those of the people. Criticizing the law establishing the Native Councils, one local newspaper stated in 1903 that it served only to "bring the authority of native rulers into disrepute and make them objects of ridicule in the eyes of their own people."[15] The Native Council Ordinance was also severely criticized by international philanthropic organizations such as the Aboriginal Protection Society, which contended that the law interfered with the internal affairs of the indigenous states, contrary to treaty agreements with Britain.[16] Thus, even at this early stage of colonial rule, a central question in the tension between colonizer and colonized was the scope of British power and the limits it placed on the rights and liberties of African subjects.

Missionaries, Humanitarians, and "Native Rights"

Debates about the personhood of the native and his/her rights and freedoms were central to both missionary activities and colonial rule in many parts of Africa. Colonization began with the ideological onslaught on the part of Christian missionaries, self-styled bearers of European civilization. With an agenda that mirrored the paternalistic character of their encounter with Africa, European missionaries set out to "convert" heathens by persuading them of their theological message and, even more profoundly, by reconstructing their everyday worlds.[17] Rights discourses were an important part of both the ideological message and linguistic forms of missionary activities in Nigeria. Such discussions about native rights in missionary circles, which were founded on Christian humanism and the notion of the "civilizing mission," provided the foundation for the more formal and codified regimes of rights that were later introduced under colonial rule. The overall impact of missionary activities in Western Nigeria has been thoroughly examined in several historical studies.[18] The discussion here is concerned with the ways in which missionary activities and the social and cultural reengineering they sought influenced popular perceptions and discussions about rights and liberties in the early colonial period.

British colonial imposition in Nigeria was preceded by the activities of European missionaries who became involved in the entire colonial project. By the end of the nineteenth century, several missionary groups had gained footholds in Nigeria, particularly in Yorubaland and the Niger Delta area. These groups included the Anglican Church Missionary Society (CMS), the Wesleyan Methodist Missionary Society (WMMS), the Southern Baptist Convention (SBC) from the United States of America, the French Catholic missionary group Société des Missions Africaines (SMA) and the United Presbyterian Church of Scotland (UP). Of these groups, the CMS was the largest and most influential with the colonial government partly because of its British connections. It had more mission stations, churches, and missionaries (both African and Europeans) than any other mission in Western Nigeria.

From the start, the Christian missions in Western Nigeria, as elsewhere in Africa, were caught up in local politics. The various denominations had diverse and frequently contradictory designs, and their activities sometimes brought them into ambivalent relations with other Europeans in the colonial stage. Some found common causes and operated openly with traders and consuls. Other "nonconformist evangelists" ended up locked in battle with secular forces for what they took to be the destiny of the continent.[19] For instance, while the CMS was able to establish strong relations with the colonial government, others like the SBC were often at odds with the government. However, generally speaking, Europeans did not always question the theory that "Christianity, Commerce and

Civilization" would work together for the great benefit of Africans. But, nevertheless, they liked to emphasize their own philanthropy and how much it set them apart in objectives, approach, methods, and morals from their profit-seeking countrymen who came for trade and political power. Many saw themselves as the moral conscience of the civilized world. The truth, however, was that missionaries, traders, and British consuls were all interdependent. The Christian missions made a considerable impact both on the trading situation and the process of British political conquest and control.

The reason for these links between missionaries and other political and commercial agents of empire lies partly in the underlying ideologies of missionary work. The ethical touchstone for missionary work, far from being purely religious, drew on the temporal model of the unfettered economy—a model that presumed the protection of the right to enter into contract and to engage in enterprise by free individuals. "Right" in the sense of good was elided into "rights" in goods, and properties of subjects into the subject of property. In the process, Christian and secular legalisms merged into one another to make for a powerfully law-centered worldview.[20] The point needs to be made, however, that missionary rights discourses were not synonymous with those of the colonial state. In fact, the former preceded the latter. Long before the establishment of effective colonial administration, missionaries and humanitarians sought to change a "backward" indigenous social and legal order to a more "civilized" and enlightened one. Early records of the CMS, including diaries and memoirs, contain numerous references to such social and legal interventions that ultimately intersected with later colonial discourses of law, rights, and justice.

One of the most important consequences of missionary involvement in law and justice was that it changed African attitude towards legal transgression. Christian religious authorities introduced, or at least strengthened, the belief that to break the law was to sin.[21] Sin was cast as a crime, and salvation and subjugation to divine law became fused with the imperatives of "civilization." The idea was spread that the point of judicial proceedings was to determine guilt and impose punishment. Transplanting British law went hand in hand with transfusing Christian guilt. Jean and John Comaroff have argued that, taken together, these axioms composed the confident bases of a universalist epistemology that allowed for only "one possible construction of the civilized subject, one *discourse of rights,* one telos of modernity."[22]

However, it may not be quite correct to characterize missionary epistemology as simply *one* discourse of rights. Missionaries also taught new ideas about the individual and humanist rights, and these were critically important in attracting slaves, women, and other subaltern groups to the alternative legal and social programs of the missions. Among these groups, the empowering language of Christian theology, and the discourse on rights underlying it, found new and varied meanings. The Christian church was seen as a source of security and refuge for communities that had endured the stress of conquest and the social disruption that accompanied early colonial rule.[23] In many parts of Africa, the activities of missionaries made concrete the ideological assault on slavery not only because they provided a more universalist vision of personhood but also because they represented an alternative idea of emancipation that slaves and other marginalized groups could themselves appropriate and deploy to varied ends. The baptismal and catechism classes at the mission stations, which became so attractive to slaves, provided them with both a place of refuge and an alternative worldview.

When Christian missionaries combined with the colonial government in the common desire to spread Western European "civilization" in Nigeria in the late nineteenth century, this effort led to significant changes in the institutions, cultural identities, and social orientations of local African communities. Early missionaries were inclined to feel that the African was in the grip of a cruel and irrational system from which he should be liberated.[24] Their experiences and observations in Africa confirmed their belief that in the African scheme of things, human life and individual liberties meant very little.[25] They therefore set about the task of "civilizing" the natives by remaking his person and changing his social orientations. European missionaries of all denominations were united in their opposition to the harsh treatment of slaves, particularly the killing and sacrifice of slaves, and actively preached against slavery and human sacrifices.

For many Africans, particularly those on the fringes of society, this message had instant appeal. In the late nineteenth and early twentieth centuries, the missionary message of a new liberal order attracted many slaves to the mission stations where they gathered to enroll in catechism and baptism classes. Such was the appeal and impact of missionary activities on the slave population that the people of Asaba in Western Nigeria called the local CMS church *"uka ugwule"* (assemblies of slaves). In another part of Southern Nigeria, Rev. James Johnson could write in the 1890s that owing to the activities of the missionaries, "slaves now realize their freedom . . . and a new dispensation has dawned."[26]

Missionary discussions about the rights and liberties of the "native" Christian convert were anchored on two main premises. The first was the assumption that conversion to Christianity and the acquisition of mission education by some Africans set them apart from the "masses of their heathen and unlettered kin."[27] In a 1925 memorandum, the colonial Resident of Oyo Province, W. A. Ross, stated: "the majority of native converts regard themselves as a separate and special community and hope that they may be so regarded by the Native Authority and be exempt from the obligations ordinarily borne by the native community."[28] Acquisition of mission education and conversion to Christianity (or at least the public demonstration of such) were perceived as indices of progress and civilization that entitled such Africans to certain liberties not necessarily availed to others. Although these entitlements were often couched in the language of rights and liberties, they were in fact more or less privileges that derived from an assumption that through Christianity and Western education the "native" attained a level of sophistication that made him more of a rights-bearing persona than others of his race.

Some African converts internalized these ideas and held themselves up to superior social and legal standards. They believed they should not be compelled to observe traditional "pagan customs" by local chiefs and elders because they enjoyed certain "Christian liberties" that were recognized by the colonial state. This sometimes became a source of arrogance and overzealousness on the part of some African Christians. It was also partly at the roots of the frequent conflicts between local

Christians and other non-Christian members of their communities as was the case in Ibowun in 1899 and Okitipupa in 1930.[29]

The second assumption anchoring notions of "native" Christian rights and liberties was the belief in a universal Christian brotherhood. Many missionaries, particularly African missionaries, shared the idea that the "native" Christian, as a member of a global Christian community was entitled to certain basic rights. They emphasized the commonalities between Christians in Africa and those elsewhere in the world. Writing in 1912, Rev. Mojola Agbebi, the African head of the CMS Niger Delta Mission, stated that "the native brethren" in Africa shared the same hopes and aspirations as "brethren in far-flung corners of the world." He also stressed the place of the African in a global community bound together in Christian humanity.[30]

Generally, missionaries were inclined to go beyond such notions as natural justice and the freedom of trade, movement, and religion, which were the essential humanistic considerations that guided treaty agreements between Britain and African rulers.[31] Missionaries created a new world order in Africa, not by military might but by belief in the transforming power of redeemed and sanctified persons, often slaves and other downtrodden members of society, whose freedom and dignity they championed.[32] Although their primary objective was the conversion of local "heathens" to Christianity, the missions realized that this objective could not be achieved until certain social and economic conditions prevailed within local communities. Among these were peace, order, and stability; the abolition of the slave trade and domestic institutions of slavery; the evolution of a money economy; and the creation of a "modern" and "civilized" society in Nigeria. Of these conditions, the abolition of the slavery was considered the most significant. It was within the context of the antislavery movement that missionary discourses about native rights and liberties became most prominent, as we shall see later in this chapter.

For their part, the humanitarians had much in common with the missionaries in their approach towards "native" rights and liberties. Generally, these were individuals and groups whose concerns for the welfare of Africans were anchored not necessarily on religion but on ethical and moral principles.

While the articulation of "native rights" within antislavery discourse by the missionaries was founded on Christian values, the
humanitarians adopted a more secular approach. Organizations
such as the Anti-Slavery Society, later the Aborigines Protection
Society (APS) and the Humanitarian League drew upon a more
inclusive language of rights in their campaigns for the welfare of
local peoples. In a speech in 1898, H. R. Fox Bourne, the secretary of the Aborigines Protection Society, publicly argued that
"native races" had an "incontrovertible right" to their own soil;
that their territory should never be acquired by force or fraud,
and that their right to personal liberty should be protected even
under colonial rule. He also argued that natives were entitled to
freedom of opinion and that Christianity and virtue could not be
enforced by the Maxim gun. An official of the Humanitarian
League, Bradlaugh-Bonner, expressed similar views in 1898:

> It is the duty of civilized nations and individuals in their
> dealings with the so-called "inferior races" to recognize the
> native's right to the use of land and its produce, to personal
> liberty and the freedom of opinion, to equal participation in
> social and political privileges, and to such enlightenment as
> may be imparted to them without compulsion.[33]

When the British and Foreign Antislavery Society and the
Aborigines Protection Society merged in 1910, its Secretary,
Fowell Buxton, declared that the main concern of the new society,
Anti-Slavery and Aborigines Protection Society (AS-APS), was
the "renaissance of slavery" and resistance to the oppression of
native peoples everywhere.[34] In the years that followed, the society launched a concerted campaign against slavery and other
forms of servitude throughout Africa. Apart from the important
role they played in the antislavery movement, humanitarian organizations such as the AS-APS took on other rights issues, particularly with regard to African land and labor rights. Appalled
by reports of forced labor and the flogging of African workers,
the secretary of the AS-APS complained to the British government pointing out that its use of forced African labor in the
colonies was tantamount to slavery.[35]

What is perhaps most significant about the activities of
these organizations is that in their discourse on rights and lib-

erties they sought to influence not only official policy in the colony but also official and public opinion in the metropole. They worked to sensitize the English public against colonial policies that they deemed inimical to the welfare of Africans. In doing so, they employed an inclusive language of rights founded on a belief in Britain's social and legal obligations to "native peoples." The notion and language of rights employed by the humanitarians drew from a more universal language of the natural rights of man and transcended the missionaries' concern for the rights of Christian converts. The journal of the Antislavery and Aborigines Protection Society, *The Antislavery Reporter and Aborigine Friend,* often contained articles and commentaries that addressed the question of native rights and liberties on a wide variety of issues. Although the language was sometimes paternalistic, it drew on a notion of rights that went beyond the racial boundaries that defined that era. The journal became a favorite of the editors of the African newspapers, who regularly culled articles from it and republished them with approval in their newspapers. The African elites who ran these newspapers clearly saw these organizations as effective champions of "native" rights.[36]

Although the AS-APS's agenda of championing African rights and welfare often pitted it against the colonial government, its members did not see themselves as opponents of Britain, the colonial government, or even the idea of empire. Their main concern was to promote the rights and welfare of Africans under British colonial rule, not necessarily to abrogate that rule or change existing power structures. Interestingly, this was true of both African and European members of the organization. At the AS-APS's inaugural meeting in Lagos, its president, the African Bishop Johnson, reminded members that King George of Britain was the grand patron of the Society. He described the Society as "a meeting of free and loyal subjects of the King seeking the welfare and advancement of His Majesty's possessions in this part of the world."[37] The humanitarians also included prominent Europeans such as Sir William Geary, a famous British lawyer, and Edmund Dene Morel, a British journalist and shipping agent who became famous for his work exposing the atrocities of the rule of Belgium's King Leopold in the Congo.[38] These individuals, along with the missionaries, were at the forefront of the early discourses of moral and legal rights in colonial Nigeria, particularly in terms of bringing concerns about individual rights more prominently into the antislavery debates of the early twentieth century.

The Antislavery Movement

The late nineteenth-century commitment of missionaries, which provided colonial powers with a moral justification for the conquest of Africa in the notion of the "civilizing mission," also rallied public support against slavery both in the colony and the metropole. Alongside the obvious political and economic considerations that drove the abolitionist movement were subtler humanist and ethical considerations founded on Christianity, liberal individualism, and a more inclusive notion of human rights employed by activists within the abolitionist movement.[39] This is true of both stages of the antislavery movement—the earlier abolitionist movement in Europe and the later antislavery push to actualize abolitionist ideals in African colonies. The language of rights within both phases of the antislavery movement had its roots partly in Christian humanism and partly in the radical philosophies of the eighteenth-century age of reason and enlightenment, with its ideas of the noble savage, natural rights of man, and the inherent values of liberty in society. Other related themes converged in the antislavery movement, such as the belief in the power of law to change the character of man, slave agitation and self-understanding, the use of petitions, evangelical social activism, the undoing of customs and other established structures, and the moral transformation of African society. All these themes, in one way or the other, were related to growing moral and ethical concerns about slavery.

Most missionaries and evangelicals in Nigeria, as elsewhere in British West Africa, saw in the antislavery campaign a challenge to the Christian to do his duty to his neighbor. Within this context of Christian humanism, antislavery became a universal movement of human rights, and the structure of profit, domination, and advantage that lived off it was challenged by this new social radicalism.[40] Missionaries, both in Europe and across the Atlantic, employed the specific language of "human rights," not just rights, to articulate their opposition to the slavery. Nowhere was this more evident than in early missionary literature. In a special issue of its journal, *The Anti-Slavery Examiner,* the American Antislavery Society in 1838 challenged slavery, not just in terms of Christian ethics but also as a human rights issue. This was at a time when the concept of human rights had not gained currency.[41] The journal, aptly titled "The Bible Against Slavery: An Inquiry into the Patriarchal and Mosaic Systems on the Subjugation of Human Rights," has been described as one of the strongest contemporary intellectual statements that we possess on the human rights character of antislavery.[42]

The fundamental point about the antislavery idea enunciated in missionary documents like these was that slaves, too, were endowed by God with certain inalienable rights, including those of dignity, honor, and justice. Such human rights and dignity could not be exchanged for slavery or yield to what was merely expedient and pragmatic. In fact, such rights needed to be reclaimed from the travesty of slavery and prejudice. Neither social custom nor racial argument would be allowed to jettison that central theocratic view of human freedom and personhood. Ideas like this, expressed in missionary journals from Europe and America, were approvingly reproduced in the many local missionary and secular journals and magazines that were established in Nigeria from the 1880s.[43]

Long before the formal establishment of colonial rule in Nigeria, missionary ideas and activities within the antislavery movement were already articulating a language of rights and liberties that fundamentally challenged local customary orthodoxies. This ideology, which has been described as "antistructure" was what the colonial state later built upon in furtherance of its antislavery agenda.[44] The ideas propagated by Christian missionaries provided intellectual support for the antislavery movement in Nigeria, where the colonial administration abolished slavery by the Slave Dealing Proclamation of 1901.[45] This proclamation abolished the legal status of slavery in Southern Nigeria, prohibiting all forms of slave dealing—trading in, selling, bartering, and transferring persons to be treated as slaves. The proclamation also invalidated all slave-dealing contracts and prescribed severe penalties for persons contravening the proclamation. "Native Courts" were expected to enforce the abolition but only where specific cases of slave dealing were brought before them.[46] This law followed the British model in India—slave dealing was outlawed and slavery was not legally recognized, but slaves were left to themselves to claim their freedom.[47]

Colonial authorities presented these antislavery laws and Britain's role in the abolition of the slave trade as evidence of the inherent goodness of her liberal traditions and her concern for the basic rights and freedoms of native peoples. They deliberately sought to legitimize colonial rule in terms of Britain's later abolitionist role rather than her active slave trading for more than half a century. The effort to define British imperial enterprise more by abolition than her legacy of slave trading was evident in an address by Governor Hugh Clifford to the schoolchildren of Lagos to mark Empire Day in 1920:

> Just as Britain had been the first of the European nations to realize and to recognize the rights of the native populations of the non-European world to equitable treatment and to claim due respect for their actions and susceptibilities . . . so now she resolved that no consideration of material gain or advantage, no dread of financial ruin, no fear of the powerful interests she was assailing, should induce her to consent to the perpetuation of systems of which her national conscience disapproved. Had she willed otherwise, there was no force in existence that could have compelled her to take the course she now voluntarily adopted. Her position as the greatest maritime power in the world was impregnable; without the aid of her navy, the [slave] trade would never have been effectively suppressed, and the general opinion in Europe was by no means strongly in favour of suppression. MIGHT was hers, and she was free to make of it what she would. She elected to employ it in the course of RIGHT—to use it, in fact, in the only manner wherein MIGHT can find its justification.[48]

This kind of rhetoric was not peculiar to colonial officials. The libertarian ideas that were believed to underscore British antislavery laws and policies were also discussed in the secular press in Lagos and other parts of Western Nigeria from the

1880s. British antislavery policies at the end of the nineteenth century represented, for many Africans, the clearest indications of Britain's commitment to protecting the rights and liberties of its "native" subjects. The *Lagos Times* in an editorial in 1882 linked Britain's antislavery position to its traditions of freedom and liberty. "Britain is a free country," it stated. "In her, personal liberty is sacred and no person's rights, however humble, can be violated with impunity. Her flag is everywhere a sign of, and guarantee of, liberty.[49]

In fact, the British control of much of Nigeria at the beginning of the twentieth century was no immediate guarantee of liberty for all. Although slavery had declined considerably by the mid-1920s, debt-slavery, or pawnship, still existed in many parts of Western Nigeria where there remained considerable local opposition by local chiefs and slave-owning classes to colonial attempts at ending the practice.[50] The desire of some local elites to hold on to their slave "possessions" drew condemnation from others who saw it as hypocritical for some privileged Africans to deny to other Africans the rights and liberties that they themselves enjoyed as British subjects. In one such critique the *Lagos Times* noted: "love and desire for slave holding have not died in us as a people, even though we pride ourselves in our own personal freedom and rejoice in the Christian name."[51] The paper stated that among the elites there had been no popular feeling against slavery and pawnship but, rather, a disposition to "treat it lightly, speak of it as indispensable to native life and excuse the guilty."[52] What the paper found most objectionable was the fact that some "liberated Africans" and their children who had been taught in Christian schools and had "found protection in the Christian name" were involved in slave trading and slave holding.[53]

Much of the antislavery debates were also underscored by disagreements over the extent of rights and liberties that domestic slaves and pawns enjoyed in African society. Some Africans and Europeans did not subscribe to the view, presented by the abolitionists, that under indigenous systems, slaves and pawns had no rights or liberties.[54] There was a longstanding position among the Yoruba elite and cultural nationalists that slavery and pawnship were benevolent social institutions for recruiting labor and assisting the needy. The

Yoruba historian Samuel Johnson opposed slavery but de-
fended the institution of pawnship from a cultural-nationalist
perspective as a respectable indigenous institution that should
be preserved.[55] Colonial officials also disagreed over pawnship
and slavery.[56]

The attempts to distinguish between slavery and pawnship as grounds for tolerating the latter centered on the rights
that pawns, as opposed to slaves, supposedly enjoyed. Johnson, in particular, stressed that freeborn pawns (as distinct
from slave pawns) did not lose their rights and privileges as
free members of the community.[57] Nineteenth-century European missionaries in Yorubaland made similar distinctions.
They argued that there were important differences between
pawns and slaves with regard to the limits of rights, which
they enjoyed. Slaves were largely denied the right to participate in certain organizations and could be alienated from the
community at the discretion of their masters. Pawns, in contrast, were not aliens to their community. They retained their
independence and political rights, while slaves lost both. It
has been suggested that missionaries made an uneasy peace
with pawnship in Yorubaland because it was virtually impossible to obtain free labor. They utilized pawnship to obtain
both labor and converts. Missionaries themselves rationalized
their positions by arguing that they had few choices in a society that looked down on wage labor.[58]

These views were largely shared by colonial officials who
made similar distinctions between pawns and slaves based on
differences in the scope of their rights. One official report
stated: "An '*Iwofa*' or 'pawn' is a free man; his social status remains the same; his civil and political rights are intact, and he
is only subject to his master in the general sense that 'a bor-
rower is servant to the lender.'"[59] Ross, the Resident of Oyo
Province, believed that there was no stigma attached to pawnship and that a pawn was a "perfectly free agent, at liberty to
regulate his own life and to follow his own pursuits when the
daily task set by his master is over."[60]

These idealized accounts clearly masked some of the more
exploitative features of pawnship. Historical evidence shows
that in many African societies pawns were denied the most
basic social and economic liberties.[61] Yet, based on the flawed

premise that pawns were distinct from slaves in terms of the rights they presumably enjoyed, colonial officials tolerated the widespread institution of pawnship and other forms of "non-slave servitude" in many parts of Nigeria until the late 1930s. In the debates over slavery and pawnship, we see how the interests of both the state and some Africans converged to shape the rights discourse and legitimize colonial policy. This debate foreshadowed the African rights/universal rights debate of the later twentieth century. While some claimed that an African conception of ethical behavior could include pawnship and other "benign forms of servitude," others saw slavery and all forms of servitude in universal terms and argued that they were unacceptable. This trend characterized other discussions about rights and liberties in Nigeria as evident in the debate over the Native House Rule.

The "Native House Rule" Debate

Two pieces of colonial legislation introduced in 1901—the Native House Rule Proclamation (later Ordinance) and the Master and Servants Proclamation—further illustrate the different ways in which the language of rights was deployed in the context of the antislavery movement. The Native House Rule Proclamation, which came onto operation in January 1902, simultaneously with the abolition of slave dealing in Southern Nigeria, was essentially a compromise between slavery and free labor. It was intended to regulate the house system of the Niger Delta communities—an indigenous social system founded on a hierarchy of house heads, slaves, and servants.[62] The law specified the reciprocal duties and obligations that the house head and members owed each other under native law and custom. The ostensible object of the law was to protect the basic rights of servants from being abused by their masters under the house system.[63] By recognizing and regulating this form of unfree labor, the law was intended to give the Protectorate of Southern Nigeria a much needed transitional arrangement until the colonial government felt able to bear the complex consequences of free labor and a free market economy.

The Native House Rule Proclamation and the Master and Servants Proclamation were widely criticized by antislavery campaigners for legitimizing indigenous forms of slavery and servitude in contradiction of Britain's declared antislavery position. The Proclamation was condemned as an official stamp of approval of customary practices of unpaid servitude given in order to appease powerful local chiefs who were partners with the colonial state under British indirect rule system of government. In a tone characteristic of such criticism, the *Nigerian Times* labeled the Proclamation the "Southern Nigeria Slavery Law."[64] Although colonial officials publicly rebuffed these criticisms, in private comments they admitted their validity. Sir Percy Anderson of the Colonial Office stated in 1911: "the effects of the House Rule Ordinance has been to render the abolition of slavery to a large extent nugatory. At best the position of a slave has been turned into that of a villein or serf."[65] The government was thus in the peculiar position of maintaining in slavery, or serfdom, a class of people whom it claimed to have freed from bondage.[66]

Much of the opposition against the Native House Rule law was articulated in the language of rights. African and European missionaries, and other opponents of the law in the colony and in Britain, saw it as a hindrance on the liberties of "native Christian converts" who were compelled to live under the House system. In 1906 the conference of Anglican Bishops and the clergy in West Africa, meeting in Lagos, forwarded a resolution against the Native House Rule law to the colonial Governor. In it they complained of injuries to "individual liberties and public morality" in the Niger Delta because house heads forbade their members from contracting marriages with persons from other houses. Later in April 1909, Bishop H. Tugwell repeated this charge when he argued that the House System curtailed among other things "liberty to marry except under grievous conditions."[67]

Strong opposition to the Native House Rule Proclamation was also voiced in Britain, particularly with reference to its implications for the rights of African Christian converts. Between 1892 and 1916 several questions were raised on the floor of the House of Commons not only about the Native House Rule Proclamation but also generally about the continued existence of slavery and pawnship in parts of Nigeria. J. King, a Member of Parliament, opposed the Native House law principally on the grounds that persons married under Christian rites had been separated against their will because of the law.[68] To the Liberal government in Britain, such allegations regarding the liberties of native Christian converts were quite serious. At a time when "commerce, Christianity, and civilization" were seen as the three cardinal objectives of the British imperial rule in Africa, official opinion was sensitive to any policy that was perceived as hindering the propagation of Christianity and civilized values in the colonies. In response to growing opposition, the colonial government first amended the Native House Rule law in 1918 and abolished it in 1920.

An important reason for the failure of the Native House Rule was the emphasis placed on the liberties of native Christian converts by missionary campaigners both locally and abroad. Underlying missionary opposition to the Native House Rule law was the assumption that African Christian converts were entitled to some rights and liberties necessary to allow them to lead proper Christian lives. Missionary campaigners worked to ensure that African converts were not encumbered by the restrictions and limitations of pagan laws and customs even where such customs had received the approval of the colonial authorities. At a time when the concern for the rights and liberties of native subjects was at best secondary to other imperial objectives, the appeal to the language of "native rights" based on their conversion to Christianity resonated powerfully, not only among missionaries but also within colonial officialdom. More so, this language appealed to ordinary Africans who began to see Christianity as a means of escaping from the restrictions imposed by unfavorable local customs and the colonial order.

Increasing pressures from missionaries, humanitarians, and parliamentarians in London prompted colonial authorities to be less tolerant of indigenous forms of servitude. By the 1930s, official toleration of the institution of pawnship shifted. Colonial officials, at least at the central level, became less inclined to present it as a benign "traditional" institution and began to extend the language of rights and liberty, once restricted to slavery, also to the discussion on pawnship. In 1938, the government in Lagos issued a proclamation prohibiting pawnship, describing it as a violation of personal

liberty.[69] Although laws like these did not immediately or totally eradicate the practice of slavery and pawnship in Western Nigeria—and some have argued that they were never
really intended to—they provided new opportunities within
the colonial legal system for people in positions of forced servitude to seek redress using the law and the language of rights
underlying it. For instance, empowered by the Slave Abolition
Ordinances, ordinary people caught in customary master-ser-
vant relations began to articulate their demand for freedom
increasingly in the language of rights and liberty. In a petition
against the *Oba* (King) of Benin to the local colonial official,
one African petitioner complained that he had been taken,
along with his wife and five children, as slaves by the king,
contrary to the law against slavery "which gave freedom and
liberty to all His Majesty's subjects."[70]

In sum, it could be said that early discussions about "native
rights" by missionaries and humanitarians in Western Nigeria
progressed along two distinct yet related lines. On one hand,
both missionary and humanitarian campaigns, as part of the
broad process of social restructuring under colonial rule, facilitated the breakdown of some African customs and forged in
their stead new notions and regimes of individual rights and
liberties. This was particularly true of missionary and humanitarian activities in the antislavery movement. However, while
missionaries employed a language of rights that tended to be restrictive and centered on conversion to Christianity, humanitarians employed a more secular and inclusive notion of rights.

At individual levels, missionary discourses about the
rights of African Christian converts provided an alternative
framework for overcoming the limitations on individual freedoms imposed by both traditional practices and the colonial
order. This alternative framework of rights founded on
Christian humanism offered rights to Africans primarily on
the basis of their conversion to Christianity. Such rights as
the freedom to marry outside the restrictions of custom, and
the freedom of movement and worship, were thought necessary to allow the native convert to lead full Christian lives
free from the constraints of pagan traditions. It would be
wrong to assume that in advocating certain rights for African
converts European Christian missionaries were demanding,

or even intended, that these converts should enjoy the full complement of rights and freedoms of Englishmen.[71] Rather, it would appear that the notion and language of rights they employed in relation to "native converts" was more in line with the ideas of the nineteenth-century ethnologist Mary Kingsley who argued that Africans were entitled to certain fundamental rights and liberties that they could exercise within their "racial" limits.[72] The significant qualification of the scope of rights to which Africans were entitled was race. But although missionary rights discourse was restricted by religion and race to certain categories of persons, it nonetheless represented a new vision of the range of rights and liberties that could ultimately be extended to everyone.

In challenging the power of local chiefs and elites who opposed complete abolition, and advocating a more liberal society that included slaves and social outcasts, missionary and colonial activities represented a disruption of the existing social order and sense of rights. With the antislavery campaign, something new and permanent was attempted in African societies, and this represented a significant break with the old political morality. As Lamin Sanneh has argued, antislavery was "antistructural" because it countered and broke down customary moral orthodoxies.[73] Antislavery did not guarantee freedom for everyone, and it sometimes even created new orthodoxies that took on elements of older oppressive structures. However, the success of antislavery was "antistructure" in that it provided new opportunities to former slaves and those most at risk to escape from old, structural constraints. It was the ethics of a second chance for such former slaves and the stress put on individual responsibility and equality before the law that gave antislavery its antistructural force and transformative power. The language of rights and liberty in which antislavery was articulated and with which it was legitimized was central to its transformative power. This is because it provided a language that subaltern groups could subsequently use to oppose and challenge prevailing social and political dogmas within and beyond antislavery.

Yet, the use of the rhetoric of rights and liberties was not limited to the antislavery movement, missionaries, and humanitarians. For the colonial state, the language of rights also proved effective for promoting specific political and social agendas. For one, it reinforced the oft-declared social obligation of the British to the "native races of the colony"—the obligation to bring civilization and enlightened government to them, to protect them in "the free enjoyment of their possessions," and to "restrain all injustice which may be practiced or attempted against them."[74] Nowhere was such paternalistic language more evident and contested than within the colonial legal system.

3

Stronger than the Maxim Gun

Law, Rights, and Justice

"Native Rights" and the Colonial Legal System

The colonial legal system was an effective instrument for fostering colonial hegemony and guaranteeing the maintenance of social order on a scale conducive to imperial interests. The discourse of rights was particularly influential in this regard. Rights talk, within the context of the colonial legal system, was one of the many discourses employed by the colonial state to rationalize and legitimize empire. But it also provided Africans with a means of articulating and promoting their interests within colonial society. Law, and the discourse of rights associated with it, was a double-edged sword. On one hand, it was a devastating weapon of conquest like no other in its capacity to repress and dispossess without being seen as doing anything at all. On the other hand, it provided the dispossessed with a means that could be used for self-protection even if not always successfully.[1] The discussion here examines the tensions and contradictions in the use of law as an instrument of coercion to consolidate British control in western Nigeria and the legitimizing rhetoric of rights, liberty, and social justice underlying this process. It probes the

circumstances that made the rhetoric of legal rights imperative for both the colonial state that employed it to legitimize
empire and African elites who subsequently appropriated it to
strengthen nationalist demands. The object is not so much to
underscore how the colonial state in Africa fell short of its
own liberal agenda—a task that others have adequately
addressed—but to examine the appeal of the language of
rights employed within this agenda and the conditions that
made it so central to the colonial project.

Although no explicit legal instruments specifically bound
British authorities to the protection of individual rights and
liberties in Nigeria, British officials generally assumed that
imperial rule was to be guided by a consideration for the basic
worth and human dignity of the colonial subject. From as
early as 1886, the social obligation of the British colonial government was made clear in several official documents ema-
nating from both the Colonial Office in London and the
various colonial administrative regimes in Nigeria. These documents included letter patent, and royal instructions issued
in 1886 and 1906. In these instructions, the British government spelled out the ostensible function of the government toward the people in the territory. This was, in part, to promote
religion and education among the native inhabitants of the
colony, to protect them in the free enjoyment of their possessions, and to "prevent and restrain all violence and injustice
which may be practiced or attempted against them."[2]

There were also similar commitments to promote equality
and fairness in dealings with "native subjects." The *Royal
Proclamation* issued in 1843 to the "African subjects of Her
Majesty Queen Victoria" promised "equality of opportunity for
selection to, and employment in, positions of profit and honor
within the British Empire, according to their loyalty, integrity
and ability without any reference whatsoever to ethnological
origin or religious creed or persuasion."[3] Although these proclamations and instructions effectively gave colonial officials wide
powers to intervene in various aspects of the social life of the
people, it also bound them morally, if not legally, to the local
protection and promotion of certain basic rights and liberties.
These aspirations were expected to guide colonial laws and
general social policy toward colonized Africans. In practice,

however, law was used more effectively as an instrument for consolidating colonial rule rather than protecting the people.

While coercion played a crucial role in Britain's conquest of Nigeria as in other parts of Africa, law clearly proved a more effective means of colonial administrative control. Force could weaken the will of the conquered peoples, but it could not make colonial rule endure. By the 1920s, the system of military conquest and repression had largely succeeded and the British authorities moved from military to civilian forms of rule. This process of consolidating and stabilizing colonial rule was founded on law and, specifically, the English legal system. Law, in the form of ordinances and proclamations administered through British-style colonial courts, became the basis for promoting British hegemony in the colony. In the hands of the British colonial administration, law was a veritable tool, stronger in many ways than the Maxim gun.[4]

Law in the management of change in colonial Nigeria took the form of local statutes. Statutes were enacted to serve a variety of purposes: to complete the process of "pacification" of the country; to secure administrative control of the country's economic resources; to ensure orderly exploitation of the country's mineral resources; to acquire land for public use; to fight fraudulent commercial practices capable of undermining the economic interests of the colonial government; to stamp out indigenous customary practices considered repugnant to European civilization; or even to deliberately implant new patterns of social behavior.[5] However, law was more than just a tool of colonial administrative control. Law also became, as several studies have shown, an arena in which Africans and Europeans engaged one another—a "battleground" on which they contested access to resources and labor, relationships of power and authority, and interpretations of morality and culture.[6] In the process, local people encountered the realities of colonialism and both they and the Europeans shaped the laws and institutions, relationships, and processes of the colonial period itself. Though engineered by colonial officials, the impact of law within the colonial state was all-embracing. Europeans used law to promote colonial hegemony; Africans used it as a resource in struggles against Europeans, and since Africans met one another in the legal battlefield far more often than they met Europeans, law also became central to the struggles amongst Africans.[7]

The British colonial legal agenda in Africa was well articulated. From as early as 1843, the *Foreign Jurisdiction Act* empowered British officials in Africa to establish legal institutions and make laws for the peace, order, and good government of the British and "those in commercial relations with them." The emphasis on commercial relations indicates the primary rationale of the Act. Law and British legal institutions were conceived as a means of realizing imperial political control and economic ambitions above anything else. The first British consuls in Nigeria carried out administration and judicial functions on the basis of this and similar laws. The first sets of ordinances and proclamations introduced were primarily directed at regulating trade and facilitating administrative control.

By the 1900s, however, the colonial legal agenda had moved beyond trade and politics to embrace social concerns. In 1900, further proclamations introduced an extensive regime of English laws and set up an English-style legal system in the newly created Southern Nigerian Protectorate. These laws formed the basis of the colonial legal system when British rule was eventually imposed throughout the country. Consequently, the sovereignty of many indigenous African states and societies became legally vested in the British crown although earlier military conquests had, in fact, made this a fait accompli. The primary objective of the colonial legal system at this stage was to serve the dual purpose of forging formal relations between the British and local peoples, on one hand, and extending British political and economic influence, on the other.

The Repugnancy Doctrine

Until the introduction of a bill of rights into the independence constitution in 1957, the main legal instrument with which the Nigerian colonial state sought to promote individual rights and liberties was the repugnancy doctrine. Although initially intended to ensure that indigenous customary rules applied in the colonial courts conformed to a certain standard of "natural morality and humanity," its application generated extensive

debates about the implications of indigenous customary practices for the promotion of individual rights and liberties. The
application of the repugnancy doctrine also raised questions
about the merits and demerits of colonial attempts to mediate
customary law with an overriding concern for European standards of morality and justice. The colonial attack on ordeals
fundamentally influenced British thinking about the nature
of African law. From their earliest contacts with Africans,
British officials campaigned against ordeals as part of their
effort to restrain parts of indigenous law they considered
"repugnant." Trials by ordeal, which had been common in
Europe until the thirteenth century, were believed to reflect
an early and primitive phase in the evolution of law. To continue to permit ordeal even within the general orbit of customary law, argued British administrators and jurists, would
be to sanction a regressive and primitive kind of law.

For these reasons, the legal system introduced by Britain
was clearly patterned along English lines. The Supreme Court
Ordinance declared that English common law, the doctrines of
equity, and the "statutes of general application" in England
were also be applicable in the colony. Local customs and traditions were, however, allowed to exist side by side with the
imported English legal system only if they met the "repugnancy test." This meant that such customs must not be "repugnant to natural justice, equity and good conscience" or
incompatible with any enactment of the colonial legislature.
The repugnancy doctrine as first introduced by the Supreme
Court Ordinance No. 4 of 1876 was intended to regulate local
customary laws and practices, which under the prevailing
legal system, operated alongside the imported English legal
system. Section 19 of the ordinance proclaimed:

> Nothing in this Ordinance shall deprive . . . any person of the
> benefit of any law or custom existing in the colony . . . such law
> or custom not being *repugnant to natural justice, equity and
> good conscience*, nor incompatible either directly or necessary
> implication with any enactment of the colonial legislature. . . .[8]

The ostensible idea behind the repugnancy doctrine was
to extend to the colony the same standards of law, rights, and

justice as prevailed in England. The doctrine was justified on the grounds that it would eradicate "barbarous," unfair, or unjust customs. On the basis of the repugnancy doctrine, the colonial courts were able to whittle off rules of customary law that had been judged "uncivilized" or "inhuman," according to prevailing British standards and values. One of the earliest and most prominent cases that applied the doctrine of repugnancy was the case of *Eshugbayi Eleko v. The Officer Administering the Government of Nigeria,* in which one of the questions which arose for determination was whether the court could allow a milder version of an alleged custom that required the killing of a deposed chief.[9] In rejecting this application, the Privy Council sitting in London held that the court could not itself transform a barbarous custom into a milder one. It had to be completely rejected as repugnant to natural justice, equity, and good conscience.[10]

This ruling is in many ways typical of colonial attitudes toward indigenous customary practices that did not conform to the applicable English legal standards. Once such customary traditions were labeled barbaric, they were rejected in their entirety. No allowance was made for their reform or modification within the colonial legal system. Many African practices failed the repugnancy test, and British officials decided such cases on the basis of their own notions of rights and justice. Even when local practices were not deemed repugnant, magistrates and judges often misunderstood indigenous law, upholding in the name of custom, practices that were not customary at all. The repugnancy doctrine coupled with the unfamiliarity of British officials with local property, labor, gender, and power relations created opportunities for litigants with assess to the colonial legal system to present local customs as they wanted them to be.[11]

Contemporary scholars are divided in their appraisal of the repugnancy doctrine. While some have interpreted it as a ploy by the colonial regime to subjugate indigenous culture and customary rules to English law, others see it as a reformatory legal doctrine. The subjugation theorists argue that the repugnancy doctrine, for all practical purposes, meant the subordination of African law and traditions to the English model. They assert the inherent subjectivity in determining what is "repugnant to natural justice, equity and good conscience" by officials who were unfamiliar with local customs in multi-ethnic African settings with varying perceptions of justice and morality.[12] Other scholars argue that the repugnancy doctrine served to civilize some obnoxious and barbarous African customary rules.[13]

While it is true that the repugnancy doctrine tended to undermine indigenous customary law and perhaps even distort its development, it also reformed certain aspects of indigenous customary practices. For instance, it became a useful principle with which the colonial authorities, through the courts, abrogated customary rules relating to slavery, human sacrifice, trials by ordeal, and even inheritance rights and child custody. In this context, the repugnancy doctrine became an important part of the discussions about rights within the colonial legal system. Colonial records and the *Nigeria Law Reports* are replete with cases where the repugnancy doctrine was applied. Perhaps the most controversial of these was the celebrated case of *Ekpenyong Edet v. Nyon Essien* in 1932.[14] In this case, the court held that it was repugnant to natural justice and equity for a man to lay claim to the biological child of another man simply because his bride wealth on the woman bearing the child had not been repaid.[15]

The facts of this case are instructive. At issue was whether the Defendant-Appellant could sustain his assertion of rights over the children of a woman to whom he had been married. The Appellant's argued that he had a customary right over the children in question because he had not been reimbursed for his bride wealth as required by customary law. The grounds for this claim were based solely on custom. Marriages in the Ibibio-Efik tradition of the litigants, as with many other ethnic groups in Nigeria, are solemnized through the payment of bride wealth. Generally, this payment creates significant proprietary interests, one of which gives the payer a superior claim over any child of the payee-bride. The custom assumes that it is irrelevant whether the bride wealth payer is the biological father. To circumvent this dilemma, the marriage had to be severed prior to the birth of a child through the repayment of the bride wealth. Because this had not been done, the Appellant claimed legal right over the children in question.[16] The court disagreed with this claim on the grounds that a custom that vests the paternity rights of a biological father on someone else is "repugnant." By this verdict the colonial courts abrogated, on the basis of the repugnancy doctrine, a prevalent customary rule that privileged bride wealth payment as the crucial determinant of paternity rights.

What is significant about this case for the purpose of our discussion is the way in which the Defendant-Appellant, through his legal representatives, articulated his customary entitlements in the language of rights. The Appellant's Statement of Claims contained several references to his "customary and traditional rights" over the child in question, which he prayed the court to uphold.[17] The language of rights had clearly become the language of choice even for making customary claims before colonial courts. The unfamiliarity of British officials with local property, gender, and power relations sometimes created opportunities for litigants in colonial courts to present local customs as they wanted them to be. One way of doing so was by articulating supposedly customary claims in the language of legal rights to which the courts were more likely to pay attention. The general assumption was that the courts were more favorably disposed to upholding claims based on English-style legal rights than those based on customary tradition. It is arguable that under precolonial African adjudicative systems, customary entitlements such as those over children in the case of *Edet v. Essien* were not conceived strictly in terms of enforceable legal rights as they later came to be argued in the colonial courts. In precolonial contexts, such claims may have been mediated by other social and moral considerations. This, however, is only conjectural and the true position is one that only detailed research into precolonial social systems and notions of rights will reveal.

The case of *Edet v. Essien* generated much debate over the effects of the colonial legal system on indigenous African regimes of rights and justice. Some sections of the local African press strongly criticized the verdict, seeing it as yet another example of the "insensitivity of the [colonial] courts towards African social values and moral safeguards."[18] Newspapers ran lengthy editorials criticizing the verdict and analyzing its "disruptive" implications for African social traditions. A few colonial officials also quietly expressed reservations about court decisions that tended to abrogate, in one stroke, widely accepted and longstanding "native" customs.

In contrast, other Africans such as the appellant in the case of *Edet v. Essien*, clearly welcomed the repugnancy doctrine and successfully used it to challenge upper-class African men and unfavorable customary practices. Most colonial officials also welcomed the verdict. To them, this was precisely the justification for the repugnancy doctrine—to whittle off "uncivilized" customary practices that violated individual rights and personal liberties. The case even formed the subject matter of a government memorandum that urged colonial administrators to be guided by the view of the court when dealing with similar cases relating to "abhorrent" African customs.[19] Ultimately, the repugnancy doctrine provided colonial authorities with one of the most effective legal instruments for their agenda of the social reengineering of African societies under the rubric of promoting native rights and liberties.

Legal Codification and Debates over Rights

Between 1900 and 1920, the colonial government in Nigeria promulgated a wide range of laws in the form of ordinances and proclamations to regulate almost every aspect of social and economic life. So widespread was the use of colonial laws that one local newspaper complained in 1911 that the country had become an "ordinance ridden colony."[20] Colonial officials seem to have been driven by a belief that law was the most effective means of administrative control and maintaining social order. The quest to assert imperial political and economic control circumscribed some of the liberties Africans traditionally enjoyed even as it introduced new regimes of codified rights patterned along the British model. The doctrine of indirect rule; the arbitrary circumscription of the powers of traditional rulers; the creation of special courts to administer unwritten customary laws and administrative orders; the exercise of the powers of political detention and deportation; and the use of laws of sedition and censorship (framed more widely than in England), all furthered British colonial hegemony but also had profound implications for the conditions of rights and liberties in the colony.

Typical of the laws introduced to further British administrative control were special ordinances passed in 1912 by the
administration of Gov. Walter Egerton in Southern Nigeria.
This series of coercive legislation included the Collective Punishment Ordinance, the Unsettled District Ordinance, the
Peace Preservation Ordinance, and the Deposed Chief Removal Ordinance. Designed primarily for British imperial administrative convenience, these ordinances significantly
affected the rights and liberties of local peoples. Measured
against the acclaimed English legal principles of "natural justice, equity and good conscience," the derogations from basic
individual and communal rights, which these ordinances im-
plied, become even more obvious. The consequences for peace
and social order were also quite significant.

Interestingly, in their opposition to these coercive laws,
African elites employed the same rhetoric of rights and liberties that the colonial authorities found so appealing in other
contexts. However, the language of rights as employed by
African elites who dominated public debates was not merely a
form of oppositional discourse. As it was to the colonial authorities in rationalizing empire, the language of rights along
with those of "self-determination" and "development" became
powerful tools for the nationalist cause. Rights talk resonated
not only in the tensions between colonizers and colonized but
also in struggles amongst African elites. Rights language was
deployed by elites in internal class struggles for political dominance and to empower themselves over other elites.

In the period between 1912 and 1920, the Collective Punishment Ordinance had widespread impact on individual
rights in the colony. Since most ordinances and proclamations
were introduced mainly to aid British administrative control,
the colonial regime, especially in the earlier years of colonial
rule, found it unnecessary to distinguish between individual
and collective responsibility for crimes and misdemeanors. By
the provisions of the Collective Punishment Ordinance, the
government legalized the practice—already widespread in the
colony—where such offences as murder and arson were treated
as the collective crimes of the entire community when individual offenders could not be identified or apprehended.[21] Under
this law colonial officials could impose fines on towns, villages,

and other communities for homicide and other crimes necessitating the use of soldiers or police. Although the Governor was obliged to conduct an inquiry before imposing collective punishments and to report them to the Secretary of State for Colonies, local officials sometimes administered collective punishments arbitrarily, and such cases were rarely reported. The law also disallowed legal appeals against orders made under this ordinance, thereby ousting the jurisdiction of both the colonial District and Native Courts from entertaining any litigation arising from its provisions.[22]

Colonial officials justified the collective punishment law on the grounds that it was founded on existing local African traditions of collective rights and communal responsibilities. "The idea of the whole family suffering for the crime of one of its members," noted one colonial official, "was probably the strongest deterrent in native communities."[23] However, in spite of attempts to rationalize the practice, its implications for individual rights and social justice were neither lost on colonial officials nor the local people. The practice of punishing whole villages for the isolated offenses of individuals acting alone, and the outright denial of any form of legal redress against such punishments, clearly contradicted the English common law principle of individual responsibility for criminal liability—a principle that was assumed to be applicable to colonial subjects by virtue of the extension of the English legal system to the colony. Here, as in other aspects of the colonial legal system, African subjects in the colony were subjected to the same lower standard of English law as "protected persons" in the protectorates even though, in theory, subjects were entitled to the same rights as Englishmen.

Colonial records, particularly the Native Court records, are replete with cases of collective punishment administered under the Collective Punishment Ordinance. For colonial officials, the ordinance provided an effective way for checking rising incidents of crime and social banditry as well as for dealing with conflicts between communities. In the most "troubled villages," judicial proceedings were held under the Collective Punishment Ordinance. Fines in cash, produce, and labor were levied, and communities were forced to construct roads as punishment.[24] Local chiefs and village heads were required to facilitate the collection of group fines or co-ordinate the undertaking of collective labor imposed on communities as punishment under the ordinance. In one case the entire population of Evureni in Warri Province was punished through compulsory fines and labor for social disturbances there in 1925.[25] Affrays between the people of Ondo Province in the late 1920s were also punished under the Collective Punishment Ordinance.[26]

The Unsettled District Ordinance of 1912 had similar implications. Under the provisions of this ordinance, the colonial government reserved for itself the powers to arrest and punish persons charged with being of "undesirable character and reputation," although no specific criteria for being undesirable were spelled out.[27] That decision lay entirely at the discretion of each administrative officer. Such wide and unquestioned discretionary power in the hands of local colonial administrators was a prescription for abuse. Given the type of cases that were subsequently dealt with under this ordinance, it became obvious that the Unsettled District Ordinance was aimed against the activities of the educated African elites, especially the new class of African lawyers who were wont to engage the colonial administration in disputes and litigations over land and commerce. In the words of one colonial report, the ordinance was aimed at getting rid of "objectionable persons trading in the unsettled districts of the interior."[28] Gov. Walter Egerton specifically made it clear that the ordinance was desired to prohibit from all unsettled districts such "aliens" as the "black lawyer" and the "Lagos agitator."[29]

The Unsettled District Ordinance made it possible for parts of Southern Nigeria to be declared Unsettled Districts in 1913. Thereafter, the government had the power to prohibit any "non-natives" or "aliens" from entering or re-entering the districts. The penalties for breach included a fine, imprisonment, or deportation. The Unsettled District Ordinance effectively constrained local African enterprise and political activism through restrictions on free movement and expression. This particularly affected the growing class of educated Africans in Lagos, Calabar, and other urban centers in Southern Nigeria where the colonial authorities encountered the stiffest opposition.

Like the Unsettled District Ordinance, the Peace Preservation Ordinance gave the Governor powers to declare any part of the Eastern and Central Provinces of Nigeria a "disturbed district." Following such a declaration, people in the affected areas could be arbitrarily searched and arrested with or without a warrant, for possessing arms and ammunitions. Within a "disturbed or unsettled district," the district commissioner exercised almost unlimited powers. He could detain any person involved in a civil disturbance for one year and impose fines of up to £1000 on anyone involved in a civil disturbance.[30]

These coercive ordinances targeted not only educated African elites but also some of the more influential traditional African rulers from whom the colonial authorities could expect serious opposition. The laws that dealt with such sensitive political matters were absolute and authoritarian in their construction and clearly contradicted the rhetoric of native rights and liberties that dominated colonial legal discourse. The Deposed Chiefs Removal Ordinance of 1917 (amended in 1925) and the Deportation Ordinance of 1939, for example, authorized the Governor to order that any deposed chief should "leave the area over which he exercised jurisdiction or influence and other specified parts of Nigeria." In fact, these ordinances merely gave a stamp of legality to what had become a common practice of the colonial government in its dealings with uncooperative and recalcitrant Africans.

The Deposed Chiefs Removal Ordinance punished chiefs and village headmen who disobeyed administrative orders with imprisonment and subsequent deportation to wherever the Governor wished.[31] Because these orders could not be appealed, they became instruments for the colonial authority to foster indirect rule and consolidate administrative control over many parts of Nigeria. These ordinances provided the basis for the deposition of Mohammed Yaji, the serki of Madagali District of Adamawa Province in 1929, and the celebrated case of Prince Eshugbayi Eleko, the head of the House of Docemo in Lagos in 1917.[32]

These coercive laws soon became the focus of attack by African critics of the colonial regime. They were seen as infringements of the rights and liberties of Africans and a contradiction of declared British imperial objectives. Driven by intense dislike of the indirect rule system and the Native Authorities established by the colonial administration, these ordinances became the focal points of elite demands for government reform. One newspaper called for a repeal of the Deportation Ordinance starting "its provisions are capable of being used to jeopardize the liberty of any person who is a marked man in any section of Nigeria."[33]

The Deposition of Chief Ordinance was particularly attacked by educated elites because of the limitations and distortions, which, in their view, it imposed on the political rights of traditional African rulers and institutions of governance. Local opposition against the ordinance stemmed specifically from the all-embracing manner in which it was written, which conveyed the impression that the Governor had the powers of an absolute dictator vis-à-vis the chiefs.[34] The educated Africans cited the ordinance as proof that the whole Native Authority system and, indeed, indirect rule was a sham in which the chiefs did not truly represent the people but merely acted as servants of the government. Concerns about the implications of the Chiefs Deposition Ordinance on the rights of local people were also voiced at the House of Commons in London. Some Members of Parliament were concerned that the Deposition of Chiefs Ordinance did not provide Africans with the right of appeal before colonial courts.[35]

Paradoxically, however, while Western educated African elites were quick to denounce laws like the Deposition of Chief Ordinance as infringements on the political rights of traditional rulers, they were, themselves, unwilling to be subjected to the authority of the chiefs whose political rights they sought to protect. In 1906 the colonial government passed the Native Court Proclamation, which extended the powers of Native Courts headed by local chiefs to include jurisdiction over cases involving "native foreigners."[36] These native foreigners, who included returnee slaves, Liberian and Sierra Leonean émigrés, constituted the bulk of the new class of educated Africans elites. These elites forcefully opposed being under the jurisdiction of the Native Courts. They petitioned the Secretary of State in London that they be excluded from the provisions of the Native Court Proclamation.

The elites' criticism was based on two principal grounds. First, they contended that the African laws and customs that would apply to them under native law were uncertain and unwritten; that the members of the Native Courts were illiterate; and that there were serious differences in language and beliefs between them and the "aboriginal natives." Second, they held that in the Native Courts, litigants generally had no right of choosing the court members who decided their cases. They argued that the court members took no legal oaths and, as such, they feared the development of irregular proceedings.[37] In short, they argued that the authority of the Native Courts would violate their rights as British subjects. This was part of the intra-African struggle by local elites to consolidate the powers of their spheres using the language of rights.

Similarly, although most educated Africans in the coastal capital city of Lagos supported the system of Native Administration in the interior provinces, they strongly objected to colonial attempts to extend the system to their domain in Lagos on the grounds that this would interfere with their rights as "British subjects."[38] But, ironically, at the same time, Lagos-based African barristers were protesting their exclusion as counsels from the Native Court system as a restriction on their rights to practice their professions.[39] It would seem the elites wanted the best of both worlds. They did not want to be subjected to the "Native" authority of traditional chiefs (whose political rights they often championed) on the grounds that it would interfere with their rights as British subjects. Yet, they demanded their "right" as Africans to participate in running this "Native" administration.

We see at play here three levels of rights discourses deployed by African elites—first, the talk concerning the political rights of chiefly authorities; second, the talk about their rights as British subjects; and third, the talk about their right to participation as Africans. Thus, the language of rights that the educated elites employed in opposing the colonial state and advocating for the political rights of traditional rulers was also easily deployed to promote their own class interests where they conflicted with those of other groups of Africans.

This paradox was not restricted to the rights discourse. The educated community in Nigeria stood between the two worlds of European and African culture, seeking to define itself within an emergent Nigerian society. Nigerian elites were not intent on reproducing Victorian society but wanted to use its discourses to meet their own ends. They were operating in a very competitive and changing society in which variable identities could be useful. For example, when politicking in the urban centers, the Nigerian elite might invoke his rights as a "subject of her Britannic majesty" and be very English. Yet, when settling family disputes or politicking in the village, the same person might appeal to his African "customary rights." The early intelligentsia thus attempted to adapt European discourses in and about Africa to their needs, to render from imposed categories something more suited to their medial position between imperial discourse and African realities.[40] Their use of the rights discourse was one example of this.

The Press and Freedom of Expression

From as early as 1900, a vigorous and articulate class of educated Africans had established control of the local newspaper press. These Africans, mainly immigrants from along the West African coast, wielded considerable influence in the country, particularly in the growing urban and commercial centers of Lagos, Calabar, and Abeokuta. By the 1930s, this group of educated Africans, mostly lawyers and doctors, had their ranks swelled by traders, skilled artisans, and other products of the missionary schools that proliferated in Southern Nigeria. For these Africans with some Western education, local newspapers provided a means to voice their opposition to the excesses of the colonial government and advance the nationalist cause. The most outstanding of these nationalist-oriented newspapers, published between 1900 and 1930, included the *Lagos Times, The Lagos Weekly Record, The Nigerian Pioneer, African Challenger, The Lagos Observer,* and *The Lagos Echo.* Of these, perhaps the most influential was the *Lagos Weekly Echo,* which was published by Liberian immigrant John Payne Jackson. The *Lagos Weekly Record* was also a determined agent in the propagation of nationalist consciousness. The major issues that attracted the paper's comments, however, were those that directly affected the elite—issues such as discrimination against Africans in the civil service, demands for more African representation in the administration of the country, and the campaign for civil and political rights of Africans.

In the early period of colonial rule, the press often supported the British administration. Many people working in the Lagos newspaper business believed that British intervention would bring significant advantage for local peoples, particularly in arbitrating the inter-group conflicts that had ravaged Yorubaland. They wanted British influence in Yorubaland to increase, believing that it would be a factor for permanent peace, as well as creating the conditions for the promotion of Christianity and Western civilization in Yorubaland. These views reflected the outlook of the educated elites who controlled the press—being products of missionary education themselves—and their aspirations for enlightened government in Nigeria. These aspirations often dovetailed with those of colonial officials. Although the early newspapers occasionally challenged colonial policies, they were almost unanimous in the opinion that British rule was a harbinger of civilization and modernization for the colony. Early newspapers such as the *Observer, Lagos Times,* and the *Lagos Weekly Record* actively advocated the expansion of British influence in Nigeria. In 1884, the *Observer* assured the British government that the "brethren on the mainland" would readily welcome their intervention.[41]

There was also the prevalent belief that, on the whole, the British fared significantly better in protecting native rights and liberties than other colonial regimes in Africa. Contrasting British colonial administration in Nigeria with the "tyranny" of the French in Porto Novo and the Germans in East Africa, the *Lagos Weekly Record* editorialized: "The English are acknowledged to be the best colonizers, and the secret of their success lies in the great consideration invariably shown by them to the people, whom they undertake to govern, affording them at the onset the full liberties and privileges of British subjects."[42]

By the 1900s, however, the placid mood of the late nineteenth century suddenly gave way to an eruption of scathing attacks. A number of factors may explain this shift. First, the cultural and anti-imperialist emphasis of the 1890s had resolved itself into more practical political agitation by the end of the century. Second, the new critical temper was an expression of the sense of frustration experienced by the educated elites in their relationship with the colonial government. The awakening anti-British mood was aggravated by the other social and economic results of British rule.[43]

Between 1910 and the outbreak of the First World War, the Nigerian press, particularly in Lagos colony, displayed an unprecedented hostility toward the colonial government. Although these newspapers enjoyed a limited readership, largely in urban centers like Lagos, Abeokuta, and Calabar, they exerted considerable influence on the policies of the colonial government and the attitudes of the growing class of literate Nigerians. The tension and hostility between the Lagos press and the colonial administration went beyond the general demands for representation in government and self rule. The educated elites (who controlled the press) were revulsed by their exclusion from government as well as by the colonial policy of dealing with traditional rulers, rather than them, as agents in the Native Authority and indirect rule systems. But, as it turned out, the contempt for the colonial administration that the newspapers demonstrated was matched by the administration's derision and hostility toward the press in particular and the elites in general. Although the attacks by the press never really posed a serious threat to the colonial government, the government realized early enough that such open attacks had the potential of stirring popular resentment and agitation that could threaten British control.

Under these circumstances, colonial officials found themselves in a dilemma—whether to suppress the press and incur the odium of attacking the British ideal of press freedom and the right to free speech, or allow unrestrained criticism and ruthlessly deal with the resultant agitation. The dangers of working against the declared ideals of free speech and press freedom were real. The notion of free speech had, by the dawn of the colonial era, been firmly entrenched in British political and legal traditions that were presumably extended to its subjects in the colony. The idea was prevalent within colonial officialdom that liberty was the source of England's greatness and that a free press was the most valuable of British privileges. These ideas, which were reinforced by the averments of eighteenth-century British liberal intellectuals, were cited by both Africans and liberal politicians in Britain, in support of press freedom in Nigeria.[44]

An important consideration that guided colonial officials on the spot in their cautious handling of the press was the ever-present concern about protecting the "good name of His Majesty's government in the colony."[45] In several memoranda colonial Governors reminded local administrative officers that in their dealings with the press, they should ensure that they do nothing to "damage and bring into disrepute, the good name of British administration in Africa."[46] Apart from the belief that a free press was necessary to achieve a "civilized" society in the colony, there was the more pragmatic viewpoint, even within official colonial circles, which saw the activities of the press not merely as a threat to the government but as one official put it, "a permissible outlet for the inevitable fumes of discontent."[47] Press freedom, it was argued, would "afford vent for the escape of the effervescence of the feelings [of the educated Africans], which if kept continually smothered, might develop into violent outbursts."[48] But although the colonial administration was cautious in its handling of the press and keen to protect its "good name," it was increasingly confronted with the challenge of maintaining a balance between upholding the ideal of free speech and accommodating the relentless attacks from the Nigerian press.

One official response to the challenge of press antagonism was the enactment in 1909 of two laws that outlined the government's strategies for curtailing the activities of the press. These were the Newspaper Ordinance of 1903 and the Seditious Offences Ordinance of 1909. Although both laws were conceived as early as 1880s, their promulgation was delayed because of the initial reluctance of the Colonial Office in London to approve them. While these ordinances did not seek outright censorship of the local press, they were intended to impose restrictions and strict regulations that would ultimately curtail press activities. In seeking the Colonial Office's approval to restrict press freedom in the colony,

High Commissioner Frederick Lugard argued that the "unrestrained licence" which the press enjoyed undermined the government's authority and had increasingly negative impacts on public order. The local newspaper press, he argued, had become too militant to be tolerated; every week, scurrilous articles full of abuse for the King's local representative were published.[49] The Seditious Offences Ordinance was expected to check this trend.

While the colonial administration sought to justify the enactment of the ordinance as an attempt to check libelous publications, local opponents of the censorship law argued that it was unnecessary because actual cases of libel in the colony had been rare. They argued that the real object of the ordinance was to restrict press freedom and limit the right to free speech. In a petition to the Governor William MacGregor against the promulgation of the ordinance, the proprietors of the Lagos newspaper press led by J.P.L Davis and Dr. J. Randle argued that in a British colony where there is no representation of the people in the administration, the press is the principal institution by means of which they are enabled to publicly express their opinions and grievances.[50] Opposition to the proposed Newspaper Ordinance was also expressed in the British Press. In an editorial in 1902, the *London Morning Leader* denounced the law as a "restriction and coercion of the press." It noted that a similar British law, the Act of George III, which required British newspapers to provide sureties of good behavior, had been considered obsolete and repealed in 1869. If such restrictive laws had been found unacceptable in Britain itself, there was no justification for introducing it in a British colony.[51]

This opposition against the Seditious Offences Ordinance was not limited to the press. The elites who controlled the Lagos press made concerted efforts to mobilize public opinion, even among the illiterate masses, in what was mainly an elite cause. In a mass protest rally against the colonial government in 1909, African newspaper proprietor Dr. John Randle urged both literate and illiterate Africans to speak up against the restrictive press laws.[52] There was a clear attempt on the part of the elites to mobilize the support of ordinary people, who had no direct stake in the matter, against a sedition bill. It was important for the elites to cultivate mass support in order to legitimize their opposition to the bill. They presented the Seditious Offences bill not just as an attack on the press but on the freedoms and liberties of all Africans. The *Lagos Standard* appealed that "no stone must be left unturned in the effort to avert the most dreadful catastrophe that has ever befallen a people."[53] In his speech at the rally, Dr. Randle conjured the imagery of slavery to stir popular opposition to the law:

> [The Sedition Ordinance] is a cruel libel on the integrity of the people of this colony to the British crown . . . It will open the floodgate of intrigue by evil disposed persons [sic] to degrade and demoralize our country . . . The only effect will be to gag the press and muzzle individuals against a fair and just criticism and *bind* the whole of the Native populations of Southern Nigeria *hand and foot,* destroying their liberties of free speech and *placing chains on their mind* and so hand them over to the despotic tyranny of the British proconsuls.[54]

However, in spite of this local opposition, the colonial government passed the Newspaper Ordinance as law in October 1903, placing a number of restrictions and administrative regulations on the publication of newspapers. This included a £250 "libel bond" that was prescribed as condition for publishing a newspaper in the colony. Since many of the early newspapers were small, privately run businesses with a limited capital base, the law made more expensive the newspaper business that had thrived in Lagos and effectively checked the tendency toward the proliferation of newspapers. The Acting Chief Justice of the colony, E. A. Speed, subsequently justified the new ordinance during the Legislative Council debates on the grounds that "it is rare to find an absolutely free press anywhere in the world."[55] Armed with press censorship and sedition laws, colonial officials successfully arrogated to themselves extensive legal powers to deal with perceived threats to law and order. On the other hand, these restrictive laws provided grounds for nationalist attacks on the government and provoked debates not only about press freedom but also generally about the limitations on rights and liberties in the colonial state.

Individual Rights and the Colonial Judicial System

As with the introduction of colonial laws, the aspiration toward protecting individual rights dominated official rhetoric
about the administration of justice in Nigeria. Colonial courts
were expected to serve no lesser function than the courts in
England. Two primary tenets of English common law were expected to guide the operation of the courts in the colony—
Nemo judex in causa sua (No one shall be judge in his own
cause) and *audi alteram partem* (hear the other side). Status
differences were not to affect the outcome of legal decisions,
and the purpose of the colonial courts was to deal with cases of
conflicts with clear-cut rights and duties established by objective investigation of only those events deemed relevant to the
pending case. Strict rules of evidence were to restrict the content of testimony that the courts could hear. Cases were to be
treated as involving a right and a wrong, with judges making
final decisions, sometime after consultation with local "experts." These principles were all elements of the modern judicial system introduced in the colony.

Several studies on law in colonial societies stress that the
European notion of justice, in which isolated cases of clear-cut
rights and duties were violated and judgments of right and
wrong were strictly enforced, simplified the complexities in
local relations.[56] Some legal scholars have argued for a distinction between African and Western European legal philosophies. They contend that in contrast to the African traditional
legal philosophy, which emphasized the maintenance of social
equilibrium rather than the rights of the individual, the European system of law and justice extolled these very rights.[57]
The concept of justice based on technical rules of law was not
in itself quite compatible with the traditional notion of justice,
which heavily hinged on moral considerations. Unlike the
English-style courts, what was sought in disputes under
traditional African jurisprudence was not the strict legal
rights of the parties but the amicable resolution of the dispute.
The duty of those who administered the law in settling disputes was to assuage injured feelings, to restore peace, and to
reach a compromise acceptable to both disputants. A litigant
came before the judge not only as a right-and-duty-bearing

persona but also as an individual involved in a complex of relationships with other persons.[58]

Although there is an ongoing debate as to how well this portrayal reflects precolonial Africans' notion of rights and justice, it was widely accepted among many Africans and European colonial officials. Colonial officials recognized that Africans did not always understand or appreciate European systems of justice. As one judge pointed out in 1906, "it is not *Law* that is required to be applied [by the courts] in Africa but *Equity:* the complex laws of England are unsuited to the primitive conditions under which people live in West Africa."[59] In recent times, the argument that traditional African systems of justice focused on compromise and reconciliation rather than retribution has been used by African leaders and intellectuals to justify the call for African countries to emphasize principles of reconciliation and restorative justice in resolving national conflicts.

In spite of the concerns about the suitability of colonial legal systems to African societies, British authorities promoted it as the best guarantee of justice and the "modern" social order for the country. The early Courts of Equity established by European merchants in the Niger Delta in the 1850s to hear cases involving commercial transactions between Europeans and Africans were based on English common law principles. Although the courts took local trading customs into account, overall their approach to law represented a shift toward Western understandings of property, contract, crime, and punishment. With the imposition of colonial rule in the 1900s, a more formal judicial system was put in place. This comprised a Supreme Court, Provincial Courts, Divisional Courts, and District Courts, which were fashioned after the British model. The Supreme Court presided over by British judges administered a blend of English common law and equity, local ordinances, and native law and custom judged not repugnant to natural justice and morality. Colonial administrative officials also presided over the District and Provincial Courts while African chiefs presided over the Native Courts patterned along customary African models. Links were provided through procedures for appeal that went from the Native Courts to the Supreme Court and sometimes to the Judicial Committee of the Privy Council sitting in London. These courts and other colonial apparatus for the administration of justice, despite their overwhelming British influence, were intended to represent a blend of both European and indigenous African standards of rights and justice.

Forming part of the Native Administration, the Native Courts were given administrative and executive powers covering a wide range of subjects. They could make rules for the "good order, peace and welfare of the inhabitants within their areas of jurisdiction."[60] As the name suggests, in creating the Native Courts, the British believed they were recreating the indigenous system of judicial organization and that the new courts would enforce native laws and customs in "the native way." However, the Native Courts did not always meet this objective. Even the term "Native Courts" was a misnomer, not only because they were creations of British proclamations but also because they were markedly different from "native" tribunals in the strict application of the term. What the Native Courts enforced was not "native law" but a mixture of European common law and customary rules.[61] Where conflicts arose between these, European ideas usually prevailed. Owing to factors such as the presidency of European officials over the courts, the prohibitive distances some people had to walk to reach the courts, and the indiscriminate grouping of diverse clans under single court jurisdiction, the Native Courts generally inspired no confidence in the people they were meant to serve.

Historians and anthropologists have also recently come to understand that what these colonial courts treated and enforced as immutable customary law was itself the product of historical struggles unfolding during the colonial period.[62] In spite of the concern with equity and natural justice, the kind of justice that these colonial courts enforced was legal justice, imbued with elements of morality but not necessarily coterminous with moral justice. For the most part, the operation of the colonial judicial system reflected inequalities in power both between colonial officials and Africans and among Africans. Inequalities in power affected the outcome of local conflicts over rules and procedures in the courts. For instance, the fact that traditional rulers served as judges in Native Courts gave them extraordinary opportunities and, in some cases, statutory authority to define and enforce rights obligations and relationships. The reliance of officials on particular individuals or groups to define tradition gave them new advantages in the competition for resources and labor, and this augmented their power.

What became evident with the operation of the Native Court system soon after its inauguration were the new powers it gave the warrant chiefs and traditional rulers who headed these courts. In the view of these chiefs and rulers who became heads of Native Courts, their new positions represented the state-sanctioned extension of their traditional powers as absolute monarchs. Under the British indirect rule system, many of these rulers suddenly found themselves presiding over Native Courts that covered areas beyond their traditional jurisdictions and areas of influence. They came to see their new positions more as opportunities for strengthening political advantage than as impartial arbiters in the administration of justice.

This became the basis of wide-scale abuse of the court system, particularly at the local level and the concern about native rights and liberties that were subsequently raised. Colonial records are replete with cases of abuse of the Native Courts and expressions of concern by colonial officials that these abuses tended to violate individual liberties and bring into disrepute the "good name of British administration in the colony."[63] One of the early issues that attracted the attention of the colonial authorities in the administration of justice and its effects on individual rights was the practice of flogging as a form of punishment.[64] Although both summary flogging and flogging as judicial punishment had been extensively used by officials in the early colonial period, the government later sought to control it, following strong criticisms from Africans and pressures from the Colonial Office as well as MPs in London.

The Lagos press was particularly forthright in its condemnation of incidents of flogging and constantly held them up as examples of poor British adminstration in the colony and insensitivity toward native rights and liberties. The newspapers published numerous cases of Africans being publicly flogged for offenses as trivial as failing to show respect in the presence of an officer or evading work. In one particularly controversial case that caught the attention of the press, Captain Huges, an administrative officer in Warri who had gained a reputation for his highhandedness, ordered that eleven Africans be flogged for alleged unwillingness to work.[65] In other reported cases, twenty young men from Agbor subdistrict were publicly flogged on the orders of the acting District Commissioner, F.O.S. Crewe-Read, for "not turning up for work," while the local chief was flogged for "not sending his people to work on the roads."[66] Nigerian lawyer Silas Dove was reported to have been publicly whipped in Onitsha in 1914 at the insistence of the administrative officer for refusing to remove his hat in the presence of the District Commissioner.[67] Although the colonial government consistently condemned these actions as "unauthorized and illegal," such incidents provoked heated debates in the Lagos press about rights and dignity of Africans under colonial rule. By the 1920s, the incidents of public flogging in the colony had become so widespread that it created concern in official quarters both locally and at the colonial office in London.[68]

Similar concerns over native rights and dignity were raised over the use of stocks for punishment and judicial sentences. The confinement in stocks as punishment for convicted offenders had been widespread in Nigeria, as in other British administered colonies, since the beginning of the nineteenth century. By 1929, that the practice had become particularly common in the Native Authority prisons in the Southern Provinces caused public concern both within and outside the colony. In November 1930, questions were raised in the House of Commons on the need to abolish stocks in Nigeria because it was inhumane and contravened the right to dignity guaranteed to all British subjects. One Member of Parliament argued, "the infliction of this kind of medieval punishment is hardly likely to add to the prestige of the British government in Nigeria."[69] Related questions were also raised about the use of chains and shackles in the colonial prison system. These questions arose against the background of growing concerns in England over the cruel and inhumane nature of the punishment. Arguments were made by the humanitarian organizations led by the London-based League Against Imperialism, as well as the Aborigines Protection Society (APS), that the use of stocks for punishment in the colony was an inhumane practice that violated human dignity and should be abolished everywhere within the British commonwealth.[70]

In the face of these criticisms, the colonial government sought to justify the punishment in stocks on the grounds that it provided one of the most effective methods of punishment and guarantee of public order available to the government. Besides, the government argued, the practice was in accordance with "native customs." One memorandum stated that the penalty is one that is specially suited to the temperament and mentality of the people and "enables a court to punish first offenders efficaciously without exposing the accused person to the contaminating influence of prison."[71] In spite of these attempts by local officials to justify the use of confinement in stock for judicial sentences, growing pressure from the local press and concerns raised in Britain ultimately forced the abolishment of the practice in 1932.

The judicial process, particularly the Native Courts, also raised concerns about native rights and social justice. Colonial officials were particularly concerned about the tendency of the Native Courts to impose harsh prison terms even in trivial cases such as civil disputes over debts. In a tour of the prisons in 1927, the Lieutenant Governor of the Southern Provinces discovered that judgment debtors accounted from between 15 and 50 percent of the inmates in many prisons.[72] This was regarded as an indication of the real dangers that abuses in the Native Courts posed to the liberties of local people.

In one case that illustrates the excesses that became characteristic of the local judicial system, one young man was convicted by a Native Court in Ijebu-Ode for possessing tools for making counterfeit currency coins. He was sentenced to twenty years imprisonment, despite the fact that the maximum sentence Native Courts could inflict was two years. This case came to public knowledge when the District Officer discovered it in the course of his routine inspection of the prisons in 1931. Alarmed by the severity of the punishment, the District Commissioner brought the case to the notice of the Governor, who ordered the prisoner's immediate release.[73] Cases like this were not uncommon, and although the colonial authorities at the central level frowned at such blatant violations of individual liberties by the Native Courts, its limited control over these courts, coupled with the fact that many local chiefs had no training on the workings of the new judicial system, resulted in widespread miscarriages of justice.

Given these and other limitations in the legal system, the colonial government introduced several laws in 1933 intended to fundamentally reform the entire colonial judicial system and in particular the Native Court system.[74] These laws provided for the dismissal and suspension of members of Native Courts who abused their powers or were found to be incapable of exercising their powers justly. More importantly, laws like the West African Court of Appeal Ordinance of 1933 provided for the right of legal appeal against the decisions of the Native Court in higher courts such as the Supreme Court and West African Court of Appeal. These reforms significantly curtailed the wide powers hitherto vested in the Native Courts and colonial administrative officers.

The basis of the 1933 judicial reforms was partly ideological. It represented a shift in colonial policy away from a paternalistic, almost static view of government to one embodying a development concept. The introduction of the right of legal appeal was considered particularly significant in the move toward modernizing the local judicial system. As the Attorney General put it: "Nothing could be more effective in checking irregularities on the part of the Native Court than the knowledge that the persons who came before it are aware that they have a right of appeal to a competent and honest court of appeal."[75]

Although constitutional protection of human rights was not introduced until independence in 1960, the 1933 judicial reforms, particularly the extension of the principle of legal appeal, marked a significant turning point in the development of institutional safeguards for the protection of individual rights and liberties in Nigeria. The reform, prompted both by the attacks against the colonial administration and its own aspiration toward enlightened governance, reflects the paradox of the colonial legal system. The colonial authorities sought to maintain a semblance of social justice and a regime of rights comparable to those in England, while simultaneously employing law arbitrarily as an instrument of coercion to meet overriding imperial objectives.

Generally speaking, British colonial administration in Nigeria as elsewhere in Africa was generally guided by a consideration for the rule of law, based on its laissez-faire conception of society and its concern about protecting the "good name" of the

government. The libertarian traditions of English common law and the system of justice extended to the colony professed a broad concern for private rights and individual freedom of action. But the introduction of the English legal system—ostensibly extending to the colony the same standards of rights, liberty, and justice as prevailed in England—did not in fact guarantee human rights conditions comparable to those in England. In the long run, the British administration like other colonial regimes denied Africans the very rights they themselves articulated as the sine qua non of modernization—enforcing, instead, "customs" for the purposes of political control.[76] This fact is hardly a matter of contention and is not the point here. The argument here is that the purported extension of English standards of law, legal rights, and justice to the colony and the official rhetoric that kept it on the agenda was—more than being an objective to which the British were seriously committed—designed to legitimize and rationalize empire.

Because of this, underlying the colonial legal regime were paradoxes and even contradictions between its professed commitment to the rule of law as a guarantee of individual rights and its coercive use of law. This created tensions between the moral claims of the colonial state and its politics. For Africans, too, the language of rights contained similar paradoxes. African elites, chiefly authorities, and ordinary people appropriated and deployed discussions about rights to various, and sometimes contradictory, ends. Educated African elites both opposed colonial laws on the basis that they circumscribed the political rights of traditional rulers and protested other colonial laws that sought to extend the authority of these traditional rulers over them.

Ultimately, the rhetoric of extending English standards of rights and justice to the colony was made necessary by the need to legitimize British colonial rule and rationalize the violence of colonialism. The articulation of a humane regime of law and rights, or at least an aspiration toward it, was seen as a powerfully legitimizing tool setting British colonial rule apart from the arbitrariness and excesses of imperial regimes elsewhere on the continent. Law was stronger than the Maxim gun, not only because it provided a more effective means of colonial control but also because within the context of the rights discourse, it provided a rationale for empire, and for the colonized, a framework for oppositional discourse. But for all its association with legalities, the rights discourse was not only a matter of law or the administration of justice. Debates about rights also extended to other economic, social, and political arenas. As the language of law and rights became more influential in public discussions, it began to feature more frequently and prominently in the debates over economic resources and social life.

4

Confronting State Trusteeship

Land Rights Discourses

Legitimizing and Oppositional Rights Discourses

Discussions about land and property rights in the colonial and immediate postcolonial period were conducted largely in relation to the liberal economic ideas and systems introduced by missionaries and the colonial state. European missionary activities provoked much of the early debates about land and property rights in West Africa. As indicated earlier, missionaries saw the inculcation of European liberal and egalitarian values as an integral part of the "civilizing mission." This mission involved changing African orientations toward property as part of the remaking of the native's conceptions of selfhood. Missionaries believed that once the principles of private property and property titles were properly inculcated in local peoples, all other bases of rights-bearing citizenship—the right to life, liberty, wife, children, and property—might take root.[1]

These ideas of propertied personhood were inherited and promoted by colonial states. In the pursuit of imperial objectives, colonial governments experimented with different regimes of social and economic rights. While the colonial period opened with widespread acceptance of the evolutionary superiority of Western concepts of individual property rights, it closed with a general atmosphere of suspicion toward individual land rights and a dogged emphasis on "customary communal rights."[2] Although these shifts were largely shaped by the exigencies of colonial administration, Africans were not passive onlookers in this process. Using the language of rights, they too challenged, negotiated, subverted, and acquiesced in the processes of colonial economic and social restructuring. In so doing, they reached beyond the terms set by the colonial state and colonial missionaries to introduce a counter discourse about property rights and economic control.

Broadly speaking, property rights discourses were patterned along two lines: legitimizing and oppositional rights discourses. The former were deployed to justify and legitimize colonial economic and social policies. As with the colonial legal system, the language of rights helped legitimize colonial economic control. This rhetoric of rights, freedom, and liberty became synonymous with colonial attempts to individualize trade and land ownership. Rights talk was deployed to justify and legitimize state trusteeship over land and other resources. The ownership of land had to be vested in the colonial state because it was a much better guarantor of equal access and right to land than ownership by a few authoritarian local chiefs. These legitimizing discourses about freedom, liberty, and rights, mainly used by the colonial state and its African allies, provide one context for examining land and property rights discourses here.

A second context in which property rights discourses were deployed stands in opposition to the first. As the colonial regime sought to consolidate its control over local resources and social life, sustained challenges emerged both from Africans and sympathetic Europeans, particularly non-state actors like missionaries and humanitarians in the colony and the metropole. This opposition was also frequently articulated in the language of rights and liberties. Colonial land policies, which restricted individual access to land and vested it in the state, were attacked as a denial of "the native's traditional rights to his own God-given resources."[3] These, unlike the legitimizing discourses deployed by the colonial state, were oppositional and anti-establishment.

However, although the paradigms of "legitimizing" and "oppositional" rights discourses provides a broad framework for our discussion, it would be a mistake to assume these two discursive contexts represent rigid, racially defined polar categories—one, colonial and European, and the other, indigenous and African—each ideologically walled off from the other. The evidence does not suggest this was the case. The understandings and use of the language of rights and liberties around economic and social issues were, for the most part, fluid and multiple. They were based on individual and group interests at different times and under different circumstances. For example, although most Africans were opposed to colonial land policies, some advocated colonial state trusteeship and agreed with the government that its acquisition of land was ultimately the best guarantee of equitable access to land. Moreover, between the poles of legitimizing and oppositional rights discourses, rights discourses emerged oriented to several other points of the compass. We can talk of "oppositional modernizing discourse" (Western-educated African elites advocating modernist land use reforms but opposing colonial ideas on how to go about this); "oppositional traditionalist discourse" (educated and chiefly elites advocating customary land tenure systems in opposition to colonial reforms); "pro-colonial nativist discourse" (chiefs who wanted to use indirect rule policies to buttress their powers and control over land); and "anti-colonial nativist discourse" (Pan-Africanists and cultural nationalists such as Edward Blyden who wanted to restore the "African personality" as a modernizing construct).

Thus, the categories of legitimizing and oppositional rights discourses provide a guide rather than a rule in our analyses of economic and social rights. It is, however, important to highlight them for two main reasons. First, for all their fuzziness, these categories reflect the ways in which many of the historical players themselves framed and understood the debates about rights in which they were engaged. Second, we need to map out the broad contours of property rights discourses in the colonial state that are sometimes lost in the attention to nuances and details. The colonial state deployed rights discourses aimed *primarily* at legitimizing imperial agendas; most Africans deployed *alternate* discourses to oppose, engage, and negotiate with the colonial state.

The Land Question

The land question was crucial to the political economy of colonial rule in Nigeria as elsewhere in Africa since the control of land and other resources was a key imperial economic objective. Yet, the land question also provided a vital arena for African challenges to the colonial state, which reinforced the anti-colonial movement. Because of the centrality of the land question and its role in defining African reaction to and engagement with colonial rule, it has absorbed much scholarly attention. In one of the earliest studies on the land question in colonial Africa, colonial anthropologist Charles Kingsley Meek wrote in 1946 that "rights over land are more jealously treasured than any other form of rights."[4] Meek argued that the land question provided a terrain like no other in the colonial period, in which issues of rights entailments and obligations were realized and thoroughly contested.[5] Although the history and politics of the land question in colonial Africa has been extensively examined, many of these studies focus on local "customary" land tenure systems and the distortions wrought on these systems by colonial land policies.[6] Few go beyond these themes to question the meanings and rationale of the underlying discourses deployed by various interest groups in the politics of land and resource control. It is important to go beyond the more obvious politics of the land question to examine how different groups within the colonial state articulated and sought to legitimize or oppose contending claims to land and other resources. Understanding this process of legitimization and opposition illuminates our understanding of the politics of resource control not only in the colonial period but also in the contemporary African state.

Land was often at the center of early conflicts between the British authorities and African rulers. Soon after the British incursion into Lagos in 1900, local British consuls claimed that the British crown had acquired ownership of all lands in the colony by virtue of the Treaty of Cession between the British Government and King Docemo in 1861. Article 1 of the treaty stated:

> I, Docemo, do with the consent and advise of my Council, give, transfer, and by these presents grant and confirm unto the Queen of Great Britain, her heirs and successors for ever, the Port and Island of Lagos, with all the rights, profits, territories and appurtenances whatsoever thereunto belonging . . . freely, fully, entirely and absolutely. . . .[7]

The wording of the treaty unambiguously attests to the transfer of "legal rights" over Lagos lands from King Docemo to the British Crown. However, as several writers have pointed out, the interpretation of this treaty provision was bound to be problematic from the beginning, because King Docemo, like many other local kings and chiefs, did not have absolute customary or legal authority over "all the lands in Lagos," which he had supposedly ceded to the British. Even in his capacity as King of Lagos, Docemo had neither feudal authority nor seigniorial rights over his chiefs, nor absolute rights over the land held in trust by them. Thus, in spite of the language of the treaty, it has been argued that King Docemo had "nothing to transfer."[8] Evidently, in staking their land claims on the basis of treaty agreements with African chiefs ab initio, the colonial state failed to take into consideration the nature of precolonial land tenure systems and the scope of the rights that local kings and chiefs enjoyed under it. This point deserves further elaboration.

In one of the most detailed studies of land tenure in Africa, Taslim Elias argued that in spite of local differences in the African land tenure systems, there were some basic principles common to all of them. First, land was not normally owned by individuals absolutely but by a community, village, or family. Land grants to individual members of the group or to strangers left the ultimate title in the family. Second, the chief or head of a village or family exercised a right of control over land as a "trustee" for his group. Land allocated to a member of a family or community could not be disposed of without the consent of the chief or family head.[9] Elias argued that African kings and chiefs had the sole authority to allocate land to the various families in the village or towns through their respective heads. It was also a chief's "right" to reallocate such land to new holders where a family became extinct through the failure to produce heirs or upon abandonment by former occupiers of the land.[10] However, these "rights" had limitations. The chief was no more than a trustee of his powers over the land of his community. He had no rights to alienate land, which, once allotted to the families, remained outside his control and subject to family ownership. Individuals did not have absolute rights over land. They did, however, possess some specific rights over the *use* of land depending on the way they acquired such lands.[11]

Although the debate continues over how well these principles reflect indigenous land tenure systems, they strongly influenced colonial land policies. The predominant idea for much of the colonial period was that "customary" African land tenure systems were based on communal rather than individual ownership of land. There was also the view that communal African notions of land rights contrasted with later European individualistic and egalitarians notions of land and property rights.

It is important to emphasize the gendered character of both the land tenure systems and discourses about land rights. Men, whether they were colonial officials, educated, Africans or traditional elites, dominated the debate about land use and ownership in the colonial and immediate postcolonial period. Women were, to a large extent, excluded until the 1940s and 1950s when a few mission-educated women began to assert their political and economic rights and independence. This patriarchal bias in the discussions over land was typical though not peculiar to colonial Africa. Debates about land use and ownership in England were also dominated by male intellectuals and ruling elites. Thus, much of the evidence and discussion here really reflects predominantly male viewpoints on the land question. I have sought to balance this by paying particular attention to women's discussions about land and property rights, although the historical evidences are few and far between.

Fostering Healthy Individualism

In the early colonial period, official attitudes toward land were largely informed by the belief in the superiority of European concepts of individual property rights over what were considered traditional African notions of communal land ownership. European colonizers took possessive individualism to be the foundation of civilized society; the corollary was that private property was unknown in "savage" Africa. These colonizers encouraged the idea of individual rights in the name of modernity and to effect the evolution of human societies from status to contract.[12] Thus, early colonial attitudes toward the ownership and use of land in Western Nigeria, as elsewhere in British Africa, were tied to European notions of individual rights in property. The notion of a right to property as necessary to human nature, a just reward for labor, and the very basis of proper political society was deeply embedded in nineteenth-century British political theory. Across the spectrum of political and legal thought, property increasingly came to be seen as meaning private property, and both liberals and conservatives were agreed that property was the basis of civilized society.[13] Based on these notions, the colonial state endorsed certain rights over land and property while refusing to recognize others. These notions also influenced its decision over what regimes of land and property rights should be accorded legal protection.

The effort to shift the locus of African economic and social life from community-orientation to the individual was not peculiar to colonial land policy. It was also at the heart of the idea of the "civilizing mission" as conceived by the state and other agents of empire. In many parts of Nigeria, early contacts with European merchants strengthened local ideas of individual ownership of land and weakened the strict rules against alienation in traditional land tenure systems.[14] The growing demand for land titles freed from the restrictions of local customs and traditions, by both affluent Africans and European traders, was satisfied by English-style grants of land by the Crown.

In 1898 the Colonial Office in London commissioned a report on Land Tenure in West Africa that concluded that communal land rights prevailed and declared individual ownership of land foreign to native ideas. Yet, colonial policy during this period centered on promoting individual rather than communal land claims. Colonial officials sought to reorient a supposedly communal land tenure system toward a more European and egalitarian model. One way of doing this was by extending the British legal system into the colony. All laws in force in England as of January 1, 1863 were deemed to also be in force in the colony and applicable in the administration of justice as far as local circumstances would permit.[15] This meant that English common law principles on land ownership and conveyance also applied to the colony. Some writers have suggested that these laws introduced the notion of individual ownership of land to some African communities.[16]

Apart from this law, other developments on the ground also moved indigenous land tenure systems toward greater alienation and commercialization. The demand for land intensified with the influx of freed slaves from Sierra Leone in the mid-nineteenth century, making land more valuable and easily alienable. As the notion of absolute ownership of land and individual ownership spread in many parts of Western Nigeria, it transformed local attitudes to land. In Abeokuta growing individualization and commercialization of land became a source of local conflict. When European firms first began to lease property in Abeokuta in the 1900s, the autonomous Egba United Government introduced a law making it illegal for anyone to sell land or mortgage houses or land to foreigners. Such transactions were only legal between "natives of Egbaland." Private individuals could only lease houses and land to non-Egba with the consent of the local head-chief, the *Alake*.[17] But far from being an attempt to restrict private land ownership, this law was actually intended to confine Europeans to the outskirts of Abeokuta and prevent them from settling in the town. It was feared that selling or mortgaging land to foreigners would result in large-scale alienation of Egbaland to Europeans.

Although the colonial government favored individual land ownership as part of its economic liberalization policy, it consented to the Egba law because it placed a check on the acquisition of land by Europeans merchants, many of whom were not British.[18] However, many locals opposed the law. In 1922, a group of middlemen and traders petitioned the *Alake* to rescind the part of the land law that forbade the sale or mortgage of land to foreigners. They anchored their argument on their rights as "citizens" of Egba to sell land to whomsoever they chose. They argued that Europeans would extend more credit if they knew they could claim property if difficulties arose. The desire of the Egba traders to use land as collateral fomented a major debate over land for many decades. In advancing these arguments, the Egba traders invoked ideas of European and Atlantic world capitalism. Their ideas of "progress" and modernization centered mainly on control over properties and accumulation of profit.

The colonial government also tried to control land through such laws as the Public Land Ordinance of 1876 and the Public Lands Acquisition Proclamation of 1903. For the most part, these laws were geared toward facilitating the acquisition of lands needed by the government for its stations and other public use. They were not intended to restrict private land ownership but, in fact, to encourage the sale of land. The Public Lands Acquisition Proclamation provided that where land required for public purposes was the property of a native community, the head chief of such community might sell and convey the land for a fee, notwithstanding any native law or custom to the contrary.[19]

This reflects the dominant colonial attitude during this period, which tended toward greater individualization and alienation of land in spite of customary restrictions. Inherent in this attitude was the policy of the colonial state to promote individual proprietary rights. Colonial officials deliberately compensated individual landowners, rather than entire communities, for lands acquired by the government. Where conflicts arose between individual and community claims to compensation, colonial officials tended to support individual claims, as was the case of Oke Agbo in 1903.[20] But quite apart from a desire to promote individual land holding, this policy may also have been informed by the need to establish an effective mechanism for limited acquisition of administrative property. Individual claims to land were likely to be cheaper and easier to settle than those of entire communities.

Private ownership and sale of land was also actively encouraged by the colonial state because it was eager to promote urbanization, the development of a money economy and private cultivation of commercial crops—key elements of its vision for a viable colonial project. The government considered that in the absence of direct taxation, the people's land should constitute the main basis of individual agricultural production and revenue for the government. Moreover, colonial officials argued that because the basis of agriculture was peasant farming, which produced the necessary surplus for export, the government was inclined to discourage large-scale land alienation and any attempts at plantation-type production, lest the masses be deprived of their land.[21] Generally, the colonial government pursued a policy that kept land ownership away from large European firms. This differed from contemporary developments elsewhere in colonial Africa, like French Equatorial Africa and German East Africa, where the colonial regimes granted large-scale land concessions to European firms for plantation agriculture. Such large-scale plantation agriculture was considered a more effective way of exploiting the agricultural potentials of the colonies to meet imperial economic objectives.

Customary Communal Rights

By 1910, the colonial state was confronted with new circumstances that changed the official attitude toward land tenure. The main concerns became how to react to the widespread sale and alienation of land in the colony and the threat of land scarcity for agriculture. This became a crucial source of conflict over land. Whereas in the past colonial officials had been eager to promote "healthy individualism" among Africans, new realities necessitated a change in policy toward greater state control. The idea became increasingly prevalent that individual and commercial dealing in land were contrary to African land tenure systems. Commercial dealings in land by supposedly community-oriented African peoples also ran against the view of African institutions sanctioned by both conservative colonial administrators and liberal anthropologists. This was not an entirely new idea. The 1898 *Report on Land Tenure in West Africa* made similar arguments. However, new realities made these views more acceptable to colonial authorities.

The government began to emphasize communalism and customary law, not individualism and a law of contract, as being more naturally African and argued that these "traditional" institutions ought to be recognized and fostered. The colonial state also began to position itself, rather than the family or lineage, as the source and guarantor of whatever rights it deemed customary. This was the beginning of the process through which the nation-state came to be seen as the ultimate guarantor of individual rights, the "guardian of propertied personhood."[22] For the colonial government, the concept of land rights became part of a delicate political balance. It reflected the gap, and sometimes contradiction, between imperial idealism and the exigencies of colonial administration. If the earlier discourse of radical individualism bore the promise, the later discourse on "customary" communal land rights bore the reality of colonial land reforms. As colonial land policy shifted, administrators and analysts began to support a model of land tenure characterized by the oft-quoted African saying that "land belongs to a vast family of which many are dead, few are living and countless numbers are still unborn."[23] Chiefs were seen, or at least presented, as the holders of land with rights of administration and allocation. Rights in land were seen as flowing downward, deriving from political authority, rather than residing in the peasantry. These ideas became canons of academic and popular knowledge about indigenous land tenure systems in Africa and were advanced to justify a new colonial policy.[24]

In line with the state policy of trusteeship, the government committed itself to protecting the indigenous inhabitants from the activities of "European and African land-sharks."[25] Governor Egerton amended the Mining Ordinance of 1912 to give the government more control over land. Under the new arrangements, the government abolished the fees, rents, and profits to which local people had been entitled under the old system. All such fees and rents became the exclusive entitlements of the state.[26] The law also denied local people the "right of objecting to prospecting licenses or mining licenses being granted for their land." Similar amendments of the Public Lands Expropriation Ordinance gave the government more powers to acquire lands for public use without owner consent. As would be expected, Africans criticized these changes. One local newspaper described the enactment of these laws as a "calculated attempt to abrogate native rights of property in land."[27]

The shift in government policy from encouraging individual ownership of land toward promoting state control based on supposedly "customary" communal land tenure systems had significant political undertones. For one, the right of Africans to use land came to be understood as being dependent on allegiance to traditional political authorities. The authority of chiefs, subchiefs, and heads of clan and family was understood and represented as being bound up with the land. Land allocation was seen as a means by which local chiefs "customarily" maintained the loyalty of their people and asserted control over them. Here, we find another probable rationale for the shift in emphasis from the individual to the community in colonial discourses on land rights. It was in the interest of the colonial state to maintain the authority of chiefs and their role as allocators of land to ensure the continued allegiance of their subjects, and the success of the indirect rule system.

These general principles were given legal endorsement through both direct administrative action and the operation of the colonial courts. Under the judicial arrangement in Southern Nigeria before 1914, land cases were accorded special treatment because of their importance for the colonial state. Land cases were put in the same category as murder, manslaughter, and serious felony cases, which were beyond the jurisdiction of the Native Courts headed by African chiefs. Such cases were reserved for the Appeal Courts and the Supreme Court presided over by European officials.[28]

One of the most celebrated cases over land rights in the colonial courts was *Amodu Tijani v. the Secretary of Southern Nigeria* in 1914.[29] At issue was the ownership of some pieces of land in Lagos that had been compulsorily acquired for public use by the government. Amodu Tijani (also known as Chief Oluwa), one of the land-owning local chiefs of Lagos, claimed that the acquired land belonged to him and his family and demanded full compensation from the government, first as absolute owner, and later (on appeal) in a representative capacity. Once again, the Treaty of Cession signed between King Docemo and the British in 1861 lay at the heart of the matter. The colonial government argued that the acquired lands were part of the territory supposedly ceded in 1861 to the British Crown by King Docemo. Opposing Chief Oluwa's claims of individual ownership, Chief Justice Sir Edwin Speed advanced the standard position of the colonial state that "customary" rights in land belonged to the community rather than the individual. He argued that Chief Oluwa's interest in the disputed land was merely a seigniorial right rather than individual rights of ownership.[30] Thus, in what seemed like a reversal of roles, the colonial state rather than African chiefs was invoking "native law and custom" to challenge the rights of an African chief to land.

In 1915 the *Tijani* case went on appeal to the Supreme Court, which held that Chief Oluwa was entitled to some compensation although not on the basis of absolute ownership rights that he claimed over the land. Although the Privy Council subsequently reversed the decision of the Nigerian courts on technical grounds, it nevertheless upheld the principle that "customary" land rights resided in the community rather than the individual. In his judgement, Lord Haldane, who had earlier canvassed Indian and Canadian aboriginal community land titles, declared that individual ownership of land is quite foreign to native ideas. He argued that in the African context "land belongs to the community, the village and the family, never the individual."[31] In spite of this decision, some commentators insisted that the notion of communal ownership of land under "customary" tenure systems was more a British invention than a carryover from precolonial times.[32]

Several writers have made the point that communal and chiefly control over land may not have been as strong, or individual ownership of land as restricted, in precolonial societies as the colonial government often suggested. Although the village was the main land-holding unit in most traditional African societies, the elders and the people did not bother themselves to define the rights of individuals to land, as there was plenty of cultivable land for everyone's needs. Although kings and chiefs had the power to revoke a land grant, they usually could only do so under circumstances of gross misconduct such as insurrection and attempted alienation. Apart from these limitations, the ordinary occupier enjoyed a large degree of security of tenure.[33] Thus, a chief occupied a position equivalent to a trustee-beneficiary under English law. He held and managed the land in trust for the members of the community. This role did not directly interfere with individual rights of access, use, and ownership of land.[34] Even traditional authorities, who had much to gain from a system based on communal rights to land, acknowledged the inalienability of individual ownership rights under precolonial land tenure systems. Writing on Yoruba land tenure in 1952, Chief Samuel Ojo, the *Bada* of Shaki, stated that although the king was usually considered the "head of the land," everyone had the liberty to use the land. The king could allot a piece of land to anybody, but once allotted, the land belonged to the person for as long as he or she lived. Upon death, his or her children inherited the land.[35]

Conflicts over the rights of individual members of a family to joint family lands also frequently came before the courts. This was another important arena in which the later colonial state, through the courts, sought to promote the idea of communal ownership of land and property. The colonial courts held that while ownership of land rested with the family, its members had *equal rights* and duties in relation to such family lands.[36] The rights over family lands were legally spelled out by the court in the case of *Lewis v. Bankole*. These include a right of each member of the family to reside in the family property, to have a voice in the management of the property and share in any income derived from it, to be consulted before any dealings on the property, and to be allocated a portion of the family land according to his needs.[37] This and other court rulings demonstrate the attempts by the colonial state to promote collective land ownership rights of families and communities while at the same time recognizing the rights of individual members to use land. Ultimately, underlying colonial land policy seems to be the basic idea of the communal nature of "customary" rights in land. But this assumption only partly explains the complex ways in which both the colonial state and African subjects deployed rights discourses in staking competing claims to land. Another explanation is the nature of the policy debates over land rights.

Asserting Land Rights: The Policy Debates

Africans responded in different ways to colonial land policies and the politics that shaped them. While some Africans opposed state acquisition and control of land as a violation of native land rights, others agreed with the government's position that state trusteeship over land was ultimately the best guarantee of customary rights. In either case, Africans appropriated and deployed the language of rights favored by the colonial state to articulate their positions and stake competing claims to land. Many people testified about land before colonial administrators and courts on the basis of customary rights because they believed their claims would only be regarded as valid if they were presented in terms sanctioned by colonial "custom." Assertions about rights in land also depended largely on when and where they were being made. People said different things at different times depending on their interests. For example, the definition of land rights during an inheritance dispute when complex questions of social expectations and family solidarity are involved could differ from the rights proclaimed in response to new economic opportunities or to challenge government-inspired land acquisition schemes. A person might invoke individual land rights if it was advantageous for him to sell or mortgage land. The same person may emphasize collective ownership of land when asserting a right of inheritance against a larger lineage group of kin.[38]

Such diversity of perspectives was quite evident in local debates on the land question in Nigeria, particularly from 1912 when the government began moving to control land in the name of state trusteeship. As law and precedence began to shape the pattern of land tenure, a vocal faction of the intelligentsia resisted what one local newspaper described as a process by which "the rights of natives in the private ownership of their lands are being assailed and the recognition of those inherent and ancestral rights are being denied."[39]

Prominent educated African elites such as Herbert Macaulay,[40] J. E. Shyngle, O. Obasa, and O. Johnson and British humanitarians such as E. D. Morel engaged in heated debates over government land policies, mainly under the auspices of the Lagos Auxiliary of the Aborigines Protection Society. O. Johnson and E. D. Morel in particular, exchanged several letters, both privately and publicly in the Lagos press, in which they disagreed over government land policies and their implications for native rights and welfare.

Johnson, like most Africans, staunchly opposed the government's acquisition and control of land, arguing that it served only to deprive the people of their ownership of and access to lands. Morel, on the other hand, believed that Johnson's opposition was informed more by cultural nationalism than by an objective evaluation of the government's land policy. Johnson, he argued, belonged to a group of Africans who "do not wish the British government to have the slightest power in dealing with the matter of land tenure."[41] Morel argued that British trusteeship over land would ultimately benefit Africans by preventing large-scale alienation of land, which could reduce the masses to the status of landless wage laborers. He advocated a system in which the British government as overlord of West African land assumed the power of protecting the people against the effects of "human folly and human ignorance" in such complex land matters.[42] Although these trusteeship arguments were not new and supported the official position, they indicate that even among advocates of native rights and welfare, fundamental disagreements arose over how best to protect native land rights.

Complex generational-, class-, and gender-related interests were also at play in the discourses of rights to land during this period. Older and upper-class men, including chiefs and village and family headmen, generally argued for communal rights in land, presenting them as customary or traditional practice. These arguments reinforced and maintained their influence and control over local affairs in the face of rapid social changes. In contrast, the younger generation, particularly Western-educated men, tended to support permanent land ownership and the individualizing of rights in land.[43] In Benin, these differences were at the core of protracted conflict between the *Oba*

(King) and a group of educated elites who, in 1933, organized themselves under the auspices of the Benin Community Association to protest against the restrictions that the *Oba* had placed on individual ownership and sale of land.[44] Another group of young men, The Benin Progressive League, also petitioned the colonial government in 1935 complaining against the "subversion of the rights of individual ownership" by the *Oba,* whom they accused of denying young men of their right to lease their land to a French Company.[45]

In spite of these differences, however, important alliances between youths and elders, and between educated elites and traditional chiefs, sometimes emerged around the land question. Educated and chiefly leaders sometimes came together under the auspices of the Aborigines' Protection Society, to assume the mandate of protecting the rights of natives to their land. When in 1907 a British merchant attempted to secure extensive timber concessions from the government in Ijebu, mission-educated reformers led by Joseph Odumosu acted in close patriotic concert with the chiefly elite led by the local chief, the *Ajuwale,* to resist, using funds raised by popular subscription. Odumosu used his newspaper and the acumen of a leading African lawyer to rally popular support to oppose the concessions while the *Ajuwale* worked to mobilize the people through "ritual and sacrifice."[46]

The incident that precipitated the strongest local opposition from both the educated elites and traditional chiefs was the proposal by the Colonial Office in 1912 to extend the colonial land tenure system in Northern Nigeria to the South. The Land and Native Rights Ordinance introduced in Northern Nigeria in 1911 was based on the assumption that land ownership was communal, with the chiefs holding it in trust for the collective benefit of the people. As in British East Africa, the colonial government in Nigeria used this principle to rationalize and legitimize its own trusteeship over land.[47] The standard argument ran thus: First, all native lands were held by the paramount chiefs and heads of the community, in trust for that community; second, all these lands subsequently came under the control of the colonial Governor, who through British conquest had become the "paramount chief," to be administered by him, according to native law and custom for the common benefit of the people.[48]

Opponents of the Land and Native Rights Ordinance and the proposal to extend it to the South argued that these principles did not reflect customary land laws of the people of Southern Nigeria. Opinion leaders in Lagos regarded the proposal as an imperial move to deprive them of the right to their own land. In several editorials and commentaries, local newspapers criticized the proposition of the British Crown to take over all lands and regulate their transfer. The *Nigerian Chronicle* argued that by "depriving the native of his right to land and vesting it in the state," the colonial government was not only destroying their customary laws but was also "reducing them from the status of proprietors in their own right into that of a peasant or a serf."[49] Such concerns over the loss of native rights in land prompted several mass meetings in Lagos to deliberate on the issue. Deputations were subsequently dispatched from the capital city of Lagos to other parts of Southern Nigeria to awaken the chiefs and people there to what was considered a grave threat to their liberties.[50] The Aborigines Protection Society dispatched a delegation composed of both Western-educated Africans and chiefs from such interior centers as Abeokuta, Ibadan, Ijebu Ode, Ilesha, and Ife to London in 1913 to protest the government's land proposals. The concern over protecting native land rights resulted in the political mobilization of new elements of the population and for the first time brought together educated Lagosians and chiefs from the interior.[51]

The series of public meetings that the members of the Lagos deputation had with the people in the hinterland over the government's land proposal provides us with unique insights into how ordinary people articulated their claims to land. Not only were these deliberations widely reported in the local press, the specific comments of various speakers were often reported apparently verbatim. One newspaper commented that the attitude of the people was one of "unbounded astonishment at the land proposals coming from Englishmen, whom they had regarded as their friends and protectors."[52] The newspaper reported that at the meeting in Abeokuta, a local chief, the *Asipa* of Egba and the official spokesman of the *Ologuns* (traditional war chiefs) summed up popular objection to colonial land reform proposals.

He recounted how the Egba fought the Oyos, the Ibadans, the Ijebus, the Dahomeans and the other foes who invaded their territories at different periods of their history and how these [people] could not succeed in taking their land from them. He asked why the British people who [sic] he thought was their friend wanted to take their land from them. They had no more slaves and pawns, and land, which was their only heritage, was also going to be taken from them by people for whom they had sacrificed their own interests to a great extent. He concluded by saying that when we were born, God gave the white man his land, the natural beauty of which is the ocean. The same God gave us our own land. They did not wish to take the white man's land from him; he too should leave them in undisturbed possessions of their God-given property . . . He said that if the proposals are carried out there will be no more trade with the white man [and] the white man must find palm oil and palm kernels from his own country.[53]

What is clearly evident from this is that for the Egba people, or at least the traditional elites who represented them, land ownership and control were fundamental rights that they would not compromise under any circumstances. This right was more important than politics (friendship with the white man) or economic considerations (the palm oil and kernel trade with the white man). It was an existential issue that defined their collective identity and integrity as a people. The importance that people attached to their rights over land was also reflected at a personal level where individuals drew on the language of tradition and "custom" to articulate diverse claims of rights in land.

Throughout the 1920s and 1930s, Africans continued to oppose and challenge colonial control over land. This intensified when the colonial government introduced the Land Acquisition Ordinance in 1937. Some of the opposition against government land control was expressed in individual and group petitions to colonial officials, as we shall see in the following section. However, the debate over land rights did not only center on African opposition to colonial control. It also centered on competing claims among Africans over land ownership and control.

Asserting Land Rights: The Language of Petitions

Individual conflicts over land were another important arena in which debates over rights were conducted. This was particularly so in circumstances where parties to a conflict requested official intervention in the matter. Getting official intervention in a land matter required making a formal request in writing, usually in the form of a petition, to colonial administrative officials. Because of limited access to the courts and the fact that many Africans found the court system too complex and expensive, petitions became the preferred way by which people sought government intervention in land disputes. The petitions in colonial archives, both in Nigeria and in London, are replete with appeals on land matters addressed to colonial officials at various level of the administrative hierarchy. My sample analysis of the archival records indicates that petitions relating to land constituted about 68 percent of all the petitions addressed to the Commissioner for Colony and the Provincial Residents between 1912 and 1950. These petitions provide a treasure trove of historical data on land-related discourses of rights.

What is significant about many land-related petitions in the colonial period is that although they were written by ordinary Africans, and sometimes by professional public letter writers who knew little of the technicalities of the law and legal language, they were characterized by the rhetoric of rights, freedom, and liberty. A few such petitions will buttress this point. In 1939, one Cyprian Ugwu wrote a petition to the Commissioner of Colony in protesting the unlawful acquisition of his family lands by the local Native Authority. He argued that although the disputed land had been freely given to the Native Authority by his deceased father for temporary use, "the right of ownership was reserved by the giver." His petition appealed to the Commissioner to protect his family's "legal right of ownership of [their] ancestral lands."[54] In a similar petition written in 1951 Aina Eko Olowo petitioned the Commissioner for the Colony complaining that he had not been paid a share of the money realized by the *Bale* (local head chief) from the acquisition of their communal land. He prayed the Commissioner to enforce his "customary rights as a citizen of Onigbongbon" to the proceeds from the land. In both cases, the petitioners had clearly taken care to emphasize that their claims were based on their rights as members of a family or community, rather than individual rights. It would be safe to assume that this was a strategy intended to give more validity to their claims and to elicit a more favorable response from colonial administrators.

Some aggrieved parties even petitioned colonial administrators to intervene in court decisions over land on the basis of what they considered judicial subversion of their customary rights. They assumed colonial administrative officials would be more attentive to these rights than the courts. In 1941 the Oloto family of Ebute Metta sent a petition to the Governor to protest a judgment delivered by the Supreme Court in favour of one Mr. Fabiyi against the family. The court had given Mr. Fabiyi the authority to sell the land and properties of the Oloto family, including the family palace, in settlement of a debt owed him by one member of the family. The petitioners protested this judgment, anchoring their arguments on collective family rights. They argued that the individual against whom the judgment was delivered had no exclusive rights over the property because "traditional lands and particularly a palace belong not to any past or present ruling chief but to the family generally."[55] Although administrative officials were reluctant to intervene in judicial matters, they clearly sympathized with such African appeals to collective rights and notions of ownership.

Land petitioners were not always aggrieved natives. Missionaries, humanitarians, and other sympathetic Europeans also wrote petitions, often on behalf of Africans claiming rights to land. Between 1914 and 1941 the British lawyer and humanitarian William Geary wrote several petitions on behalf of Africans and missionary groups to the Commissioner of Colony and the Secretary of State for Colonies in London protesting arbitrary government's acquisitions of land.[56]

The outbreak of the Second World War affected the discourses about land rights. During the war and in the postwar years, petitioners sought government intervention in land matters by anchoring their demands on Allied propaganda, which portrayed the war as a fight for freedom from Nazi tyranny. An interesting example of this is a petition sent to the Governor in 1941 by the Farmers Protection Society protesting against the government's price-control policies and proposals to acquire the farmlands of some of their members. The association invoked native treaty rights and the ongoing war with Germany to make its case. While praying for the success of British arms against "Hitler, enemy of liberty, civilization and democracy, to whom a treaty is merely a scrap of paper," the petitioners implored the Governor to protect their own treaty rights to their "ancestral lands."[57] Such references to the war and treaty rights were not limited to petitions over land or economic issues. As we shall see later, references to the "war for freedom and liberty against Hitler" also characterized petitions relating to political and civil rights in the postwar period. This was part of attempts by Africans to use the same rhetoric of rights and liberty that characterized British wartime propaganda to articulate their own political and economic aspirations.

Rights, Development, and State Trusteeship

As the nationalist movement gathered momentum in the postwar period, the notion of customary communal land rights, which had been used to rationalize state trusteeship over land in the heyday of colonial rule, found new meanings in state development agendas. The various strands that had earlier contributed to the hostility toward individual rights in land became interwoven with the new development ethos. Colonial officials assumed that freehold rights tie the hand of the government in all schemes of agricultural advance. It was also assumed that only effective state ownership assured judicious land use and maximized the exploitation of land for economic development.[58] These ideas about state trusteeship and development, which shaped colonial land policies, were to become recurring elements in the discourse about land rights in Nigeria.

When Nigeria attained independence in 1960, the new government, like the colonial regime it succeeded, sought to assert control over land, both in the name of protecting African customs and facilitating development. While the idea that state control of land promoted communal African custom was an

old one, the development ethos was relatively new. Nevertheless both ideas converged in the attempts to accord the state
even more powers over land. A customary veil was drawn over
the national confiscation of land and the circumscription of
individual rights to land. The problem with restricting individual rights in land in the public interest was more easily solved
where the rights were seen to be only rights of usage and enjoyment granted by the group to the individual.[59] Besides, the
demands of a planned and directed economy—a cardinal aspiration of the nationalist postcolonial government—were perfectly consistent with the old communal concept of customary
law. Since development was seen essentially as a state initiative, state trusteeship over land was considered fundamental
to the process of national development. These ideas have continued to guide state policies toward land in the postcolonial
period as they once did under colonial rule.

The idea of communal rights in land, which has provided
the basis of state trusteeship, has served the interests of the
postcolonial state and powerful constituencies within it, just as
much as it served those of the colonial state. Immediately before
independence and since then, hostility in the name of custom toward the emergence of individual rights in land, combined with
the development ethos, have facilitated the state's efforts to reinforce its power over land rather than the rights of individuals.
This trend, which is evident in many African nations, has restricted the rights and access of ordinary people to land and has
contributed to the dominance of the state over society.[60]

The most significant demonstration of how colonial ideas
about communal land rights and the development ethos have
combined to define state trusteeship over land in postcolonial
Nigeria was the promulgation of the Land Use Decree (later
Land Use Act) in 1978. This law vested the governor of each
state in the country with control over all lands in the state
just as it had been under colonial rule. The land was to be
"held in trust" by the Governor and administered for "the use
and common benefit of all Nigerians."[61] The language of the
decree drew extensively from colonial texts and laws such as
the Public Land Ordinance of 1876, the Public Lands Acquisition Proclamation of 1903, and the Land and Native Rights
Ordinance of 1911.

Like these colonial laws, the Land Use Decree of 1978 gave the governor exclusive authority to grant "statutory individual rights of occupancy," while local authorities were empowered to grant "customary rights of occupancy."[62] The decree also made it clear that the ultimate ownership rights over land continued to reside in the state and that lands could only be transferred, assigned, mortgaged, or improved with the permission of the governor who could also revoke a right of occupancy for "overriding public interest."[63] This law, which is still operational in Nigeria, remains, in many ways, a legacy of the politics of colonial land policy and the discourses of customary rights underlying it.

Interestingly, the ostensible rationale for the introduction of the Land Use Act was also strikingly similar to the pro-trusteeship arguments made earlier by humanitarian activists such as E. D. Morel, which many Nigerian intellectuals found objectionable at the time. The Land Use Panel, which recommended the Land Use Act, was mandated by the government to recommend a formula that would benefit the vast majority of the people.[64] Like earlier colonial land ordinances, the main justification advanced for the Land Use Act was that it would make access to land easier both for the citizens and the state. It would also protect the right of all Nigerians to use and enjoy land. But, as several studies have shown, far from making land more accessible to citizens, the Land Use Act has mainly strengthened the control of the state and ruling elites over land to the disadvantage to ordinary citizens.

Pro-trusteeship arguments by Morel and other humanitarians were criticized and dismissed by Nigerian elites as detrimental to their rights and interests in the colonial period, but were vigorously canvassed by ruling elites in the postcolonial dispensation to justify state land control. The only change was the political context. In the postcolonial dispensation, state land trusteeship has served the interest of ruling Nigerian elites who hold political power. These elites, once outsiders and opponents of colonial government, have become state-insiders with access to state resources that they have an interest in protecting.

But what does this tell us about the nature of the land rights discourse? First, it indicates that it is more useful to understand the debates over land rights in terms of conflicts of interests rather than a clash between customary regimes and colonial trusteeship. In this case, it is evident that arguments for and against state trusteeship over land in both colonial and postcolonial dispensations have been determined more by the interests of individuals and groups at different times than by the intrinsic tension between customary and noncustomary systems. Second, it demonstrates the way in which rights discourses changed over time. It shows how Nigerian elites have moved from using rights talk to challenge colonial land control to using it to defend the status quo. In some ways, this complicates one of the central arguments of this book. Rights discourses were used to promote complex agendas. They were used not only to legitimize the status quo but also to challenge it. But here we see that the "legitimizers" and the "challengers" were not always different interest groups, i.e., colonizers and colonized. We see here that those who used the rights discourse to oppose an established order at one point could also use it to defend the same order at another point. This process also illustrates how the discourse of rights became Africanized. African political elite not only appropriated colonial rights talk to challenge colonial control but ultimately internalized and shaped it to serve their own needs in the postcolonial period.

Women, Land, and Property

An important issue that deserves attention in the debates over land is the property rights of women. Most societies in Nigeria were predominantly patriarchal and patrilineal. Early ethnographic data on the Yoruba and Benin indicates that ownership of land and property was mainly the preserve of men. Women's access to land was often restricted to use rather than absolute ownership.[65] The same rules applied to property. Under customary rules of succession, it was widely accepted that a woman—whether a daughter or a wife—could not inherit landed properties from her father or her husband.[66] These customs were recognized and generally upheld by colonial officials. One colonial judge ruled in 1947 that a woman was not entitled to share in her deceased husband's estate because under customary law devolution of property followed blood rather than marriage lines. More significantly, stated the judge, "she herself is an object of *inheritance*."[67]

Several scholars have sought to explain the limitations imposed on women's proprietary rights in terms of the sociopolitical and economic structures of both precolonial and colonial African societies.[68] We cannot explore all the arguments here, but it suffices to point out that colonial officials were even more ambivalent about the land rights of women than they were about those of men. Colonial customary law simply did not accommodate the idea of women as landowners. Claims by women in the name of custom were viewed with impatience and seen as an impediment to the development process, because the interpretation of women's rights to land was often limited to use, not ownership. Even then, such rights were based on social status connected with marriage. In most cases, a woman acquired rights to use land in her husband's place of residence through marriage—rights that were forfeited if the marriage dissolved.[69]

As others have argued within the context of colonial East Africa, the rightlessness of women that resulted from the development of the colonial land regime was part of the overall story of the interweaving of individualization, protective and communal ideologies, the development ethos, and the facts created by the early colonial land grab.[70] Whatever limited rights to land women traditionally had were further circumscribed by the transformations brought about by colonial policies and land tenure systems. This was particularly true in Southern Nigeria where there was a clear male bias in European gender practices and assumptions.

However, African women, like men, were not passive onlookers in the transformation of indigenous land tenure systems by the colonial state. They challenged and took advantage of these changes. African women were able to use colonial administrative and judicial systems to assert their land rights within a changing society. In a petition to the Resident of Benin Province in 1940, Maria Olomu requested the Resident's intervention to restore her ownership of a piece of land that she alleged the Chiefs of Umuezi had taken from her and unlawfully transferred to a

European firm, the United Africa Company. The tone of Maria Olomu's petition provides no indication that she felt any less entitled to the land she claimed because of her gender or social status. Her emphasis was on the justification of her claim and her rights as a British subject. Part of her petition read:

> I feel, as one of the British protected individuals of the British Empire, that I have the right of freedom and in these days, I am sure that the gospel of "might is right" is no more preached, but equality of rights and fair play . . . I appeal for your intervention in the interest of fair play which had been ideally represented by the British Government; which your Honour duly represents as a virtuous woman with bandaged eyes holding impartial scales.[71]

Although the petition does not provide much information about her personal background, there is some indication that Maria Olomu belonged to a small group of women in Nigeria in the 1930s and 1940s who had acquired missionary education and were beginning to break the traditional and colonial barriers on women to assert their rights in economic, social, and political matters. Her petition is significant in many regards. First is the mere fact that it was written by a woman. Colonial records indicate that very few women in the 1940s wrote petitions on matters relating to land and property. As we shall see in the discussion of social rights discourse in the next chapter, most petitions from women in this period dealt with domestic and matrimonial issues.

Second, unlike most petitions in this period that were written by professional public letter writers, the tone and format of her letter suggests that Maria Olomu wrote the petition herself.[72] The language of the petition was also remarkably different from the generic phraseologies that characterized petitions written by professional public letter writers. Maria Olomu's references to "might and right," equality, fair play, and "the virtuous woman with bandaged eyes" indicates an attempt to draw attention to her position of weakness as a woman in a male-dominated society. However, as would be expected, the colonial Resident refused to intervene in this matter and advised Maria Olomu to enforce her rights through the law courts.[73] Apparently, the Resident was not inclined to intervene in a land matter on the side of one woman against a group of influential chiefs and a European firm—both powerful constituencies of the colonial state.

Colonial administrators made little or no attempt to mask their ambivalence toward women's proprietary rights. While they were willing to intervene in social issues like marriage or to abolish customary marital practices deemed repugnant to women, there was no such concern for women's access to economic resources. One colonial report on "The Rights of Women" in Nigeria submitted to the League of Nations in 1936 simply stated that it was not customary for women to hold land and landed property among the "tribes" of West Africa.[74] This attitude toward women's proprietary rights differed markedly from colonial positions on social rights issues like marriage, divorce, and inheritance. On these matters, the state, following the lead of earlier missionaries, demonstrated a greater tendency toward decisive intervention.

Land and property were important issues in the debates about rights because they were central to people's daily lives and economic struggles within the colonial state and with each other. Land was also at the heart of the attempts by the colonial state to exercise greater control over economic resources, and this process was characterized by complexities and contradictions. Colonial land policies turned and shifted according to the local exigencies. For the colonial state, the rhetoric of rights was useful for promoting its land policies—so useful, in fact, that it could be deployed to promote two contradictory policies at different times. While the first decade of colonial rule was dominated by ideas about the evolutionary superiority of Western liberal concepts of individual land and property rights, it closed with a general atmosphere of suspicion of these rights and an emphasis, instead, on "customary" communal rights.

For much of the period of colonial rule, British administrators elaborated models of African societies that linked the integrity of the family, community, and tribe to collective control of land. Concerned that uncontrolled expansion of private property right would undermine chiefly powers and its system of indirect rule, the colonial state restricted individual ownership and emphasized communal customary rights in land. This became the basis of the colonial and postcolonial policy of state ownership and trusteeship of land. Also significant in the debates over the land was the way in which Africans used the rhetoric of rights through the courts and in petitions to articulate their own interests in land matters. This process of appropriating and deploying rights talk was not limited to the land question. It was also evident in the debates over social issues like marriage, divorce, and inheritance.

5

Negotiating Inclusion

Social Rights Discourses

Negotiating Social Inclusion

C olonial discourses about social rights centered mainly on familial and communal matters. The key issues were marriage, divorce, polygamy, child custody, betrothals, inheritance, and demands for social inclusion. Because of the wide range of social issues over which rights discourses were deployed and the difficulty of addressing all of them within this limited space, I have isolated a number of salient themes to guide the discussion here. These include marriage and divorce, debates about family rights, and the agitation for social inclusion by marginalized groups within colonial society. Archival records suggest that these were the dominant social themes generating public discussions over rights.

As in economic matters, colonial authorities sought a reorientation of African social life along a more "modern" and liberal European model. Colonial social policies such as those relating to marriage and divorce, child custody, and inheritance were justified on the grounds that they protected the rights of women, children, and other vulnerable groups from patriarchal customs, some of which were considered "repugnant to natural justice, equity and good conscience." They argued that women should be free to choose their husbands and not bound by customary practices of forced betrothals, exchange marriage, and widow inheritance.[1]

Many Africans opposed and resisted these changes, seeing them as disruptive to local customs and the prevailing social order. However, others welcomed these changes and took advantage of them. Women in particular, welcomed colonial liberal marriage and divorce policies and exploited them to assert their independence and escape patriarchal control. Men also invoked the language of rights, but to assert their customary matrimonial prerogative to regain some of the control over women lost in the early colonial period. Likewise, marginalized social groups such as communities of former slave used colonial discourses of freedom, rights, and liberty to demand state intervention in enforcing their social and political integration into society. In complex and sometimes contradictory ways, various groups asserted, opposed, and negotiated social interests and agendas using the rhetoric of rights and liberties.

Marriage and Divorce

Marriage and divorce were two related themes on which there were extensive debates over women's rights. Much of these discussions were conducted within the context of missionary and colonial notions of the "civilizing mission." As we saw in Chapter 3, early missionaries identified religious conversion with cultural transformation and called on African converts to embrace Western social practices as well as Christian religious beliefs. Rights discourses within this context centered on missionary and colonial attempts to make modern rights-bearing subjects out of native peoples by changing their social attitudes and practices toward a more "civilized," moral, and enlightened outlook. European missionaries tried unceasingly to reform local notions and practices of matrimony through the language of legalism and rights.

European missionaries in Nigeria, particularly among the Yoruba, preached the merits of monogamy and the vices of the indigenous practice of paying bride wealth and "buying" wives.

They emphasized the freedom of all God's creatures to enter into contracts of their own freewill including the contract of matrimony. Whether preaching from the pulpits or teaching in the classrooms, European missionaries sought to inculcate a legalistic view of selfhood in the "native," presenting the marital bond as a sacred contract and an ensemble of enforceable rights and duties. Both the "rite and the rights" entailed in Christian unions became increasingly important in the construction of relations and identities.[2] For its part, the colonial government sometimes encoded these notions in specific legal obligations, particularly with regard to marriage. In Nigeria as in most of British Africa, colonial marriage laws stipulated that Christian unions should be monogamous and should rest on new property and inheritance rights.[3]

As with its land policy, colonial attitudes toward marriage changed significantly over time. In the early years of colonial rule, European officials regarded polygamy and arranged marriages as repugnant and misguided. District officers and judges looked with sympathy on women who testified before them that they had been forced into marriage against their will and readily intervened to "liberate" them. Later on, however, official attempts at improving the lot of African women shifted to a preoccupation with curbing their "loose morals," believed to have been adversely affected by colonialism, by bringing wives under the tighter control of their husbands.[4] This shift in emphasis was also partly due to local opposition and resistance, particularly from men, against earlier colonial attitudes toward marriage and divorce. Thus, while the colonial period opened with official concern toward liberating women from the constraints of customary marital practices, it ended with greater concern about restoring "traditional" social and moral values. The pursuit of the latter meant abandoning, or at least de-emphasizing, the former.

Here, too, the dual frameworks of legitimizing and oppositional rights discourses are useful analytic categories. Using the rhetoric of women's rights and liberties, the colonial state initially sought to "reform" traditional marital practices as part of a larger program of social transformation. On one hand, discourses about women's rights validated and legitimized the colonial social agenda to break down patriarchal customs that were considered oppressive to women. On the other hand, those who stood to lose their influence and control over women—particularly elderly and upper-class men—also invoked the rhetoric of rights to articulate their opposition to these new ideas about women's empowerment. They, too, invoked customary rights, traditional family values, or, as one male petitioner put it, "the right and liberty of the human family" to challenge liberal colonial policies on marriage and divorce.[5]

From as early as the 1880s, colonial authorities began putting in place laws intended to change local attitudes toward marital relationships. They emphasized the rights of women to have a say in the choice of their husbands and to be able to divorce their husbands under certain conditions. The Marriage Ordinance, introduced in 1884, contained a provision that permitted children over the age of twenty-one to marry without their parents' consent. This was intended to check the practices of child betrothals and arranged marriages that were prevalent among the Yoruba and to "give women the liberty of entering into the contract of matrimony on their own terms."[6] Similarly, the Native Court Ordinance of 1914, which restricted the Native Courts to making rules that were "not opposed in letter or spirit to the ordinances of Nigeria," had important implications for indigenous practices relating to marriage. The application of the Native Court Rules under the direction of colonial administrative officers almost entirely abrogated indigenous customs regarding marriages, divorce, and custody of children and replaced them with practices that European officers regarded as moral and more in accordance with the principles of natural justice. For example, unlike the practice in precolonial times when a girl often had no choice in the contraction of marriage, the Native Court Marriage and Adultery Rule required her expressed consent. Under the Rules, girls married as children could legally renounce such marriages upon maturity.

Colonial authorities also worried about the African custom of "widow inheritance,"[7] or *levirate* marriages, which was common to many communities in Nigeria. Among the Yoruba, the younger brother or the eldest son of a deceased man customarily "inherited" the deceased's property and his wives, the latter being considered chattels.[8] Although this custom also permitted a widow to redeem herself from such marital obligations by refunding the bride wealth paid by her late husband, colonial officials generally saw the practice as immoral and repugnant, mainly because it was thought to violate women's liberties. Laws were subsequently enacted to discourage these practices. Women were also given jural status and the right to pursue litigation in the Native Courts. All these changes relating to marriage, divorce, and "widow inheritance" disrupted the prevailing social order and faced strong opposition from men. Although these colonial rules were sometimes subverted, a general fear of prosecution progressively weakened parental and other male control over young women.

Women took advantage of these new circumstances to assert their freedom and independence in matters of marriage and divorce. One newspaper commented in 1945 that "wives of modern times, whether literate or otherwise, are becoming conscious of their rights and are increasingly prepared to assert them."[9] Women effectively used the colonial arguments about women's liberties and the need to change "immoral" customary marriage practices to escape from marriages that displeased them. This trend was further encouraged by the Native Courts' propensity to grant divorce based on absence of true consent in marriage contracts as required by colonial law. It has been suggested that colonial divorce laws encouraged divorce among African women by making it easier for them to nullify customary marriages. This is based on the premise that in traditional African societies divorce was very rare and only the gravest crimes by a husband—not poverty or misfortune—were acceptable grounds for divorce. The colonial administration changed this tradition and legislated, in effect, that the "ability to pay from £5 to £12 to the husband of a woman was the only condition necessary for divorce."[10]

The attitude of the courts toward divorce reflected the greater scope accorded the personal status of women in society. As one colonial administrative officer put it, the law and the courts were intended to "liberate [women] from the old positions of servitude to which they were doomed."[11] Colonial officialdom viewed marriage without consent and without the option of divorce as de facto slavery.[12] For this reason, colonial courts were exceedingly liberal in their approach to requests from African women for divorce. This was often in defiance of the traditional code of behavior, which made marital separation difficult and rare. In many ways, the colonial courts became battlegrounds where women challenged patriarchal authority. Writing in 1930, N. A. Fadipe captured the reaction of African men to these developments when he stated disapprovingly: "Women who wanted to renounce their husbands simply went up the hill to the officer or the court of the [British] Resident Commissioner to sue for divorce. Young girls have availed themselves of the opportunity offered by the law and courts to defy tradition by rejecting unwanted marriage proposals imposed on them by their parents."[13]

Some of the divorce petitions written by women to colonial officials give us an idea of how women exploited colonial institutions and policies toward marriage to escape the control of men. In one such petition to the Resident officer of Agbor District in 1935, one woman, Nwanokpa, complained about her forceful seizure by the *Obi, or* king, of Uteh-Okpu as a wife, in replacement for her late sister who had been married to the *Obi*. She alleged that she had been forced into the *Obi's* compound against her will and had undergone "abundant cruelties" and only narrowly got the chance to escape from the *Obi's* custody. She requested the intervention of the Resident so that she "may be set at liberty."[14] In response, the Resident directed that Nwanokpa's allegation be promptly investigated. The District Officer subsequently reported that upon investigation he had found the material facts of Nwanopka's petition to be true and that he had taken steps to protect her liberties. He had also advised the woman to contact the Resident if she "had any further trouble."[15]

Another example of colonial attitudes toward marriage and divorce is the celebrated case of *Ekpenyong Edet v. Nyon Essien,* which came before the courts in 1932. In this case, the court upheld the position that it was "repugnant to natural justice, equity and good conscience" to allow a man to lay claim to a child of another simply because his bride wealth paid on the woman bearing the child for the other man had not been repaid upon divorce.[16] In adjudicating such marital matters, colonial administrative officers, with their English backgrounds, placed more emphasis on individual rights and tended to grant divorce to women much more easily than was the case under precolonial African legal systems. This explains why marital cases dominated the civil cases heard in the colonial courts. In a 1934 memorandum, the District Commissioner for Ekiti stated that 70 percent of the civil cases in the district are "concerned with divorce which were granted in most cases." In nearly all the cases, the petitions came from wives against their husbands.[17] In one court alone, out a total of 125 petitions for divorce in 1924, divorce was granted in 123 cases.[18] These statistics reflect the complex gender and generational struggles that took place within the framework of colonial legal and social systems.

Patriarchy, Family Values, and Public Morality

While women generally welcomed colonial changes to marriage practices, most African men strongly opposed them. The Marriage Ordinance, in particular, provoked pubic outcry when it was introduced in 1884. Elders complained that by permitting children over the age of 21 to marry without their parents' consent the state was weakening parental control and working against traditional family values.[19] In Abeokuta, this concern was raised repeatedly at the meetings of the local council. Council members complained that as a result of European civilization, parents had lost control of their children and societal decay had set in. The *Alake* lamented that in the old days, a girl who ran away from her husband would have been "promptly shackled and returned to him."[20] Under British rule, parents could no longer resort to such measures, and for some council members, the lack of such coercive measures contributed to the high divorce rate. The chiefs also complained that young men had lost respect for them and were having adulterous liaisons with the wives of the elders and chiefs or wooing girls away from their betrothed.[21] They were concerned that colonial liberal policy on divorce was leading to a breakdown of public morality and traditional social values. These male complaints are important because they add another layer to our understanding of how Africans engaged with the process of colonial social transformation.

While several writers have examined the ways in which women used colonial institutions to free themselves from traditional male control, they often overlook or give too little emphasis to men's counterstrategies for challenging these changes and renegotiating their control over women.[22] One example of the counterstrategies is that former husbands insisted that their bride wealth or dowry be returned to them upon divorce—a customary request that colonial officials were often not as eager to grant as women's requests for divorce.

Bride wealth return was both a social and economic issue. Many men put themselves in debt, often becoming pawns (*iwofas*, among the Yoruba) to raise the necessary funds for marriage. The strong connection between indebtedness and marriage, particularly in periods of economic depression, hardened many men to divorce. It was economically easier to take back an errant wife than to become entangled in an effort to reclaim the original bride wealth. However, if the wife could not be convinced to return, the husband was strongly inclined to demand bride wealth return.[23] Apart from economic value, the return of the bride wealth was important to men because customarily it was considered a condition for the nullification of marriage. Without the return of the bride wealth, a woman was still considered bound to her husband even if they were separated. Any liaison she had with another man before returning the bride wealth was, therefore, both adulterous and sacrilegious. Because of these deep-seated traditional beliefs, the issue of bride wealth return became a major source of grievance among men. If women had the right to divorce, they reasoned, men had a right to have their bride wealth returned. Most men could not understand why colonial officials were so eager to grant women's requests for divorce and yet so ambivalent about their own demands for the return of their bride wealth. One local chief reportedly asked a District Officer in exasperation whether the colonial government had paid the bride price on their wives.[24]

Since marriage, accumulation, and indebtedness were so intertwined, men had a vested interest in limiting their wives' ability to leave them for another partner. The need to control wives and daughters also intensified with the rapid changes in the colonial economy, which placed a premium on access to labor and credit.[25] In the 1920s, cases of men seeking the refund of their bride wealth became so common in the Abeokuta

Native Courts that the King, *Alake* Ademola, attempted to redress the situation by reviving the old local custom of *dipomu,* which empowered him as King to detain women in the palace until their bride wealth was refunded.[26] Although in the past, the practice of *dipomu* enabled both men or women who were experiencing crises to seek refuge in the palace, the system introduced in the 1920s was limited only to women involved in matrimonial disputes. Women could be brought to the palace either by their parents or their ex-husbands for being unable to refund their bride price following a divorce.[27] This modified practice of *dipomu* was clearly an attempt by traditional authorities, working within the ambit of the colonial Native Authority system, to stem the high divorce rates. It was also an effort by elders and upper-class men to reassert control over women and lower-class men. It represented an attempt by men to use traditional institutions to mediate the disadvantageous effects of colonial policies and institutions on their power and control over women.

Concern about the breakdown of traditional family structures was not limited to the chiefs. Educated African elites also voiced their concern over the high rate of divorce in the colony and its implications for family values and public morality. In one editorial in 1908, a prominent African newspaper, *The Lagos Standard,* lamented that woman who had been "living peaceably under their husband have been forced out by the proclamation of freedom."[28] Such views were widespread throughout the colonial period.

In their criticism of the prevalence of divorce in the Native courts, some leading Nigerian intellectuals of the period even argued that the practice of divorce was alien to indigenous culture and was a European creation. Samuel Johnson argued that divorce was "practically non-existent" among the Yoruba before European incursion, while N. A. Fadipe suggested that Yoruba women in the nineteenth century were more or less locked in their marriages.[29] These arguments were made within the context of widespread concern among both traditional and educated male elites about the rising divorce rates and nostalgia for the old order in which men exercised more control over women. In fact, as recent studies have shown, divorce was not as alien to

Yoruba society as Johnson and Fadipe suggested. Although public opinion weighed against divorce, estrangement between spouses were known and accepted.[30]

European and African Christian missionaries also took up the issue of the prevalence of divorce in the Native Courts and its implications for public morality. At the annual conference of West African bishops in 1935, the Bishop of Lagos was mandated to hold discussions with government officials on what they considered "an alarming and disturbing trend." The bishops' concern was that Native Courts, under the supervision of colonial officials, were granting divorce without proof of genuine separation. They argued that the mere repayment of bride wealth was insufficient for the dissolution of marriages.[31] Similar concerns were raised in 1937 at the synod of the Anglican Church, where church officials complained that divorce had become so easy to obtain that it has "become a very real danger to the morality of the people."[32]

Even among colonial officials there was unease over the long-term effects of colonial policy toward marriage. Some colonial administrators regarded the high rate of divorce as a serious threat to the social solidarity of the community. In 1943 a senior colonial judge, J. Jackson, decried the effects of colonial policy on indigenous marriage practices, pointing out that native custom regarding marriage, divorce, and the custody of children had been "almost entirely abrogated by administrative directions." He noted that in marriage, the free will of the woman, which was a matter of little or no consideration under native custom, had become a cardinal principle. To secure a divorce in a Native Court had become "as simple a matter as buying a railway ticket."[33] The Chief Justice, A. R. Pennington, was similarly concerned that the rate of divorce in the Native Courts might engender "a wholesale degradation of the marriage status according to native law."[34]

Concerns such as these within official circles prompted a quiet review of the government policy toward divorce and official intervention in marital and other domestic affairs.[35] This shift in policy is evident in several administrative documents issued between 1925 and 1930. In one memorandum to District Officers in the Yoruba provinces, the Senior Resident of Oyo Province, W. A. Ross, stated:

I have to invite your attention to my written and constantly repeated verbal instructions in regard to adultery and divorce cases . . . The Yoruba are naturally a very moral people and before the breakdown of native and parental authority the moral standard was quite high. With the establishment of the native courts and fixed dowry fees, parental and patriarchal control over morality has greatly diminished and wives and woman are dealt with in the Native Courts as property for barter or the security for a deposit. This is entirely foreign to Yoruba thoughts. The Obas and Chiefs are constantly complaining that the system introduced by us has made divorce so easy and the morals of the people distinctly lax. I entirely agree with their view. . . . Generally speaking litigants should not be allowed to lay their matrimonial grievances before the District Officer, and orders in regard to matrimonial cases should not be sent by the District Officer to the Native Council except in very rare circumstances. Any complaint in such cases should be dealt with only in the presence of the Judges of the native courts, and as far as possible the District Officer should refrain from interference in matrimonial cases.[36]

The instruction that cases of adultery and divorce be dealt with only in the presence of the Judges of the Native Courts, was clearly an attempt to restore the traditional influence and control of African men, particularly chiefly authorities, over marital practices. This was borne out of the recognition by colonial officials that their system of indirect rule would never succeed if rural chiefs lost control over women. This became something of a patriarchal coalition formed by African chiefs and colonial officials with the intent of creating state and ideological structures to bring women under control.[37] What, we might ask, happened to earlier colonial ideas about promoting the rights of African women and liberating them from the constraints of repressive African traditions? It would seem that these ideals, which were used effectively to legitimize colonial rule at one point, were ultimately overshadowed by the overriding exigencies of the British colonial administration in alliance with African chiefs and powerful male interests within the society. The rhetoric of women's rights had been toned down for political expediency.

What is most significant to our concern with discourses of social rights here are the ways in which men, like women, invoked the language of rights to restore some of the control over women that they had lost in the early colonial period. This was particularly evident in the demands by husbands for the return of their bride wealth or their runaway wives. In several petitions to colonial administrators and cases brought before Native Courts, men requested official intervention in enforcing their "customary matrimonial rights."[38] A typical statement of claim in such cases read: "The plaintiff is claiming the restitution of *conjugal rights* on the Defendant who deserted away from lawful husband."[39] Colonial records indicate that cases of men demanding the return of runaway wives and the return of their dowry constituted the majority of civil cases in Benin District between 1905 and 1918.

Apart from using the Native Courts to assert their claims, men also petitioned colonial administrators directly, requesting official intervention to enforce their matrimonial or conjugal rights. In one such petition in 1939, O. B. Okereke, an Efik clerk, requested the Commissioner for Colony to intervene in the repatriation of his "run-away wife" who had left him on the instigation of a nurse employed with the government's Department of Medical Services. He alleged that the nurse had encouraged his wife to divorce him because of his objection to his wife's employment in the department. According to Okereke, the nurse even promised to help his wife refund the bride price, telling her that she could earn her living independently. He complained against the nurse's interference in his "domestic and private matter," which had subsequently deprived him of his "comfort and happiness." He, therefore, sought the intervention of the Commissioner in the repatriation of his wife "in the interest of the rights and liberty of the human family."[40] The matter, which appears to have dragged on for some time, was eventually resolved when the Director of Medical Services, to whom the petition was referred by the Commissioner, called a "peace meeting" between Okereke, the accused nurse, and some leaders in the local Efik community.[41] Remarkably, there is no evidence that Okereke's wife, who was at the center of the conflict, was either invited or represented at the peace meeting.

In a similar petition titled "Restitution of Marriage Rights" addressed to the Commissioner for Colony in 1940, Robert Madukwe, a security guard employed with the colonial government, sought official intervention to effect the repatriation of his wife "of Christian marriage" who had absconded to live with another man.[42] What is significant about Madueke's petition is that the petitioner anchored his petition not only on his "marriage rights" as a Christian and as a British subject but also on his loyalty and service to the British Crown. He emphasized that he was a veteran of the First World War who had received the King's medal for meritorious work.[43]

These petitions and several related cases brought before the Native Courts for "wife repatriation" and "return of dowry" provide us with interesting insights into the gendered nature of rights discourses in the colonial period. They represent another layer in the complex ways in which the rhetoric of rights was deployed over social issues like marriage and divorce in the colonial period. As in other arenas of colonial intervention, legitimizing discourses about civilization, morality, natural justice, rights, and liberties were deployed to legitimize colonial attempts to transform indigenous marriage practices and free "native women" from the bondage of patriarchal African customs. African women drew upon these notions and used them effectively, within the framework of colonial legal and administrative institutions, to escape male control. But, as we have seen, the language of rights deployed over issues of marriage and divorce was not only a tool for legitimizing specific social agendas. It was also an instrument of opposition and negotiation. Men, who mostly bore the brunt of colonial marital reforms, also used the language of rights to renegotiate and reassert their positions within a changing society.

These insights improve our understanding of the gendered and generational tensions that characterized the process of social change in colonial and early postcolonial Nigeria. Also, significantly, they underscore the limitations of the suggestion made in some quarters that human rights scholars go beyond the confines of "rights talk and culture talk" and embrace instead a "language of protest."[44] In some contexts, the language of rights provides a broader and more useful framework for understanding oppositional discourses than the language of protest. As evident here, the language of rights was not only a means of protest. It was much more. It was variously invoked as a means of legitimizing the status quo, opposing it, and even negotiating it. This multiple use of rights talk was not limited to issues of marriage and divorce. Africans also used the rhetoric of rights and liberty to resist social exclusion and demand greater integration into colonial society.

The Idumuashaba Agitation

The Idumuashaba agitation provides a unique perspective into how ordinary Africans used the language of rights to articulate social demands in the colonial period. The Idumuashaba (Idumu-Asaba) community in southwestern Nigeria had, since precolonial times, been the section of Issele-Uku used exclusively for the settlement of war captives, bondservants, and slaves. As in many other Igbo societies, even after the abolition of slavery, the people of Idumuashaba continued to be derogatorily referred to as *Oshu* (slaves).[45] They suffered discrimination and social stigmatization and were denied certain entitlements and privileges within the larger community. But, beginning with the formal abolition of slavery in the colony in the early 1900s, the people of Idumuashaba began a concerted campaign to redress their social conditions. In the eyes of the law, they were no longer slaves. But, in the eyes of their community, they still suffered the social ostracism of slavery, which is what they wanted so desperately to redress. They wanted acceptance and social inclusion. Between 1905 and 1945, the Idumuashaba people, led by a vocal group of mission-educated and literate indigenes acting under the auspices of the Idumuashaba Family Union, wrote several petitions and instituted several court actions to bring attention to the plight of the Idumuashaba people.

In 1905, the elders of Idumuashaba paid to the *Obi* of Issele-Uku the sum of £12.10.0d and 18 bullocks as "ransom" to propitiate the gods and free them from their slave status. But in spite of an earlier agreement to do so, the *Obi* refused to perform the necessary customary rites and rituals to "cleanse" them. Seven years later, the elders of Idumuashaba sent another delegation to *Obi* Esemene I, requesting that they be granted the full rights and liberties enjoyed by other citizens of Issele-Uku.[46] Dissatisfied with the response of the *Obi,* the elders appealed to the colonial Native Court. One of their main complaints was the prohibition of intermarriages between them and the other people of Issele-Uku. They implored the Court to proclaim this prejudice repugnant and contrary to British law against slavery. The European District Officer who presided over the case did not agree with their submission. He delivered a judgment in favour of the *Obi* on the grounds that the *Obi* was acting in conformity with native law and custom. Protesting the decision in a subsequent petition to the Chief Commissioner, the Idumuashaba elites stated that they found it "ridiculous" that slave stigmatization could be condoned in a British territory or countenanced by its administrative officers.[47]

In 1936, at the request of the Idumuashaba Family Union, the local colonial government held a public inquiry into the issue of slavery at Issele-Uku, where representatives of the Idumuashaba people presented their case once again. They stressed that the continued prejudices and discrimination against them within the larger Issele-Uku community had made them second-class citizens, and they requested the government's intervention to restore their rights as British subjects. Colonial officials were not convinced that there was much the government could do to help the Idumuashaba people under the circumstances. They perceived the problem as one of social custom and tradition that was best dealt with by the local Native Authority. But the Native Authority was headed by the *Obi* and his chiefs, who were not inclined to change such deeply entrenched social customs. In 1937, the leaders of Idumuashaba sent a more detailed and earnest petition to the colonial government. The petition, whose language is as instructive as its content, outlined their grievances and the remedies they sought.

> [W]e are treated most disdainfully as outcasts; and even that condition is aggravated by our exclusion from the exercise of civic rights as well as the enjoyment of our native privileges and social equality . . . We are constrained to state that, left to

himself, the Obi will never entertain our request for freedom and for the full privilege of exercising our civic rights. . . . Our desire, which we fervently pray may be conceded, is for the authority of His Majesty's Government to secure and establish for us our freedom and rights as free people unencumbered by limitations; that the derisive expression "oshu" in allusion to any one of us in public or private may be prohibited; that the enforced taking of an oath of servitude—administered at the Isu Indichie (juju place) [sic], to every offspring of Idumu Asaba—be declared unlawful, and banned; that the headman of our quarter may be accorded a seat in the Issele-Uku Native Court as a Sub-Chief and for all such reforms and rights to which the improved conditions will entitle us. . . . [A]ll assessed persons among us are regular taxpayers; we are law abiding, industrious, and with ambition innate in the minds of good citizens everywhere in the world. We need and we seek the full protection of Government as a unit of the Protected Subjects of His Britannic Majesty KING GEORGE VI in the Colony and Protectorate of Nigeria—a rich gem in the crown of Imperial Britain, on whose soil (or possession) [sic], no slave breathes.[48]

The petition ended with a suggestion by the petitioners as to how the government might go about introducing the necessary reforms to end the long-held prejudice and discrimination against the Idumuashaba people as slave descendants. They suggested that this could be done by oral announcements made publicly at mass meetings of inhabitants of all the communities of Issele-Uku. They suggested that the *Obi* and all his chiefs be required to be present, with "European Representatives of Government protected by a platoon of policemen."[49] Evidently, having lost faith in the *Obi* and the local Native Authority, the Idumuashaba petitioners were requesting more direct government intervention, backed by the coercive power of the state, to protect their rights and liberties.

The language of these petitions reveals much. Apart from the frequent references to rights and liberties, the writers make an effort to state the grounds for their demand for these rights. There is clearly an attempt to legitimate their rights demands on several levels. First, they emphasize that they are "law abiding, industrious," good, ambitious and tax-paying citizens of their community—attributes which, in their reckoning, earn them the rights and freedoms they demand. Second, they stress that they are "protected subjects of His Britannic Majesty" entitled to the same rights accorded British subjects and protected persons elsewhere. Finally, they make subtle reference to British antislavery policy and the obvious contradiction of this policy that their case presents.

In employing the language of rights and liberty to make their case, the petitioners appeal mainly to the libertarian ideals that they thought would resonate with colonial officials. There is no mention of customary native or communal entailment that dominated African rights claims in other contexts. For the Idumuashaba petitioners, the language of custom would hardly have been useful since they were challenging customs that mandated their social exclusion. In demanding the abrogation of these customs, it was more useful to appeal to British egalitarian notions of individual rights and liberties. This deployment of rights talk was a creative use of the same language of rights employed by the colonial state to legitimize its policies and agendas. But the Idumuashaba petitioners did not simply redeploy colonial rights rhetoric; they adapted it to suit their demands in their confrontation with both the colonial state and local customs.

In his reply to the Idumuashaba petitioners, the Resident of Benin Province, N. C. Denton, stated that he found no grounds for intervening in the matter because all legal disabilities imposed on the Idumuashaba people had been removed except for intermarriages with people of other sections the community. However, since such intermarriages were not forbidden under any penalty, there was not much the government could do about it. He maintained that social equality could not be attained by an order of government as the petitioners had requested and that the government could not compel men and women to enter into contract of marriage.[50] While assuring the petitioners that the British government would not countenance an involuntary state of slavery in the colony, he opined that the spread of education would, in the course of time, remove the conservatism of the townspeople and end their prejudice against the Idumuashaba people.[51]

This response reflected official thinking at the time. While the government was willing to enact laws abolishing slavery

in the country, it believed that the social residues of the long
tradition of slavery in Africa could not be abolished by legal
fiat. That would only come with time and the gradual changes
in social attitudes that were bound to come with the spread of
Western education, Christianity, and "civilization." Thus, although
antislavery laws prescribed stiff penalties for trading and holding slaves, they were silent on prevalent institutionalized discrimination against former slaves and people of slave descent.
This was thought to be beyond the scope of government regulation for, as the Resident put it, "government cannot decree
social equality."[52] Moreover, it was assumed that there were
already adequate provisions in the legal system for redressing
social grievances like those of the Idumuashaba people. Because colonial officials saw slavery only as a labor system, they
tended to underestimate the social and political restrictions
that slave status imposed on affected individuals and communities. This may explain why the Resident, in his response,
simply advised the Idumuashaba petitioners to obtain legal
redress in the Native Court.[53]

The attitude of the Resident toward the Idumuashaba petitioners suggests that there was nothing the government
could do for those who were legally free to leave the communities that kept them in social bondage but who, in practice,
could not or would not do so. No court of law could free them
from their social servitude or allow them to enjoy all the rights
and privileges of other sections of society.[54] The postabolition
problem of slavery in Idumuashaba, as in many other parts of
Africa, was not one of emancipation but rather one of incomplete assimilation. It was also an issue of parties seeking to
protect or challenge entrenched class interests that ensured
that in spite of the abolition of slavery some communities
continued to regard ex-slaves and their descendants as social
inferiors, denying them certain rights and privileges.

The responses of colonial officials to their grievances were
clearly not what the Idumuashaba petitioners had expected.
The petitioners did not see the discrimination and prejudice
they suffered as a result of their slave status as being merely
a matter of social grievance over local customs and traditions.
Rather, they saw these issues as an affront to their fundamental rights and liberties and they expected the government

to actively intervene on their behalf. As they pointed out in a subsequent letter, the government's attitude to their petition was indicative of a lack of full appreciation of the social discrimination that they suffered and its implications for their rights both as human beings and as British subjects.[55]

In February 1945, the Idumuashaba Family Union sent yet another petition to the Resident of Benin Province and the Chief Commissioner of the Western Provinces restating their grievances in terms similar to those used seven years earlier. This time, the language of rights and freedom that they employed was even stronger and the justification for demanding the intervention of the government to protect their rights and liberties more compelling. The petition read:

> We earnestly entreat that the Obi be urged to give us our complete freedom—freedom to live as others; freedom to speak and freedom to mix with the other sections of Issele. We urge that the Obi of Issele and his chiefs be forced to put a stop to all principles and policies that have hitherto marred or hindered our rights as citizens of Issele . . . We are fully aware of the fact that our Empire (the British commonwealth) is presently engaged in a titanic war against Hitlerism. We on our side share greatly in men and materials in the struggle. Several of our youths are in the front fighting to suppress oppression. . . . Our sufferings and experiences under Obi Osemene II, who continues to undermine our rights and freedoms, justify our action—for world peace would mean nothing to our gallant sons who today give up their lives that humanity might survive in peace, whilst some who may survive, return to find themselves and their future generations still being regarded as slaves and wickedly ostracized in the land of their fathers. Consequently, peace under our present state has no significance for us.[56]

The reference to the efforts of the "gallant sons" of Idumuashaba in the fight against Hitlerism as a justification for their rights demands is significant. References to the Second World War and Allied propaganda about the war being fought to free the world from the oppression of Nazism and Hitlerism characterized most local petitions in the 1940s and the postwar era. African petitioners were quick to appropriate the rhetoric of rights, liberty, and global peace, which the Allies

employed in the propaganda war against Nazism, to justify
their own local rights demand.

The impacts of the Second World War and the rhetoric of
universal human rights that characterized local politics during
the period are examined in greater detail in the next chapter.
What is of interest here is the gap between official attitudes toward slave stigmatization and those of Africans who were directly affected. This gap reflects the difficult challenge, earlier
outlined, that faced the colonial authorities caught between demands for wider antislavery intervention by the government
(like those of the Idumuashaba petitioners) and other groups
opposed to the extension of antislavery policies to the supposedly customary social sphere. These latter groups sometimes
articulated their opposition to the extension of colonial antislavery measures to African caste systems on the grounds that
it could jeopardize the traditional social order in local communities. This was the basis of the counterargument made by the
chiefs of Issele-Uku in response to the allegations of discrimination and exclusion by the Idumuashaba petitioners.[57]

Under these circumstances, colonial officials, even where
they privately sympathized with the plight of the Idumuashaba
people, were unwilling to act on their demands.[58] The Idumuashaba people were a small, even if vocal, group within the
larger Issele-Uku community. Colonial officials worried that
acceding to their demands would stir wider social dissent and
upheaval within the Issele-Uku community. The government
chose not to stir the hornet's nest even when legitimate concerns of rights and liberties—which it considered central to its
antislavery policy—were involved. In a final reply to the
Idumuashaba petitioners in June 1945, Resident L. L. Cantle
stated rather curtly: "You know that slavery does not exist
under British rule. If anyone calls you a slave you may at once
take action in your courts against him for 'defamation of Character' and recover damages."[59]

Although the Idumuashaba people failed in their bid for
government intervention, their petition campaign spanning
four decades demonstrates the ability of Africans to appropriate and deploy in diverse ways the same language of rights
and liberty that was so central to British imperial agenda. It
is important to stress, however, that, more than simply appro-

priating colonial rights talk, the Idumuashaba petitioners adapted it to meet their own needs. They extended rights talk beyond the limits of colonial usage, invoking the language of rights and liberty within antislavery in a wider sense than did the colonial administration.

For the most part, the colonial regime in Nigeria used the language of rights and liberty to justify and legitimize antislavery and other social agendas but only to the extent that it found convenient for maintaining administrative control. However, some Africans, like the Idumuashaba petitioners, were able to appropriate this language of rights and extend it to their demands for wider antislavery intervention in ways that the government did not originally intend or envisage. For them, the rights agenda articulated within antislavery could not be guaranteed by just the enactment of laws abolishing slavery. Further government intervention to guarantee the social equality of ex-slaves and people of slave descent with others in their communities was a necessary part of this agenda. Such adaptive reuse of rights talk was not peculiar to the Idumuashaba petitioners. The ability of local people to appropriate for their own ends the language of rights originally deployed to justify colonial agendas is characteristic of rights discourses in many African contexts.

The Idumuashaba petitions have another significance that needs to be emphasized. These petitions provide unique insights into how Africans used the language of rights and liberty in this period to articulate at a communal level their demands for social justice. They also demonstrate how these rights-based demands intersected with the exigencies of colonial administration. The evidence from the Idumuashaba petitions suggests that long before the Atlantic Charter and the Universal Declaration of Human Rights (UDHR) in 1948 the language of human rights was a dominant feature of entitlement claims within the colonial state.[60] This language of rights was not always localized but sometimes drew from global or universal ideals. For instance, the Idumuashaba petitioners stated that world peace would mean nothing to them if their "gallant sons," sacrificing their lives in the war against Hitler so that humanity might live in peace, continued to be deprived of their full rights upon return from the battlefields. This appeal to a universalist ideal of justice shaped much of the discussion about rights during the late colonial period early postcolonial period.

The Right to Family Life

By the 1950s public discussions about social rights in Nigeria had taken a different turn. They became more formal and intertwined with the political debates about decolonization, independence, and nation building. In 1957 a commission of inquiry, set up by the colonial government to inquire into the fears about oppression and marginalization by minority ethnic groups in the country, recommended the inclusion of a bill of rights in the independence constitution. The commission recommended a bill of rights as the best way to protect the rights of minority groups in a multiethnic and democratic country. The presence of a bill of rights, it stated, defined beliefs widespread among democratic countries and provided a standard to which persons whose rights are infringed could appeal.[61] The bill of rights subsequently included in the Nigerian constitution made extensive provisions for a wide range of "fundamental human rights" that were guaranteed to all Nigerians.[62] Perhaps the most significant of these was the right to "private and family life."[63] The constitution guaranteed, among other things, a legally enforceable right to "private and family life."[64]

Although the inclusion of a bill of rights in the constitution was borne out of the increasing global awareness of human rights following the Second World War and the adoption in 1948 of the UDHR, the provision for the right to family life was unique to the Nigerian constitution. There were no similar provisions in either the UDHR or the European Convention for the Protection of Human Rights and Fundamental Freedoms, which were the models for the Nigerian bill of rights.[65] The inclusion of the right to family life in the independence constitution was clearly an attempt by Nigerian politicians and intellectuals to uphold what they considered customary African social values and regimes of rights in the constitution. By providing a guarantee of family life, it was thought that "traditional" African family and community-oriented values, which were thought to have been circumscribed by colonial rule, could be transposed into the modern nation-state. The constitutional right to family life was intended to represent a synthesis of Western and traditional values—African traditions incorporated in a bill of rights patterned after Western models.

Ironically, the debates over family rights and the need for constitutional guarantees to protect them were reminiscent of earlier colonial debates over the need to regulate African marital and family relations in order to ensure that they conformed with "customary" models. In a 1941 editorial titled "The Sanctity of Family Life," the *West African Pilot,* a newspaper owned and edited by the nationalist activist and politician Nnamdi Azikiwe, who later became the president of Nigeria, stated:

> In our social evolution as a people, among the things that must be held sacred and jealously guarded is a respect for family life . . . If the whole country is to move forward, as it definitely must, the beginning must be made from a recognition of the sanctity of family life with a set determination to battle against anything that must come to shatter the tranquility of the family.[66]

Arguments like these about the ideals of traditional African family life and the need to uphold them in an independent state were often articulated in the language of "human rights," which had gained currency in the 1950s and 1960s. If membership of an extended family was a "fundamental right" protected by the community in traditional African societies, in modern society it was the duty of the state to protect this right.[67] It was argued, for instance, that extended family membership among the Yoruba gave the individual certain enforceable rights—the right to succession to the family property that is held in common, the right to be supported in times of scarcity, and the right to claim societal and psychological help at moments of need. The problems associated with old age, infirmity, widowhood, and being orphaned were also primary concerns of the family to which individuals were entitled as of right.[68] These and similar arguments provided the bases for including the right to family life as a fundamental human right in the national constitution.

However, the constitutional provision for the right to family life was more that just a reaffirmation of traditional social values. It had profound legal implications since it was interpreted by the courts to mean that a person's exclusion from membership of an extended family was a violation of his or her fundamental human right to family life under the constitution.[69] Another legal implication of this provision for the existing social order was that it became illegal and unconstitutional for a family to expel any of its members either by physical force or in the sense of alienating them, disowning them, and denying them the right to participate in family activities.

As would be expected, this constitutional guarantee of the right to family life proved quite problematic when it came to actual enforcement. Before this law, it was a common practice, particularly among the Yoruba, for family heads or family councils to sanction erring members with expulsion and exclusion from family activities. But with the introduction of the constitutional right to family life, new situations arose in which expelled family members challenged their expulsion in the courts on the grounds that their expulsion violated their fundamental human right to family life. In most of these cases, the courts tended to find the "customary" grounds for the expulsion of a petitioner from his extended family insufficient to warrant the expulsion.

In cases where the grounds for a person's expulsion from his family constituted a criminal offence under Nigerian criminal law, the courts ruled that the relevant section of the criminal code, rather than the traditional sanction of exclusion from the family, should be exclusively applied. In other cases where the particular act warranting a family member's expulsion was considered one of "mere social disgrace to the family," the courts also reversed family orders to expel erring members for being unconstitutional. One of the leading cases on the right to family life was *Aoko v. Fagbemi* in 1961 in which the applicant committed adultery and was expelled by the elders of her family.[70] Adultery was considered a crime under Yoruba customary law but not under the English common law model adopted at independence. The expelled family member then applied to the High Court for an injunction against her expulsion from the family on the grounds it would violate her fundamental human rights as guaranteed in the constitution. The court allowed her application on the grounds that her expulsion would indeed constitute a violation of her constitutional rights.

This and similar decisions of the Nigerian courts created conflicts between the new constitutional human rights regime and long-standing customary law regimes. Ultimately, constitutional rights provisions could not provide expelled family members with the relief they sought in the courts. Although the courts ruled that family members should not be expelled, they were powerless in actually enforcing the reintegration of expelled members back into their family. It became clear that the courts simply could not mandate social conduct or regulate family life. In the case of the Yoruba village of Ishogba, for example, a court injunction in 1962 to stop a number of family expulsions proved to have no practical effect. The expelled members were shunned and ostracized by their own families and the larger community. They were eventually compelled to leave their homeland for other locations. Many sought refuge in the anonymity of urban centers to start a new life. Other expelled members later chose to come to terms with their family and pay reparations in order to gain readmission.[71]

In the end, the constitutional and legal guarantees of the right to family life, introduced to promote family life and traditional social values, may have served only to complicate family relationships. In fact, it soon became clear even to the most ardent supporters of the constitutional right to family life that legal regulation of informal social relations by the state, even when done under the rubric of "human rights," was impractical. Eventually, the right to family life provision was removed from the bill of rights.

The constitutional provision for the right to family life was partly borne out of a sense of cultural nationalism and the quest by the Nigerian intelligentsia to reaffirm African social values in the period leading up to independence. As we have seen, similar ideas about native customs informed earlier colonial attempts at social restructuring, and rights talk was useful to both colonial officials and African elites at different times and for different reasons. The language of rights, whether deployed in the context of "liberating women" from oppressive marital traditions (as in the early colonial period) or in the context of guaranteeing the right to family life (as in the late colonial period), promoted and legitimized specific social agendas. As colonialism drew to a close, rights talk began to assume new meanings and significance for African elites; it shifted from being mainly a means of engagement with the colonial state to a means of validating nationalist agendas. Here again, we confront the paradox of colonial rights discourse. Rights talk originally deployed by the colonial state to legitimize its social agenda of civilizing and modernizing the native, ultimately provided these same natives with a complex discursive terrain in which they could challenge the state, construct competing entitlement claims, and, ultimately, negotiate their own positions within a changing society.

6

Citizens of the World's Republic

Political and Civil Rights Discourses

We want to prove ourselves men, gentlemen, and loyal citizens of not only the empire that offers us protection but *citizens* of the World's Republic. . . . *Civis mundi sum; civis mundi sum!*[1]

—*The Lagos Standard,* November 2 and October 10, 1917

Colonial Politics and the Rights Question

I f politics is conceived broadly as the tactics and strategies of gaining, contesting, and negotiating power, then most discussions about rights are ultimately political in nature. However, this chapter focuses specifically on the issues and debates that dominated the struggles for political influence and control. It explores the debates about rights and liberties that characterized the political process of policy-making, nationalism, and constitutionalism in the colonial and immediate postcolonial state. Two important events shaped these discourses—the First and Second World Wars. The first war had far-reaching political consequences that contributed to the rise of organized nationalist movements in Africa. The loyalty and contributions of Africans to the Allied cause during the war produced a new

141

sense of entitlement that was often expressed in the language of rights. In Nigeria, vocal elites were no longer content with their status as colonial subjects and British-protected persons. They demanded their rights as "full citizens of empire."

The second war had even more significance for discussions about political rights. The emergence of the contemporary human rights movement has been linked to certain outcomes of the war, particularly the UDHR, which has become central to the definition of human rights. In Nigeria, as elsewhere in the colonized world, the language of universal rights in the Atlantic Charter and the UDHR became an important part of the nationalist rhetoric and a model for the constitutional rights regime introduced at independence. Much of these debates centered on two issues. The first was the concern of African chiefs and their supporters among the Western-educated elite about the erosion of their political power under British rule. The educated elite opposed British intervention in local politics and sought to defend the political rights of chiefs and their subjects against colonial excesses. In 1894 one local newspaper lamented the "spectacle of native chiefs and tribes being hunted down and made fugitives by colonial authorities."[2] Putting aside their sometimes-acrimonious differences, Western-educated Africans allied with local kings and chiefs to promote what they construed as the political rights of Africans as the reach of British power expanded. The second issue that raised widespread concerns about political rights was educated Africans opposing their exclusion from colonial administration. Although these issues affected two distinct groups of Africans, both converged in early debates about colonial rule and the limitations it placed on political participation by Africans.

The exclusion of educated Africans from meaningful roles in the central government was an explicit policy of British colonial administration, particularly in the early colonial period. This policy was based on the assumption that these educated elites were alienated from the people and so could not adequately represent them. As the colonial Governor Frederick Lugard put it, "The interest of the large native population should not be subject to the will of a small minority of educated and Europeanized natives who have nothing in common with them and whose interest are often opposed to theirs."[3] Lugard's successor, Governor Hugh Clifford, expressed the same view when he described the National Congress of British West Africa, a nationalist political organization, as a "self-selected and self-appointed congregation of educated African gentlemen."[4]

The denial of the political claims of educated Nigerians was based on the view of the colonial authorities that they lacked a cultural connection with the "unsophisticated masses." However, there were other important factors at play in the tension between the colonial authorities and the educated elites, particularly in the operation of the Native Authority system. The Native Authority system, which arrogated much power to chiefs, was introduced at a time when the educated elite, brought up under Western ideas and conscious of their rights, began to demand participation in all aspects of local government. They saw their exclusion from government as denial of their rights on two grounds. First, it was a denial of their right as Africans to participate in the management of their own affairs. Second, and perhaps more importantly, it was a denial of their "right" as a class of educated and enlightened Africans to lead their people. "The intelligentsia of this country," wrote one newspaper contributor in 1916, "have a right to represent their people; to govern the majority in order to safeguard the interest of the whole and create a situation where the greatest good can be done to the greatest number."[5]

The grievances of the elites were compounded by the extensive powers that the colonial authorities gave to chiefs under the Native Authority system. In many cases, the precolonial checks and balances to chiefly powers were either removed or ignored under the Native Authority system. Some traditional rulers were designated "Sole Native Authorities." Subject only to the supervision of the colonial Resident, they had absolute powers over local administration. This was a recipe for discord and conflict. It led to tensions over political power between Western-educated elites and the colonial authorities, between educated elites and the chiefs who ran the colonial Native Authorities, and even among the chiefs who constituted the Native Authority administration. In these struggles over political power, entitlement claims were often articulated in the language of rights.

Colonial officials argued that the system of indirect rule through African chiefs ensured African participation in governance. Educated African elites responded that the limitations of chiefly powers under the system effectively made African chiefs instruments of colonial domination rather than true representatives of their people. However, although the intelligentsia rejected the ideas and institutions of empire, they did not always reject the ideals of empire. They still needed and pursued the advance of British imperial power, with its commitment to social and economic reordering. Despite their continuing advocacy for the rights of Africans in the management of native affairs, most elites favored some form of British overrule. The emphasis at this stage was not on the right to self-determination or complete independence as it became in the 1940s but on the right to political participation in colonial administration. Between the alternatives of the British colonial status quo or incorporation by another European empire, the intelligentsia remained ardently pro-British. "The Natives of Africa," wrote the *Lagos Weekly Record* in 1892, "love the Queen not only for what she is, but for what she represents—the freest and best system of government the world has ever known."[6] The prominent African lawyer Osho Davis wrote in 1914, "Our cry is not against British justice, as we are bred to it and love and admire it, but against the endeavor being made to deprive us of that justice."[7]

The main reason for these pro-British sentiments was the elite's belief that even under colonial overrule they could be beneficiaries of the full rights of British subjects. This was possible, however, only when colonial officials upheld traditional British values. Writing in 1908, Bandele Omoniyi, a British-trained doctor, called for continued adherence to the true British school of colonial policy, which "admitted the capacity of Africans to enjoy full political and civil rights."[8] For these elites, there was no contradiction in their defense of the political rights of African chiefs while at the same time advocating British ideals and their own rights as British subjects. To them, both agendas were compatible. Indigenous political systems and enlightened British rule each had a place in their vision of a modern and civilized polity. These sentiments that appealed to both the "traditional" rights of the African and his acquired rights as British subject would be ardently reiterated during the First World War.

Citizens of Empire: War, Liberty, and Justice

The most palpable effect of the First World War was that it strengthened the African's sense of belonging to the British Empire. In declaring war against Germany, Britain seemed to most Africans under its rule to be fighting Africa's battles against a symbol of ruthless colonialism. In the period leading up to the war, stories of the brutality and repression of German colonial rule in East Africa were widely reported in the local press and the war was seen partly as a battle to liberate Africans burdened by German colonial rule. British propaganda portrayed Germany as "the most tyrannic, oppressive, and illiberal" colonial power, as opposed to England, the most liberal and accommodating colonial power. Germany had come into the non-European world in 1884, argued British colonial governor Hugh Clifford, solely for the purpose of exploitation and as "a roaring lion seeking whom she may devour."[9]

Local newspapers threw themselves into the effort to "conquer and vanquish" Germany, presenting a picture of a progressive British Empire united against a common foe.[10] The *Lagos Standard* commented in 1916 that the war was a "titanic struggle" in which "might and brute force are arrayed against Right and Justice."[11] Even newspapers like the *Record,* which were critical of the colonial government, dropped their anti-imperialist roles and urged the public to "think imperially" by supporting the Nigerian Overseas Contingents Comforts Fund. "Our destiny," wrote the *Lagos Standard,* "is indissolubly linked with England and we must rise or fall with her."[12] The *Nigerian Pioneer* commented that Germany's successes in the previous century had made her drunk with power and that "with dreams of still greater greatness, she suddenly and ruthlessly attacked other countries in utter disregard for the very fabric of civilization."[13] In contrast, Britain was presented as the beacon of liberty and the ideal of imperial rule. The *Lagos Weekly Record* wrote about the "benign influences of British imperial rule, whose watch words are liberty and progress."[14] Although some discordant voices questioned popular support for the war, most of the African intelligentsia remained solidly behind British war efforts.

VICTORY IS VITAL!

GERMANS WOULD ROB
WEST AFRICANS OF THEIR PRODUCE

BRITAIN'S FAIRNESS

Happy family life

Modern transport

You come and go in safety

SLAVES UNDER HITLER

You would not receive cash payment for your produce

You would have no money for goods and could not buy where you wished

Germans would take your produce and give you no goods in return

Figure 6.1. "Victory Is Vital!" (Colonial Government propaganda poster, circa 1943)

But if the war against Germany promoted a stronger sense of patriotism and commitment to empire among the Nigerian intelligentsia, it also provided new grounds for questioning and challenging colonial rule. British involvement in the war encouraged educated Africans to believe that all nationalities, however small, had a right to their independence and to the sanctity of their treaties. Britain was understood to have declared war on Germany in defense of the treaty guaranteeing the political independence and territorial integrity of Belgium. African elites took seriously the British wartime resolution affirming her "inflexible determination to continue to a victorious end the struggle in maintenance of the ideals of Liberty, Justice and Freedom"—ideals that were said to be the common cause of the allied powers.[15] The statements of President Wilson of the United States and Prime Minister Lloyd George of Britain affirming liberty and self-determination as justifications for the war were echoed by Nigerian elites. The *Lagos Standard* quoted with approval President Wilson's statements concerning America's aims in the war: "liberty, self-government freed from alien dictation, and unhampered development."[16]

Special weight was also given to Lloyd George's statement in 1918 that the principle of self-determination was as applicable to the colonies as to occupied European territories, even though subsequent qualifications made it clear that his statement did not refer to African territories.[17] In spite of these inconsistencies, the idea remained strong among Nigerian elites that Britain's war against Germany was a war for the principles of honor, freedom, and liberty, as the *Lagos Standard* indicated in an editorial in 1918.

> "We are fighting," says the Governor General "for the observance of treaties which the Germans regard as scraps of paper to be disregarded when they no longer serve their advantage. We are fighting that there may be, remaining the world, some regard for the liberty to live our lives in freedom in our own way . . . The right of all men to live in peace and the sanctity of the pledged word.[18]

Although these statements were originally made in relation to the political conditions in wartime Europe, many Nigerian commentators extended them to their own status as colonized peoples. The *Lagos Weekly Record* advised that any treaty of lasting peace after the war must affirm that the native inhabitants of tropical Africa have rights, however obscure, which must be respected and that European nations also have obligations toward the native.[19] These ideas about the political rights of Africans, articulated from a global perspective, intersected in complex ways with a more radical racial discourse of African rights coming from across the Atlantic.

Race, Rights, and the Black Atlantic

Although racial discourses from the United States and other parts of the Atlantic world had influenced educated Nigerians from the early nineteenth century, the First World War ushered in a period of even greater influence of these ideas. The Nigerian intelligentsia was influenced by black Atlantic race and rights discourses in two main ways. One was through the writings and activities of African Americans who advocated black empowerment. Another was through the influence of Nigerians who had studied in the United States and returned home to propagate the Atlantic race discourse. This group of Nigerian intellectuals drew parallels between the conditions of the "American Negro" and the "colonized Native."

Much of the Atlantic race discourse centered on rebutting the scientific racism of the early twentieth century. It was also aimed at challenging well-developed American racial doctrines, resurgent after the post-Civil War reconstruction, which provided the basis for disenfranchisement and official discrimination against African Americans.[20] These issues were widely addressed in local newspapers and discussed extensively among Nigerian intellectuals. The Nigerian press seemed to have been particularly preoccupied with reporting and commenting on developments concerning African Americans. This interest became even greater with the return in the 1940s of American-trained Nigerian intellectuals such as Nnamdi Azikiwe, Mbonu Ojike, and Ozuomba Mbadiwe, who became actively involved in the newspaper press.

In Nigeria, as in the black Atlantic, the intelligentsia turned to race pride to defend themselves against an increasingly prejudicial power structure. The stress on racial pride and solidarity informed the growing Pan-African sentiments that animated the diaspora by the end of the century. W.E.B. Du Bois, one of the leading African American intellectuals of the period, emphasized the collective destiny of the African race. He argued that "negroes must strive by race organization, by race solidarity, by race unity" to establish their place among the races of the world.[21] Writings of Pan-Africanists such as Du Bois and Marcus Garvey struck a chord with many educated Nigerians, and the message of emancipation and empowerment underlying them resonated in the pages of local newspapers.

African intellectuals gave local meaning and relevance to the Atlantic ideas about liberty, equality, black consciousness, and rights, which they promoted through their control of the newspaper press. The publisher of the *Lagos Weekly Record,* John Payne Jackson, gained a reputation as a determined agent in the propagation of native rights and racial consciousness. His pungent criticisms of the colonial government which touched on the rights and welfare of Africans were published in lengthy editorials in his newspaper.[22] He urged Africans to be aware of their "common nationality" and jointly safeguard their liberties. "Liberty," he wrote, "was never conferred upon any nation"; it had to be won through "sacrifice, martyrdom and patriotism."[23]

The convening of the First Pan-Africanist Congress in Paris in 1918-1919 by W.E.B. Du Bois and Blaisé Diagne further stimulated the spread of these Pan-Africanist sentiments in Nigeria. The congress aimed at impressing on the victorious Allied powers the importance of Africa in the world and demanded a "Charter of Rights" for Africans, including the right to participate in their government.[24] The demands of the congress struck a chord with Nigerian intellectuals such as Earnest Ikoli and Nnamdi Azikiwe, who championed similar ideas in the 1930s and 1940s. In Du Bois and other Atlantic Pan-Africanists, they found allies who could voice their concerns about political marginalization and visions of empowerment on a world stage. Azikiwe, who later became president of independent Nigeria, was particularly influenced by the Atlantic race discourse. From the time he returned to Nigeria in 1934 from his studies in the United States,

Azikiwe generally thought and acted along universalist and racial lines. His writings, an eclectic adaptation of nineteenth-century black Atlantic ideas, illustrate the ways in which African engagement with the black Atlantic race discourse invigorated local debates about rights and empowerment.[25]

By drawing diasporic affinities and connections between the Atlantic Pan-Africanist/race discourse and their own concerns about segregation and racial discrimination at home, Nigerian intellectuals found universal themes that reinforced their own positions. References in the press to "Jim Crow colonial policies"[26] and comparisons of racial segregation in Lagos with the experiences of the American negro in the "ghettos of Harlem"[27] were part of this process of discourse integration. The Atlantic context not only inspired anticolonial sentiments but also reinforced the basis of the assertion of African rights by the Nigerian intelligentsia. The influence of Atlantic ideas on the rights discourse became particular evident from the 1920s onward as Africans became more assertive in their demands for political reforms.

Influenced partly by Atlantic Pan-Africanist ideas, the developments among African American groups in America, the nationalist ferment in India and Ireland, and the climate of idealism generated by the war, a few educated Africans in the British West African territories organized the National Congress for British West Africa (NCBWA) in 1920. This set the stage for later nationalist organizations such as the Nigerian National Democratic Party (NNDP) as well as the Nigerian Youth Movement (NYM), which proclaimed as its political goal, "a complete taking over of the government of Nigeria into the hands of the indigenous people of our country."[28] The NYM demanded universal suffrage, an end to color prejudice, admission of Nigerians into the colonial legislature and civil service, and abolition of the indirect rule system and its replacement by "a form of indigenous local government."[29] Other nationalist organizations such as the National Council of Nigeria and the Cameroons (NCNC) the Action Group (AG) emerged during the Second World War to demand independence more forcefully. They took advantage of a wartime political environment of increased political awareness among ordinary Nigerians. Although the war provided the colonial government with an opportunity to enhance its influence and power, it also strengthened the local nationalist movement and an emergent universal human rights movement.

War Rhetoric and Anti-Imperialism

As with the First World War, most Nigerians supported Britain and Allied campaign against Germany during the Second World War. The colonial state extensively deployed anti-German propaganda in a way strikingly reminiscent of the First World War. In both official and public circles the moral battle lines were clear—Germany and the evil force of Nazism against the forces of good represented by Britain and the Western democracies. Governor Bernard Bourdillon emphasized that the British Empire was fighting for "the right of the ordinary man in every part of the world to live out his own life in freedom and peace" and that the struggle was against those who believed in force and brutal repression of freedom.[30]

These views were shared within the nationalist movement where there was a consensus that Nigeria should unequivocally identify herself with the forces of good—the Allied Nations. The *West African Pilot* stressed the loyalty of Africans to the British Empire and their willingness to make the ultimate sacrifice of "shedding their blood in order that the ideals of liberty, democracy and peace might thrive in the world."[31] But, in spite of their support for British war efforts, Nigerian elites continued to push their demands for political reforms and challenge state policies. Opposing the government's proposals to introduce censorship laws during the war, the *West African Pilot* stated that no pretext, not even the war against Nazism, should be used to restrict the cherished press freedom that prevailed in the British Empire. To do so, it argued, would be to go against the very same principles of freedom for which the war was being waged.[32]

Allied propaganda that the war against Germany was being fought to preserve democracy and to ensure that every man in every part of the world might live in freedom and peace provided a basis for Nigerians to demand that these same ideals be extended to them. Since Africans as citizens of the British Empire were being called upon to fight, Britain must not deny these Africans those democratic rights for which the war was being fought.[33] The *Daily Service* in an editorial in 1940 asserted that to be secure against "Hitlarism," democracy and liberty must be universal. It stressed the importance of extending to Africans and other "weaker peoples" the same ideals of freedom and liberty for which the war against Hitler had been waged.[34]

Nigerian intellectuals were attempting to link their political demands with global issues associated with the war. They used war rhetoric and, particularly, Allied propaganda, to press their political agenda by increasingly articulating their demands in terms of universal rights and "global liberty" rather than merely their rights as citizens of empire. They criticized the colonial government by drawing parallels between it and the excesses of Nazism in Europe. Objecting to the composition of the colonial Legislative Council in 1942, the Nigerian Youth Movement stated the Council was reminiscent of the "tyranny of Nazi Germany."[35]

Wartime discussions about rights and liberties within the nationalist movement were further stirred in the early 1940s over the interpretation of the Atlantic Charter, which raised further concern among Nigerian nationalists over Britain's postwar intentions for the colony. What became known as the Atlantic Charter was not originally intended as a formal document; it was a press release on the outcome of a meeting in 1941 between Prime Minister Churchill and President Roosevelt at Placentia Bay aimed at drawing up a common declaration of purpose concerning the Second World War. The "charter" declared that both leaders "respect the right of all peoples to choose the form of government under which they will live" and that they wished to "see sovereign rights and self-government restored to those who have been forcibly deprived of them."[36] The charter, which has been described as the first major document of global significance to affirm the right to self-determination in both humanistic and universalist terms, was subsequently incorporated by reference in the Declaration of the United Nations and the UDHR.[37]

The Atlantic Charter became the focus of global discussions

and debates about the right to self-determination soon after it was issued. Public discussion over the charter centered on its famous third clause, which affirmed "the right of all peoples to choose the form of government under which they will live." This statement excited the hopes of colonial nationalists everywhere, who saw it as an unequivocal recognition of their right to self-determination and independence. However, they cautiously welcomed the charter, fearing that its ideals would turn out to be no more than mere platitudes.[38] The *West African Pilot* stated that the charter might turn out to be "just one of those human instruments nobly conceived but poorly executed."[39]

These fears were confirmed in November 1942 when Churchill stated in the House of Commons that he and President Roosevelt had only European states in mind when they drew up the charter and that the charter was intend as a guide, not a rule.[40] Even more controversial was his widely quoted remark that he had not become Prime Minister to preside over the liquidation of the British Empire. "Let there be no mistake in any quarter," he proclaimed, "we intend to hold what we have. I have not become the King's First Minister to preside over the liquidation of the British Empire."[41] To further complicate matters, a different and contrasting interpretation of the charter soon came from Roosevelt, who maintained that the "Atlantic Charter applies to all humanity."[42] Roosevelt's liberal interpretation of the provisions of the charter was more in tune with the expectations of the Nigeria intelligentsia, who responded to Churchill's statements with disappointment and vehement criticism.

In a 1941 editorial titled "Even Mr. Winston Churchill!" the *West African Pilot* described Churchill's statements as a dishonor to Africans who had sacrificed their lives for the Allied cause.[43] The newspaper demanded a clarification of Britain position on the Atlantic Charter. Although Churchill subsequently explained that the Atlantic Charter was not incompatible with the progressive evolution of self-governing institutions in Nigeria and elsewhere in the British Empire, this clarification did not satisfy an already incensed and disappointed intelligentsia. Dismissing Churchill's explanations in an editorial titled "Churchill's Consistent Inconsistencies," the *Daily Service* stated:

> Winston Churchill is a bundle of contradiction. He believes
> in "liberty and freedom for all men." He is at the same time
> a die-hard imperialist. Imperialism and liberty are by no
> means coterminous. Churchill believes in ruling irrespective
> of the will of those who are ruled and yet he decries dictator-
> ship of the world by Great Powers.[44]

In an editorial titled "The Atlantic Chatter," the *West African Pilot* lamented that Africans had been hoodwinked into believing in the promise of the "Atlantic Charter" which it claimed did not exist at all. What existed was an Atlantic *Chatter* rather than an Atlantic *Charter*. "A *charter* is a document bestowing certain rights and privileges; *chatter* on the other hand, means to utter sounds rapidly or to talk idly or carelessly." For Africans, the promise of the Atlantic Charter was nothing but idle talk among Western powers.[45]

Criticism of Churchill was not limited to Nigeria. Perhaps the most trenchant criticism came from across the Atlantic. American criticism, not only of Churchill's statement but also of the whole imperial project, unleashed a trans-Atlantic debate over the ethics of colonialism. In 1941 Wendell Wilkie, a Republican presidential candidate, called for an end to colonialism and the "rule of people by other people."[46] The notion that the war settlement should include a deal for colonized peoples also figured prominently in postwar schemes advanced by private American individuals and organizations.[47] The League of Colored People at a conference in London drew up a "Charter for Colored Peoples" that it called upon the United Nations to adopt. The charter affirmed the same "political, economic, educational and legal rights" of all persons, irrespective of color. It demanded that indigenous peoples of all dependant territories be granted full self-government at "the earliest possible opportunity."[48] As would be expected, the Nigerian intelligentsia enthusiastically received this "alternative charter."[49]

Even within the usually conservative British press and political circles, there was stiff opposition to Churchill's position on the Atlantic Charter. The *Times* of London questioned the rationale for Churchill's qualifications of the Charter while the

Manchester Chronicle urged him to rethink his position; otherwise, the Atlantic Charter would become, for millions of people, a symbol of hypocrisy.[50] The anti-imperialist British Labor Party and its close associate the Fabian Council Bureau also strongly opposed Churchill's interpretation of the charter. Labor spokesmen, both inside and outside parliament, demanded the application of the spirit of the Atlantic Charter to the colonies.[51]

These international objections to Churchill's statements on the Atlantic Charter reverberated in Nigeria and fortified the intensity of the criticism heaped upon Churchill by Nigerian intellectuals. Commenting on Britain's position on the charter, the nationalist leader Nnamdi Azikiwe urged Africans and other colonized peoples to prepare their own blueprint of rights themselves instead of relying on those who are too busy preparing their own.[52] Azikiwe did, in fact, go about preparing his own blueprint of rights. In his *Political Blueprint for Nigeria*, published in 1943, he listed the basic rights that should be guaranteed to every "commonwealth subject." These included the right to health, education, social equality, material security and even the right to recreation.[53] He recommended that the Virginia Bill of Rights, which served as a model for the American constitution, should also serve as a model for preparing the Nigerian constitution. The Virginia Bill of Rights, he argued, was ideal, because "it embodies all the basic rights for which democratic-loving humanity had fought to preserve in the course of history."[54]

Azikiwe's *Blueprint* became the basis of the Freedom Charter, a statement of rights drawn up by his political party the National Councl for Nigeria and the Cameroons (NCNC) in 1943. The Freedom Charter is historically significant because it included the first comprehensive regime of fundamental human rights in Nigeria. The Charter affirmed a wide range of political, economic, and social rights for all Nigerians. It included a condemnation of slavery, servitude, and imperialism; an affirmation of the right to life and dignity of the human person; the equality of all persons; the right to basic education and health; the right to free expression and association; and the right to recreation and leisure. The Charter particularly stressed the right to self-determination. Alluding to the Atlantic Charter, it affirmed the "right of all peoples to choose the form of

Figure 6.2. Akinola Lasekan, "Yes, She Would Look Best in this New One." (*West African Pilot,* December 7, 1948)

government under which they may live."[55] Azikiwe and the NCNC justified the Charter as a document founded on African political experience and expressive of the aspirations of African people.[56] The party demanded the adoption of the Charter to replace the existing colonial constitution.

A major significance of the Atlantic Charter was that it partly inspired the creation of the United Nations and provided the basis for the Universal Declaration of Human Rights in the postwar era. The inauguration of the UDHR marked the first time in history that certain fundamental rights and freedoms were set forth at a global forum of nations as inalienable universal values to which *all* individuals are entitled simply by virtue of their humanity. At its adoption, the UDHR was heralded as a "a milestone in the road of human progress."[57] Eleanor Roosevelt, one of its chief architects, stated that the Declaration had the potential of becoming "a Magna Carta for all humanity."[58] This optimism was in spite of the fact that half of the world's peoples were still under colonial domination. Also, most colonized peoples were not represented at the United Nations and had no opportunity to make any input into the preparation of the UDHR. The exclusion of the voices of colonized peoples in the process of drawing up the UDHR remains one of the strongest challenges to its claim to universality.[59] Yet, the UDHR has been widely acknowledged as the cornerstone of the contemporary human rights movement.

The precise extent to which the Second World War, the Atlantic Charter, and the UDHR affected the nationalist movement and, ultimately, the decolonization process in Nigeria is difficult to assess. Taken together, these developments marked a critical phase in the nationalist movement. Nigerian nationalists acknowledge that the Atlantic Charter exposed them to new ideas and increased popular support for their cause.[60] The language of universal rights underlying discussions about the Atlantic Charter provided a framework for the Nigerian intelligentsia to articulate and legitimize their demands for political reforms within the colonial state. However, it would be erroneous to conclude that the Atlantic Charter or the

Figure 6.3. Akinola Lasekan, "The People's Choice" (*West African Pilot,* July 2, 1949)

UDHR marked the beginning of an entirely new tradition of "human rights" distinct from previous notions or discourses of rights. The historical evidence from this part of Africa does not support this assumption. Although there was a change in the pattern of rights discourses during and following the Second World War, this change did not mark the beginning of an entirely new tradition of rights talk. If anything, discussions about rights and liberties in the period of Second World War were built on a long tradition of colonial rights talk in which Africans were fully engaged. Postwar rights discourses, despite their more universalist appeal, were part of a historical continuum. They were part of a long tradition of rights discourses in Nigeria that dates back to the early Christian missionary humanism, the antislavery movement, the colonial legal system, and debates about rights within the context of empire during the First World War. In appealing to "universal human rights" to advance their demands for self-determination in the 1940s and 1950s, Nigerian nationalists were not drawing on something entirely new. The language of rights and liberty that they deployed was neither novel nor unique to their time. It was another phase in the adaptive appropriation of a language of rights that had been deployed at various times in the past by the colonial state and various groups of Africans for different reasons. What needs to be examined is how Nigerians, following in this tradition, deployed the language of "universal rights," which gained currency in the postwar era to advance nationalist agendas.

Placing the Universal Declaration of Human Rights

In appraising the impact of the Second World War on the decolonization process in Africa, one question that arises is the extent to which postwar developments such as the establishment of the United Nations and the adoption of the UDHR influenced the nationalist movement. How much influence did the UDHR really have on the decolonization process in Africa? This question is important given the widely held assumption that the UDHR is the foundation of the contemporary concept of human rights and that its adoption by the

United Nations in 1948 marked the beginning of a human rights revolution that has redefined our understanding of ethics and justice.

Questions over the impact on the UDHR on the status of colonized people arose even while the Declaration was still being drafted. The irony that a declaration purporting to be a "Magna Carta for humanity" was being drawn up at a time when half of the world's population was still under colonial domination was inescapable. Perhaps to address this odd reality and remove any ambiguity over whether the provisions of the Declaration applied to colonized people, the drafters of the Declaration included a clause that stated quite categorically: "The rights set forth in this Declaration apply equally to all inhabitants and non-self governing territories."[61] Not surprisingly, some countries were uncomfortable with such a categorical statement affirming the applicability of the Declaration to colonized peoples. There was concern that this would provide new grounds for nationalists and anticolonial activists to assail the legitimacy of colonial rule and other forms of political domination. White minority-ruled South Africa, one of the countries that opposed the Declaration, was concerned about the implications for its policy of racial segregation.[62] Its delegate stated that the text of the Declaration went beyond generally accepted rights. He argued that the right to participate in government was not universal; it was conditioned not only by nationality but also by qualifications of franchise.[63] In the end, the General Assembly deleted the clause specifically affirming the applicability of the Declaration to colonized peoples and replaced it with a less specific one: "Furthermore, no distinction shall be made on the basis of the political, jurisdictional or international status of the country or territory to which a person belongs, whether is be independent, trust, non-self governing or under any limitation of sovereignty."[64] It was also emphasized that the Declaration was not legally binding on United Nations member states that had adopted it. It was purely a "moral force" intended to serve as a "guiding light to all those who endeavoured to raise man's material standard of living and spiritual condition."[65]

But, in spite of its lack of legal force, few doubted that the UDHR was an important landmark in an emerging global human rights movement. Eleanor Roosevelt thought that the Declaration would be of importance comparable to the 1789 French Declaration of the Rights of Man and the American Declaration of Independence.[66] As it turned out, the UDHR proved to be even more significant than these documents. Its influence reverberated across colonized Africa where people demanding the right to self-determination welcomed its adoption by the United Nations as a vindication of their cause.

In Nigeria, nationalist leaders were cautiously optimistic about the impact of the Declaration on their aspirations for independence and self-rule. The *West African Pilot* hailed the Declaration as "a courageous initiative," stating that while its principles would be difficult to implement by the "imperialist powers" that subscribed to it, the fact that they have enunciated these principles and accepted them in theory, was sufficient to provide oppressed and colonial peoples everywhere with a tribune for their political demands.[67] Writing on the significance of the UDHR in 1949, Eyo Ita, a leading nationalist politician, remarked that the Universal Declaration of Human Rights provided a new yardstick with which peoples of all lands could measure the success or failure of their political systems. To him, the UDHR was a direct condemnation of imperialism in all its forms. Its universal language ushered a new global era in which Africa was no longer "an isolated asylum of slavery and oppression."[68] Evidently, the UDHR provided an internationally accepted moral, if not legal, standard of rights to which these nationalists could appeal in their demands for independence from European colonial powers.

However, it is important not to overstate the influence of the UDHR on postwar rights discourses in this part of Africa. For one, the introduction of the UDHR did not stimulate the kind of impassioned debates about the right to self-determination that followed the Atlantic Charter. One possible reason for this may be because after the Second World War the Nigerian intelligentsia tended to focus more on domestic issues and their internal struggles for independence rather than on developments on the international front. Besides, with no representations at the United Nations in 1948, most Nigerians did not see the organization as a forum for African voices or those of other colonized peoples.

Another reason for caution in evaluating the significance of the UDHR is that it seems to have had very limited influence on constitutional developments in the country and the rights-based demands of Nigerian nationalists. Rather than the UDHR, the document that dominated postwar discussions about rights in Nigeria was the Freedom Charter put forward by the Nigerian political party the NCNC in 1943. The NCNC Freedom Charter, which was one of the most comprehensive statements of rights produced by Africans in the colonial period, preceded the UDHR.[69] The Charter was seen as being more relevant to African needs and aspirations than a declaration of rights crafted thousands of miles away by a body dominated by Western powers.

The point here is not to deny the influence of the UDHR on the rights discourse in Nigeria as elsewhere in the colonial Africa. Rather, my argument is that the immediate impact of the UDHR on the rights discourse in the African context need not be overstated. This call for caution is in response to the tendency within human rights scholarship to ascribe too much to the UDHR and too little to other longstanding traditions of rights discourses that have shaped the contemporary human rights movement in Africa and elsewhere. Although the UDHR had some influence on the political rights discourses within nationalist movements in Africa, it did not launch a significantly new tradition of rights discourse in the colonial context. The lack of African representation at the United Nations, the non–legally binding character of the Declaration, and the dominance of European colonial powers at the United Nations all combined to engender skepticism toward the UDHR in many parts of colonial Africa. The most that can be said of the UDHR in this regard is that it provided a model for the regime of constitutional rights that was adopted at the end of colonial rule.

Decolonization and Constitutional Rights

One fallout of the Second World War and the resurgence of African nationalism in the postwar period was that Britain was forced to make important political concessions toward granting independence to its colonies in Africa. The political reforms inaugurated in the late 1940s signaled the beginning of the decolonization process in many parts of British colonial Africa. In Nigeria, colonial administrators made major constitutional reforms in 1946 and 1951, allowing for more African representation in the government. The 1951 reforms marked the first time that Nigerians were directly involved in drawing up a constitution for themselves. Nigerian elites saw it as an opportunity to express long-held views on their expected role in the new political dispensation. The constitutional reforms stimulated the formation of local political parties, which in turn increased the level of popular participation in Nigerian politics. Important debates shifted from the confines of colonial officialdom to the nascent political organizations. But with this increased political participation also came increased ethnic and regional rivalries.[70]

The nationalist movement, which until then had united Nigerians from all ethnic groups against colonialism, began to assume a more ethnic and regional character. The new political parties that emerged placed greater emphasis on regional and ethnic concerns rather than on national interests. Most of them were essentially ethnic organizations. The Action Group (AG) evolved from a Yoruba cultural movement in 1948. Its stated objective was "the inculcation of the idea of a single nationalism throughout Yoruba land." The founders of the party openly declared it to be a regional party aimed at organizing within its fold all nationalities in the Western Yoruba-dominated region of Nigeria. Similarly, the Northern People's Congress (NPC) was a purely Northern political party, dominated by the Muslim Hausa-Fulani ethnic group. Membership of the party was limited to people from the Northern region; the party's declared objective was to seek regional autonomy within Nigeria. The third major party was the Igbo-dominated National Council of Nigeria and the Cameroons (NCNC, later the National Council of Nigerian Citizens).

Although these regionalist parties jointly negotiated with the British government over constitutional changes leading up to independence, cooperation among them was often the result of expediency rather than an emerging sense of national unity. For the most part, political groups fashioned their agendas on the basis of regional, rather than national, interests. Once it became clear that political independence was within reach, the tenuous sense of national unity and consensus that had sustained the anticolonial movement gave way to rigidly parochial ethnic and regional interests. In championing their various regional causes, some political leaders even questioned the viability and desirability of a Nigerian nation. Ahmadu Bello, the leader of the Northern People's Congress, characterized British amalgamation of Northern and Southern Nigeria in 1914 as a mistake, while Obafemi Awolowo, leader of the Action Group, famously stated that Nigeria was not a nation but a "mere geographical expression."[71]

With growing regional sentiments among the dominant ethnic groups, leaders of minority ethnic groups began to demand either for separate states of their own or for constitutional safeguards to prevent their domination by majority ethnic groups in an independent Nigeria. These concerns were based on the fact that leaders of the numerically dominant ethnic and cultural groups—the Hausa-Fulani, the Yoruba, and the Igbo—effectively controlled the major political parties. Minority groups were justifiably concerned that independence from British colonial rule would only be replaced by permanent Hausa, Yoruba, or Igbo domination.

To address these concerns, the British government in 1957 established a commission of inquiry headed by Sir Henry Willink, a former minister of the British cabinet, to ascertain the facts about the fears of minorities ethnic groups in Nigeria and to propose means of allaying those fears. In its report, the Willink Commission identified two main grounds for the fears of suppression and political marginalization among minority ethnic groups in the country. First was the use of physical force by the major political parties to intimidate smaller political groups. In the view of the commission, this trend was a grave threat to national stability and inter-ethnic harmony. A second reason for the fears of the minority groups was the tendency of regional governments, secure in their majority, to disregard the wishes of the minority ethnic and political groups. But, in spite of these observations, the Commission rejected the idea of creating more states out of concern that it would "create more problems as great as it sought to cure." It suggested, instead, that a Bill of Rights modeled after the European Convention on Human Rights be included in the independence constitution as a way of promoting national integration and guaranteeing minority rights. Following this recommendation, the constitution introduced at independence contained elaborate provisions guaranteeing to every Nigerian certain basic human rights and fundamental freedoms.

The recommendation of the Willink Commission was not the first time that a bill of rights was recommended as the panacea for growing ethnic rivalries in the country. In 1953 the Northern Elements Progressive Union (NEPU), a minority political party, proposed that the colonial government should include a bill of rights in the constitution as a safeguard against the oppression of minority groups.[72] The Colonial Secretary, Oliver Lyttleton, objected to this proposal on two grounds. First, he argued that fundamental rights could only be exercised where they did not affect the fundamental rights of other people. Any list of rights would, therefore, be so hedged around with reservations that it would be meaningless. Second, he questioned the efficacy of such a bill in actually guaranteeing minority rights. He argued that he had never known of any similar declaration to be incorporated in a British constitution. Although there was such a declaration in the Indian and Sudan constitutions, it had not made for greater freedom in those countries. In contrast, the Dominion of Canada, which had no such constitutional provisions for fundamental rights, had a much better record of protecting human rights.[73] In any event, the proposals for a constitutional bill of rights were jettisoned.

The adoption of the recommendation of the Willink Commission marked official acknowledgement of the need for constitutional guarantees of minority rights in a diverse multi-ethnic society like Nigeria. The new bill included elaborate provisions for the right to life and liberty, the right to freedom of movement and peaceful assembly, and the right to protection against retrospective legislation. Other recommendations of the Commission toward allaying the fears of minority groups included the establishment of a strong police force that would not be subject to any regional control, equal sharing of financial responsibilities between the regional and federal governments, and the setting up of a council to monitor the economic and social development in minority areas.[74]

However, the Commission did not pretend to believe that the inclusion of a bill of rights in the constitution would completely solve the problem of the minorities in respect of their fears of oppression; it stated that the bill should be included nevertheless because the presence of such a statement "defines beliefs widespread among democratic countries and provides a standard to which appeal may be made by those whose rights are infringed."[75] The Commission acknowledged that a government determined to abandon democratic courses will find ways of avoiding them but stated that constitutional guarantees are "of great value in preventing a steady deterioration in standards of freedom and the unobtrusive encroachment of a government on individual rights."[76]

While there was agreement among Nigerian politicians over the inclusion of a bill of rights in the constitution, there remained fundamental differences over other recommendations of the Minorities Commission. For one, the Commission's recommendation against the creation of more states was criticized by some sections of the Nigerian political class. The Action Group wanted the problem of the minorities settled before independence by the creation of more states for ethnic minority groups. The NPC and the NCNC, on the other hand, were opposed to the creation of more states, because it threatened to split their power bases. The question of states' creation and minority rights became so contentious and divisive among the political elite that the British Secretary of State for Colonies warned that if it remained unresolved it would delay British plans to grant the country's independence in 1960.[77] When it became apparent that the disagreement threatened to delay the granting of independence, the Action Group compromised its position and agreed to shelve the creation of new states for minority groups. This was in spite of protestations from minority groups insistent on the creation of new states in which they would be protected from domination. In the end, the contentious issue of minority rights protection was conveniently swept under the carpet to expedite independence.

In retrospect, it is unfortunate that the minority question was not resolved and the burgeoning discourse on human rights not fully explored before independence. This meant that Nigeria entered her era of independence with a constitution that did not satisfactorily address the expressed fears and grievances of diverse groups of people and the questions about how best to protect their rights. This fact, coupled with the failures of the emergent political leadership class, made the question of protecting minority ethnic groups from dominant groups the central issue at stake in the debates over political and civil rights in the late colonial and immediate postcolonial era.

Independence and Fundamental Human Rights

Following the recommendation of the Willink Commission, the independence constitution introduced in 1960 contained elaborate provisions guaranteeing to every Nigerian certain basic human rights and fundamental freedoms. These provisions for "Fundamental Human Rights" were partly based on the UDHR and the European Convention for the Protection of Human Rights and Fundamental Freedoms, which, at the time, was perhaps the most comprehensive legal provision for human rights in the world.[78] The basic rights guaranteed in the constitution included the right to life, freedom from inhuman treatment, freedom from slavery and forced labor, the right to personal liberty, the right to fair hearing, freedom of conscience and religion, freedom of expression, freedom of peaceful assembly and association, freedom of movement and residence; freedom from discrimination, and the right to family life, which we have examined in detail in the previous chapter.

Although most Nigerians welcomed the inclusion of a bill of rights in the constitution, some criticized its theoretical and practical limitations on two main grounds. First, the bill was only a statement of civil and political rights; it did not make sufficient provision for social and economic rights such as the right to education and work, which many thought the state should also protect. Second, all the rights provided for were so limited by provisos that they were made nugatory for all practical purposes.[79] For example, while the constitution guaranteed the right to "dignity of the human person" and "freedom from torture, inhuman or degrading treatment," it exempted from these guarantees any punishment that was lawful and customary in any part of the country as of November 1, 1959. This proviso meant that customary practices such as trials by ordeal and colonial laws on flogging, which otherwise would have been considered violations of the constitutional right to human dignity, were not because they had been "lawful and customary" before November 1, 1959. This proviso also effectively legitimized such practices as punishment in stocks, which many considered abhorrent and inhuman, but which were quite prevalent in the colonial era.

There were similar debates over the qualifications placed on the guarantee of "freedom from discrimination." The constitution prohibited discrimination of any person on grounds of his or her ethnic group, place of origin, and religious or political opinion. However, in its definition of discrimination it exempted any law that imposed restrictions on certain persons in "special circumstances" that were "reasonably justifiable in a democratic society."[80] In the interpretation of legal experts and the courts, this rather vague clause meant that institutionalized discrimination against certain groups of persons such as women (with regard to property rights) and children born out of wedlock (with regard to inheritance rights) under prevailing customary law, did not fall within the scope of the constitutional guarantees of "freedom from discrimination" since any such discrimination could be regarded as based on the "special circumstances" of these persons.[81]

These qualifications, or "claw back clauses," in a bill that was supposed to guarantee the "fundamental human rights" of all Nigerians say a lot about the nature of political debates about rights during this period. This was a time when Nigerian politicians, eager to consolidate their political bases in preparation for taking over power from the colonial government, seemed preoccupied with advancing ethnic, gender, and class interests. Under such circumstances, instituting a regime of constitutional rights that guaranteed the equal and unqualified rights of all Nigerians was symbolically significant but not politically expedient. In public, nationalist politicians declared their commitments to promoting equal rights for all citizens. They promised that independence would usher in a new era, unlike the colonial past, in which all citizens would be guaranteed their fundamental human rights and treated equally before the law.

In fact, such absolute guarantees of human rights were perceived as threats to strongly held cultural and religious beliefs. In spite of its official rhetoric of freedom and liberty, the NPC, the main political party in the predominantly Muslim Northern region, vehemently opposed the extension of voting rights to women in that region when universal adult sufferance was first introduced in the country in 1954. The party objected on the grounds that women's franchise would compromise the religious and moral values of the Islamic societies of the north.[82] It claimed that it was not totally opposed to women's voting rights but that women would be given franchise only in "God's time."[83] Other more progressive political parties, such as the NCNC and the AG, which had insisted on universal adult suffrage throughout the colonial period, could have put pressure on the NPC and the colonial government to extend women's franchise to Northern Nigeria. They did not. Rather, they compromised their position to accommodate the NPC in order to "ensure a consensus for independence."[84] Again, as with minority rights, the crucial issue of women's franchise was pushed aside as powerful male-dominated constituencies scrambled for political power in the lead-up to independence. This typifies the kinds of class and gendered compromises made by Nigerian political elites in the discourse about constitutional rights.

The content of constitutional guarantees of rights depend not only upon the range of the rights guaranteed but also upon the scope and sweep of the qualifications made to them. It is obvious that rights cannot be guaranteed in absolute terms if for no other reason than to protect the rights of other persons. But, in the case of the Nigerian bill of rights, it was clear that the qualifications made to the guaranteed rights went too far. In practice, these qualifications often negated the very essence of the constitutional rights guarantees. More so, these qualifications were the result of class- and gender-centered political compromises rather than the exigencies of protecting the rights of others. Ultimately, such political compromises undermined the spirit of the bill of rights and reflected the real tensions arising from the attempts by political elites to balance public aspirations for equal rights in the postcolonial dispensation with entrenched class and gender interests.

Beyond Rights Talk: The Challenge of Enforcement

Apart from the qualifications in the bill of rights, there was also the more practical problem of enforcing the bill. In recommending the inclusion of a bill of rights in the constitution, the Willink Commission recognized that such a bill could not provide an absolute guarantee against violations of human rights either by the state or other individuals. It acknowledged that constitutional safeguards do not in themselves provide complete and indefensible security for human rights and liberties even though they do "make the way of the transgressor, or the tyrant, more difficult."[85]

True to this assumption, the provisions of the constitution did not always protect individuals from violations of their fundamental rights, particularly those perpetrated by the state. For one, many colonial laws and policies, which had been criticized by nationalist politicians as oppressive and undemocratic, were either retained or revised and re-enacted by the government soon after independence. Nigerian politicians soon found out that these laws, which colonial officials used so effectively to wield absolute control over the colony, could also be useful for strengthening their own political power. Some of these laws included the Official Secret Act of 1962 and the Sedition Offences Act of 1963, which became convenient tools with which the government sought to suppress the press, smother political opposition, and stifle public dissent. These were originally colonial laws that had reincarnated in the postcolonial era to serve precisely the same functions as they did under colonial rule. In many cases, they conflicted with constitutional human rights guarantees.

The first major test of the bill of rights came soon after independence in 1961. A prominent opposition politician and professor, Chike Obi, was charged with sedition for publishing a pamphlet in which he criticized the corruption and intolerance of the ruling government of Abubakar Tafawa Balewa. The offending publication was a booklet titled *The People: Facts You Must Know*. Although the government described the booklet as a seditious document intended to incite the people, it was in fact no more than an innocuous tirade against the government.[86] For this, Obi was arrested, tried, and convicted for sedition. He subsequently appealed his conviction on the grounds that his fundamental rights to freedom of expression in the Nigerian constitution had been violated. Obi's appeal, which was closely followed by the public and the press, was considered a test case of the capability of the judicial arm of government to enforce guaranteed constitutional rights in the postcolonial state. At issue was the proper interpretation of the section of the constitution that guaranteed freedom of expression vis-à-vis the related proviso which stated: "Nothing in this section shall invalidate any law that is reasonably justified in a democratic society."[87] The question at issue was whether the government's sedition law could be considered reasonably justified in a democratic society. In the end, the court, which was hardly independent of the ruling government, dismissed Obi's appeal on the grounds that his conviction under the sedition law was indeed reasonably justifiable in a democratic society.[88]

This and similar cases vindicated the fears expressed in many quarters that the extensive qualifications placed on the bill of rights made it practically ineffective. Indeed, the bill proved to be more of a rhetorical device with which elite politicians, like colonial officials before them, sought to legitimize their political authority, rather than an instrument of actually protecting individual rights and liberties. What soon became evident in the immediate postcolonial era was a change in the pattern of rights discourse in the country. The use of rights talk shifted from the nationalists, who had extensively deployed it in the colonial era, to a new postcolonial antigovernment opposition movement. The irony here is that having attained power at independence, nationalist politicians who had used rights talk to challenge the colonial state found themselves at the receiving end of the same rights-based opposition that they had mounted against the colonial state.

Here, we see how rights discourses were used to further specific class interests and agendas under different political situations. The promising adaptation of rights ideas by Nigerian elites in their opposition to the colonial state would seem to have fallen apart soon after independence. Rights talk, once wielded vigorously and effectively to oppose and challenge colonial domination, was thrust aside by nationalists when they attained power. The new bearers of rights talk were opposition groups and antigovernment critics such as Chike Obi for whom it now held more relevance. These groups drew on both local traditions of rights talk and an emerging universal human rights discourse to challenge the government.

Another major test of the constitutional bill of rights came in 1962 when a political crisis engulfed the country, raising the most serious human rights concerns since independence. The crisis was provoked by bitter rivalry among the major regional political parties and their struggle for supremacy at the central government. In the Western region, a minority government, in spite of public protestations, sat tight in power sustaining its hold by widespread rigging of elections, the intimidation of political opponents, and the harassment of the press and the judiciary. The result was a complete breakdown in law and order, which the central government responded to by declaring a state of emergency. But, far from restoring calm and order, the imposition of a state of emergency escalated the crisis, leading to further repression and widespread human rights abuses by state security agents.[89] Under these emergency conditions, coercive and repressive laws were introduced and used to sustain authoritarian political control. Laws such as the Emergency Powers (General) Regulations, the Emergency Powers (Requisition) Regulations, and the Emergency Powers (Protected Places) Regulations gave the police and other security agents unlimited powers to summarily arrest and detain persons who were considered threats to public order and security.[90]

By 1966, just six years after independence, this culture of authoritarianism and government repression had become firmly entrenched. A group of military officers overthrew the elected civilian government and established a military dictatorship in the country. But even the military found the language of rights essential for establishing its legitimacy at home and abroad. Like colonial officials and the elected local politicians before them, they too recognized the mobilizing and legitimizing power of rights language. The successive military regimes that ruled the country after independence were openly repressive and authoritarian, but they all persistently declared their commitments to protecting and promoting human rights. Soon after the military regime of General Aguiyi Ironsi came to power, it suspended the constitution, including the bill of rights, and vested all governmental authority in a body of unelected military officers known as the Supreme Military Council. This effectively ended democratic constitutional rule in the country.

Yet, even General Ironsi, a military ruler not known for his political sophistication, soon became a champion of rights talk. He pledged a commitment to promoting fundamental rights and freedoms for all citizens even as he enacted laws and pursued policies that severely restricted these rights. He courted a sceptical and critical press by stressing his belief in press freedom. As a demonstration of this he revoked the ban on some newspapers that had been placed by the preceding civilian regime. He even went so far as to prescribe penalties for interfering with the distribution and sale of any newspaper in the country.[91] All these were touted as evidence of the military regime's new commitment to human rights and a departure from the political chaos of the past. In fact, these were largely cosmetic changes that pale into insignificance when compared with the scale of human rights violations that came to characterize this and other military regimes in the country. If anything, the pretense of a commitment to human rights was part of a strategy of rights talk that proved quite effective in wining military regimes some legitimacy and public acceptance. But, as we have seen, such manipulative use of rights talk was neither new nor unique to military dictatorships. This was only a new a phase in a long tradition of deploying rights talk for political ends that often had little to do with actually protecting the rights and liberties of ordinary people. This tradition of rights talk as a means of winning political legitimacy, even in the face of state authoritarianism and repression, came to characterize decades of military dictatorship in Nigeria and elsewhere in Africa.

7

The Paradox of Rights Talk

The historian's job is to simplify and complicate—to simplify the complicated and to complicate the simple in an unending process.[1] This work has been inspired by the need to both simplify and complicate the history of the rights discourse in a colonial African context. I have sought to discern broad patterns in the discussions about rights and liberties in Nigeria since the 1900s while at the same time exploring the intricacies, nuances, and contradictions in these discussions. Underlying this has been the need to put the contemporary human rights discourse in historical context by looking at longer-standing debates about rights in colonial Africa. Understanding these earlier traditions of rights discourses is central to understanding current debates about human rights in Nigeria as elsewhere in Africa. In particular, it helps us to better understand and place in historical context the creative tension between the particular and universal in our understanding of rights—a theme that has dominated the debate over the universalism and cultural relativism of human rights. This study indicates that before the postwar universal human rights "revolution" there was a thriving colonial discourse of rights, which has in many ways shaped contemporary notions and discussions about human rights in Africa. This colonial rights discourse may originally have been produced to legitimize empire, but it was also one in which Africans were fully engaged. We have seen here how various groups within the society— European colonial officials, missionaries, chiefs, Westernized African elites, excluded social groups, and women—all employed the language of rights to serve varied social, economic, and political ends.

The earliest bearers of rights talk in the colonial context were the European missionaries, who in many ways prepared the ground for colonial conquest. Underlying early missionary and colonial encounters with Africans in Nigeria were important debates over rights and liberties. Colonial incursion and expansion in the 1900s prompted discussions over "native" treaty rights and British "rights of intervention." While local rulers sought to maintain their influence and autonomy by emphasizing their rights under existing treaty agreements with Britain, British colonial authorities justified their intervention in local politics in the name of protecting the rights and freedoms of "native" subjects under British jurisdiction. This was one of the many paradoxes of colonial rights discourse—that both conqueror and conquered found it necessary to invoke rights talk, albeit from varying perspectives, to justify or escape the imperial order.

There were also extensive discussions about native rights within the context of the antislavery movement. Although slavery had been officially abolished by the time Britain established full control of its African colonies, its legacies had not been completely wiped out in many parts of the continent. Missionaries and humanitarians employed the language of rights and liberties in their continued campaigns against slavery and pawnship. While missionaries appealed to a notion of native rights founded on Christian humanism and based largely on conversion to Christianity, humanitarians focused on a broader and more inclusive notion of rights founded on British liberal ideals and the colonial legal system.

Even the colonial legal system was itself an arena in which Europeans and African engaged in wide-ranging debates over rights and liberties. The libertarian traditions of English common law and the system of justice extended to the colony professed a broad concern for private rights and individual freedom of action. In practice, however, imperial political and economic imperatives were more pragmatic considerations in the process of colonial administration. This raises a crucial question: If the colonial state fell so dismally short of its own liberal agenda, why did the rhetoric of rights, justice, and liberty remain so appealing to colonial officials? My argument is that the ostensible extension of English standards of law, legal rights, and justice to the colony and the official rhetoric that kept them on the agenda was a powerful device for rationalizing and legitimizing empire.

In this sense, British colonialism in Nigeria, as perhaps elsewhere in Africa, was a double gesture. On one hand, it justified itself in terms of difference and inequality: The greater enlightenment of the colonizer legitimized his right to rule and to civilize. On the other hand, that legitimacy was founded, ostensibly, on a commitment to the eventual erasure of difference in the name of a common humanity. But if this difference and inequality had actually been removed, the basis of colonial rule itself would have disappeared. It was not. Instead, colonialism promised universal rights but kept the ruled in a state of subjection. If the discourse of radical individualism and "native rights" bore the promise of colonialism, the discourse on the subjection and imperial control bore the *realpolitik*.[2] However, the paradox of legal rights talk was not limited to the colonial state. Underlying African engagement in the discourse on law and rights were similar paradoxes. Educated African elites opposed colonial laws on the basis that they circumscribed the political rights of traditional rulers, yet they objected to colonial laws intended to strengthen these traditional institutions by expanding their power over the educated elites. It would seem that for the elites rights talk was acceptable only to the extent that it did not circumscribe their own political interests. Just as it had been for colonial officials, rights talk proved to be an equally effective instrument with which African elites consolidated political power within the postcolonial state.

The question of rights also resonated in discussions over economic and social issues. The two central issues at the heart of the colonial state's attempt to exercise greater control over economic resources and regulate social life were land and marriage. As with colonial law, this was a process characterized by contradictions. Colonial rule opened with ideas about the evolutionary superiority of Western concepts of individual land and property rights; it closed with a general atmosphere of suspicion of these rights and an emphasis, instead, on "customary" communal rights to land. Afraid that uncontrolled expansion of private property rights would undermine African chiefly powers and its administrative system of indirect rule through chiefs, the colonial state restricted individual ownership and emphasized communal ownership in land under the control of chiefly authorities. This became the basis of the colonial and postcolonial policy of state trusteeship of land. However, this process of state appropriation of land in the name of trusteeship did not go unchallenged. Africans also used the rhetoric of rights in the press and in petitions to colonial courts to challenge trusteeship policies and articulate their entitlements to land.

I have argued that discourses of land rights developed along two broad lines—legitimizing and oppositional rights discourses. While the former focused on justifying and legitimizing colonial trusteeship policies, the latter centered on opposing colonial land policies and emphasizing instead African rights to ownership and control over their land. In drawing this conclusion, I have been careful not to lapse into the old Manichean paradigm of colonizer versus colonized that has dominated African historiography for so long. The limitations of this model have been too well documented to bear detailed restating here. It tends to be too simplistic, elides the agency of subaltern historical actors, and stands in the way of a fuller, more nuanced understanding of historical events. I have also been attentive to the contentious debate over the place of structure and agency in colonial historiography. Does the broad structural framework of "legitimizing and oppositional rights discourses" obscure the historical agency of Europeans and Africans who do not fall neatly into these categories?

Mindful of these concerns, I emphasize that the paradigms of legitimizing and oppositional rights discourses need not be seen solely as representing rigid, racially defined polar categories ideologically walled off from each other. Salient nuances and complexities underlie these categories. However, based on the historical evidence, I find this paradigm a useful framework for understanding and explaining the nature of colonial rights discourses over land. Almost all Europeans involved in the land rights discourse (including humanitarians such as E. D. Morel, who was sympathetic to the African cause) advocated colonial state trusteeship as the best way of protecting individual rights and access to land. In contrast, the overwhelming majority of Africans (including traditional chiefs who had much to gain from a trusteeship system based on the notion of communal ownership of land) opposed colonial trusteeship policies and advocated instead individual rights of ownership. While we can speculate on whether this clear dichotomy was simply a coincidence or was a reflection of entrenched political and economic interests, what is clearly evident is that Europeans and Africans saw the issue of lands rights from different and opposing perspectives. Thus, while I have tried to be cognizant of the agency of less prominent historical actors, there is compelling empirical basis for using the legitimizing and oppositional frameworks in explaining the discourse over land rights.

Similar patterns are evident in colonial debates about marriage and divorce. The colonial period opened with official concern about liberating women from the constraints of customary marital practices. By the end of the first decade of colonial rule, however, the colonial state had become more concerned with what it considered the breakdown of public morality and began to focus on restoring "traditional" African social and moral values. The pursuit of the latter meant abandoning or at least de-emphasizing earlier ideas about liberating African woman. But unlike land rights discourses, there was no clear divergence in the positions of the colonial state and its Africans subjects. Many African women welcomed initial colonial liberal divorce laws and effectively exploited them to escape male control in patriarchal societies. On the other hand, chiefly authorities and upper-class men vehemently opposed these policies and blamed them for the breakdown of public morality. Their opposition and pressure partly accounted for the eventual reversal of colonial policy on "native" marriage and divorce. One of the most significant findings of this study with regard to the debates over marriage and divorce are the complex and creative ways in which ordinary Africans, both men and women, used the language of rights in divorce petitions to articulate their interests and strengthen their cases before colonial adjudicators.

Much the same can the said of the discussions about political rights. We have seen how the outbreak of the First World War in 1914 ushered an era in which Nigerians increasingly began to articulate their political aspirations in terms of their rights as full citizens of empire. British wartime propaganda, which presented the war against Germany as a fight for liberty and freedom, became an important part of the early nationalist narrative. Nigerian intellectuals demanded that these same ideals of justice and freedom be extended to them. As in the realms of economic and social life, the language of rights became a language of choice for politically challenging and negotiating with the colonial state. In the same way, the Second World War and the rhetoric of universal rights that underscored allied wartime propaganda provided new standards of universal rights to which the Nigerian intelligentsia appealed in their demands for political reforms. The Atlantic Charter, the United Nations Charter, and the Universal Declaration of Human Rights reinforced the language of universal rights. The universalist ideals of the UDHR, in particular, provided further impetus for the nationalist movement and a model for the regime of fundamental human rights that was adopted at independence in 1960.

The rhetoric of rights was more than merely an instrument of colonial hegemony or a means of legitimizing the status quo; it was also a means of challenging, negotiating, and, ultimately, ending it. Nigerian intellectuals drew on the language of rights dominating Atlantic race discourses and wartime propaganda to articulate their own political demands. They appropriated the rhetoric of rights for varied ends, deploying it to challenge the colonial state. Paradoxically, the rhetoric of rights was as crucial in the fall of empire as it was in its rise. Rights discourses facilitated domination at one moment and liberation at another. Yet, the use of the rights discourses by African elites was not limited to their engagement with the colonial state. Nigerian elites deployed rights discourses not only to oppose and challenge the colonial state but also for intraclass conflicts and internal struggles for political power. This was particularly so in the postcolonial period. With independence, rights talk began to assume new meanings and significance for the nationalist elite who now constituted the ruling class. It shifted from being mainly a means of challenging the colonial state to becoming a means of validating postcolonial nationalist projects such as redressing the distortions of colonialism and promoting traditional African family values.

Much time and effort was spent articulating vague ideals such as the constitutional right to family life, while more important human rights issues, such as institutionalized discrimination against women and "illegitimate" children, were overlooked as part of class-centered political compromises. The promising adaptation of rights ideas by Nigerian elites as a means of moderating state power during the colonial period completely fell apart after independence. Rights talk, once wielded effectively by the elites to challenge colonial power, was thrust aside once they attained power. New subaltern groups such as opposition parties, ethnic minority advocates, and non-governmental organizations became the new bearers of rights talk.

In spite of the dominance of the educated elite in the rights discourse, what is also evident from this study is that rights talk was not an exclusively elite affair. Ordinary Africans were also well engaged in debates and discussions about rights. In their petitions to colonial administrators, ordinary and often illiterate Nigerians, using the services of professional letter writers, deployed the language of rights to express their grievances and demand redress. This is particularly evident in the agitation of the Idumuashaba, a community of slave descendants, for social inclusion. In several petitions to the colonial government between 1912 and 1945, the Idumusahaba people demanded that the government go beyond the legal abolition of slavery to actively enforce their social integration into the society. Their petitions provide unique and revealing insights into how ordinary Africans were engaged in rights discourse. They also demonstrate how the rights-based demands of ordinary people intersected with the exigencies of colonial administration.

At the beginning of this book, I indicated that discourses of rights and liberties in Nigeria, as elsewhere in colonial Africa, were so widespread and diverse that it is impractical, if not impossible, to thoroughly examine all their many facets in one study. This book merely scratches the surface of what may well be the tip of a huge iceberg of future historical inquiry. I have examined in some detail how British colonial traditions and other external ideas such as the Atlantic race discourse and European wartime propaganda influenced discussions about rights in Nigeria. There are, however, two important aspects of the rights discourse that this book has not fully engaged for reasons of space and scope.

The first is the precolonial dimension of the rights discourse. My focus on colonial rights discourse in this study is not to suggest that formal discussions about rights and liberties in Africa began in the colonial period. I recognize that many African societies had long traditions of rights talk that predate European contact and that understanding these precolonial traditions of rights discourses in their oral and scripted forms is crucial to a full understanding of the rights movement in Africa.

Another equally important aspect of the rights discourse that this book has been unable to fully accommodate is the influence of rights discourses produced in the colony, on the metropole. How did debates about rights and liberties in colonial Africa affect the rights discourse in Britain and other colonial metropoles? In what ways did the impassioned debates about "native rights" in British newspapers and among liberal and conservative politicians in Britain shape British self-image as the epitome of enlightened imperial rule and the beacon of liberty to colonized peoples? Examining these questions is important because it draws attention not only to the place of Europe in Africa but also to the reciprocal place of Africa in shaping developments in Europe during the colonial epoch. As other studies have shown, colonialism was as much involved in the making of the metropole and the identities and ideologies of colonizers as it was in remaking peripheries and colonial subjects.[3] The story of how the rights discourse in colonial Africa resonated in the metropoles of Europe and spread the ideology of the colonizers is a story that needs to be told. Apart from its significance for imperial history, such studies will bring fresh insights to human rights scholarship. It will mark a departure from the hackneyed trend of emphasizing the influences of human rights discourses as produced in the global North on the South. In this case, the emphasis will be on the counterinfluences of human rights discourses in the South on the North and the contributions of non-Western societies to the development of the contemporary human rights corpus. This, hopefully, will be subject of another project.

Notes

Chapter One:
The Subject of Rights and the Rights of Subjects

1. The main significance of the UDHR is that it took the unprecedented step of identifying a core set of rights to which every person is entitled by virtue of being human and acknowledging that the protection of these rights is a global responsibility.

2. Michael Ignatieff, "The Rights Revolution," Massey Lectures, University of Toronto, November 7, 2000. Also see Michael Ignatieff, *Human Rights as Politics and Idolatry* (Princeton, N.J.: Princeton University Press, 2001).

3. Ronald Dworkin, *Taking Rights Seriously* (Cambridge, Mass.: Harvard University Press, 1978). See Chapter 4.

4. For instance, it has been suggested that rights discourses were central to the construction of ethnic identities in colonial Africa. See John L. and Jean Comaroff, *Of Revelation and Revolution*, Volume 2: *The Dialectics of Modernity on a South African Frontier* (Chicago: University of Chicago Press, 1997), 400–401.

5. For an exposé of this developing aspect of Africanist studies, see Bonny Ibhawoh, "Human Rights and Cultural Relativism: Reconsidering the Africanist Discourse," *Netherlands Quarterly of Human Rights* 19, 1 (2001): 43–62.

6. Ralph Austin, "Human Rights and the Moral Economy of Colonialism," unpublished conference paper presented at the Symposium on Law, Colonialism and Human Rights in Africa, Stanford University, May 1999.

7. Makau Mutua, *Human Rights: A Political and Cultural Critique* (Philadelphia: University of Pennsylvania Press, 2002), 11.

8. A classic example of this approach to post-colonial discourse analysis is Edward Said, *Orientalism* (London: Routledge & Kegan Paul, 1978).

9. Sara Mills, *Discourses* (London: Routledge, 1997), 107.

10. Margaret Macdonald, "Natural Rights," in *Theories of Rights*, Jeremy Waldron, ed. (London: Oxford University Press, 1984), 27–29.

11. Burns Weston, "Human Rights," *Human Rights Quarterly* 6, 3 (1984): 259.

12. Orlando Patterson, "Freedom, Slavery, and the Modern Construction of Rights," in *Historical Change and Human Rights: The Oxford Amnesty Lectures 1994*, Olwen Hufton, ed. (New York: Basic Books, 1995), 158.

13. The classic statements on natural rights theory include Locke's *Second Treatise* and Thomas Pine's *The Rights of Man*.

14. Lewis P. Hinchman, "The Origins of Human Rights: A Hegelian Perspective," *Western Political Quarterly* 37 (March 1984): 12.

15. Ibid., 12–13.

16. Josiah A. M. Cobbah, "African Values and the Human Rights Debate: An African Perspective," *Human Rights Quarterly* 9 (1987): 314.

17. Patterson, "Freedom, Slavery, and the Modern Construction of Rights," 176–77.

18. Article 1 of the Charter of the United Nations.

19. These include the International Covenants on Civil and Political Rights and the International Covenant on Social and Cultural Rights, which came into effect in 1976.

20. Such regional conventions include the American Declaration on the Rights and Duties of Man; the European Convention on the Protection of Human Rights and Fundamental Freedoms; and the African Charter for Human and People's Rights, also known as the Banjul Charter.

21. Pieter Boele van Hensbroek, *Political Discourses in African Thought 1800 to the Present* (London: Praeger, 1999), 13–14.

22. Patterson, "Freedom, Slavery, and the Modern Construction of Rights," 135.

23. Rhoda Howard, "Group versus Individual Dignity in the African Debate on Human Rights," in *Human Rights in Africa: Cross-Cultural Perspectives*, Abdullahi Ahmed An-Naim and and Francis M. Deng, eds. (Washington, D.C.: The Brookings Institution, 1990) and Rhoda Howard, *Human Rights in Commonwealth Africa* (Totowa, N.J.: Rowman & Littlefield, 1986), 19.

24. Jack Donnelly, "Human Rights and Human Dignity: An Analytic Critique of Non-Western Conceptions of Human Rights," *American Political Science Review* 76 (1982): 303.

25. See, for example, Lakshman Marasinghe, "Traditional Conceptions of Human Rights in Africa," in *Human Rights and Development in Africa*, Claude E. Welch Jr. and Ronal I. Meltzer, eds. (Albany:

State University of New York Press, 1984) and Alice L. Conklin, "Colonialism and Human Rights, A Contradiction in Terms? The Case of France and West Africa, 1895–1914," *The American Historical Review* 103, 2 (1998): 419–42.

26. Even this point is subject to dispute. At the signing of the UDHR in 1948, many countries in Africa and Asia were still under colonial rule and were not members of the United Nations. They were, therefore, not party to the drafting of the original document, although most of these nations subsequently ratified the declaration.

27. Patterson, "Freedom, Slavery, and the Modern Construction of Rights," 156.

28. Mahmood Mamdani, ed. *Beyond Rights Talk and Culture Talk: Comparative Essays on the Politics of Rights and Culture* (New York: St. Martin's Press, 2000), 93.

29. See Michel Foucault, *Discipline and Punish: The Birth of the Prison* (New York: Pantheon Books, 1977), 27–28.

30. Patterson, "Freedom, Slavery, and the Modern Construction of Rights," 133.

31. See An-Naim and Francis Deng, eds., *Human Rights in Africa;* Issa Shivji, *The Concept of Human Rights in Africa* (London: Codesria, 1989); Bonny Ibhawoh, "Between Culture and Constitution. Evaluating the Cultural Legitimacy of Human Rights in the African State," *Human Rights Quarterly* 22, 3 (2000): 838–60.

32. The term "traditional African society" can be problematic. If the term refers to precapitalist, communal stage of slave and feudal modes of production, the historical attributes that we identify as being traditionally African may, in fact, not be peculiar to Africa since this stage of social development was common to most societies. Our conceptualization of African tradition here, therefore, is in a dynamic sense. It is refers not only to the social attributes of the precapitalist stage of development but also the more "modern" social changes and continuities in African traditions.

33. Osita C Eze, "Is the Protection of Human Rights and Democracy Strange to African Traditions?" in *Human Rights and Democracy in Africa*, Tunji Abayomi, ed. (Lagos: Human Rights Africa, 1993), 82.

34. Donnelly, "Human Rights and Human Dignity," 303–16.

35. Makau Wa Mutua, "The Banjul Charter and the African Cultural Fingerprint: An Evaluation of the Language of Rights and Duties," *Virginia Journal of International Law* 35, 2 (1995): 347.

36. Rhoda Howard, "Group versus Individual Identity in the African Debate on Human Rights." Also see Jack Donnelly, *Universal Human Rights in Theory and Practice* (Ithaca: Cornell University Press, 1989).

37. Welshman Ncube, "Universality and Cultural Relativity of Human Rights," 8.

38. Mahmood Mamdani, "The Social Basis of Constitutionalism in Africa," 360.

39. Keba M'Baye, "Organisation de L'Unite Africaine," in *Les Dimensions International de Droits de L'Homme* (Paris: UNESCO, 1987), 651.

40. References to "Western values" in the human rights discourse can be confusing in that it often presents a picture of an undifferentiated West—what J. G. Carrier has called the "Occidentalised West." The Occidentalized West is an imagined entity that ignores the vast areas of Western life that conflict with its vision. Other writers have taken this point further to argue that just as "orientalizing" was a part of imperialism and colonialism, so is "occidentalizing" a part of the emergence from colonial rule and cultural power. See J. G. Carrier, *Occidentalism: Images of the West* (Oxford: Claredon Press, 1995), 28.

41. B. Fine, *Democracy and the Rule of Law: Liberal Ideals and Marxist Critiques* (London: Pluto Press, 1984), Chapter 2.

42. For a more detailed analysis of some of these arguments, see Issa Shivji, *The Concept of Human Rights in Africa;* Y. Khashalani, "Human Rights in Asia and Africa," *Human Rights Law Journal* 4, 4 (1983); Dunstan M. Wai, "Human Rights in Sub-Saharan Africa," in *Human Rights: Cultural and Ideological Perspectives*, A. Pollis and P. Schwab, eds. (New York: Praeger, 1979); L. Marasinghe, "Traditional Conceptions of Human Rights in Africa," in *Human Rights and Development in Africa*, Welch and Meltzer, eds.

43. Thandabanto Nhlapo, "The African Customary Law of Marriage and the Rights Conundrum," in Mamdani, ed. *Beyond Rights Talk and Culture Talk,* 137.

44. Josiah Cobbah, "African Values and the Human Rights Debate: An African Perspective," *Human Rights Quarterly* 9 (1987): 321

45. Makau Wa Mutua, "The Banjul Charter and the African Cultural Fingerprint," 363.

46. For a more incisive exposé on the Asian values and human rights debate, see William Theodore De Bary, *Asian Values and Human Rights: A Confucian Communitarian Perspective* (Cambridge, Mass.: Cambridge University Press, 1998); Joanne R. Bauer and Daniel A. Bell, eds., *The East Asian Challenge for Human Rights* (New York: Cambridge University Press, 1999).

47. The Bangkok declaration argues, in essence, that the notions of human rights enshrined in the UDHR have not and have never been universal, and have no roots or sanction in the traditions of most countries of the world. It states that if these ideas are to be

taken seriously, they must be expanded to include other non-Western notions of human right.

48. El-Obaid Ahmed El-Obaid and Kwadwo Appiagyei-Atua, "Human Rights in Africa: A New Perspective on Linking the Past to the Present," *McGill Law Journal* 41, 819 (1996): 819–54.

49. This point has also been repeatedly made with reference to the argument for "Asian values" in the discourse on the cultural relativism of human rights. Xiaorong Li, " 'Asian Values' and the Universality of Human Rights," in Patrick Hayden, *The Philosophy of Human Rights* (St. Paul, Minn.: Paragon House, 2001), 397–408.

50. Rhoda Howard, "Is There an African Concept of Human Rights?" in *Foreign Policy and Human Rights: Issues and Responses*, R. J. Vincent, ed. (Cambridge: Cambridge University Press, 1986), 11–32, and Rhoda Howard, "Evaluating Human Rights in Africa: Some Problems of Implicit Comparisons," *Human Rights Quarterly* 6, 4 (1984): 160–79.

51. Jack Donnelly, "Cultural Relativism and Universal Human Rights," *Human Rights Quarterly* 6, 4 (1984): 413–15.

52. Martin Chanock, "Culture and Human Rights: Orientalising, Occidentalising and Authenticity," in *Beyond Rights Talk and Culture Talk,* Mamdani, ed., 2.

53. Marianne Jensen and Karin Poulsen, *Human Rights and Cultural Change: Women in Africa* (Copenhagen: Danish Centre for Human Rights, 1993), 6.

54. Ibid.

55. Mamdani, *Beyond Rights Talk and Culture Talk*, 3.

56. Nivedita Menon, "State, Community and the Debate on the Uniform Civil Code in India," in Mamdani, *Beyond Rights Talk and Culture Talk,* 77.

57. Ibid., 1.

58. It is significant to note that most of the attributes that are now frequently ascribed to the West, as "Western values" are, in fact, relatively recent developments in the West. Democracy and universal adult suffrage and the full range of individual-centered political and civil rights were not instituted in many parts of Europe until the middle of the twentieth century. Only a century ago, many of the communal attributes now described as Asian or African values could also easily have applied to societies in Europe and North America.

59. Nhlapo, "The African Customary Law of Marriage and the Rights Conundrum," 137.

60. Bonny Ibhawoh, "Human Rights and Cultural Relativism: Reconsidering the Africanist Discourse," *Netherlands Quarterly of Human Rights* 19, 1 (March 2001): 61.

Chapter Two:
Right, Liberties, and the Imperial World Order

1. The Berlin West Africa Conference was a meeting of representatives of fourteen European countries convened by the German chancellor Otto von Bismarck in 1884 to settle the problems arising from the European quest for African territories. The conference formalized the European scramble for Africa.

2. J. F. A. Ajayi, *Christian Missions in Nigeria 1841–1891* (London: Longman, 1965), 55.

3. NAI, CSO 5/1/15. "Treaty of peace, friendship and commerce with the Kingdom of Ife," dated May 22, 1888.

4. Samuel Johnson, *The History of the Yorubas from the Earliest Times to the Beginning of the British Protectorate* (London: Routledge & K. Paul, 1966), 640.

5. *Lagos Weekly Record,* September 7, 1897.

6. *Lagos Standard,* September 11, 1897.

7. Johnson, *The History of the Yorubas,* 640.

8. *The Lagos Standard,* June 2, 1909, 5.

9. *The Lagos Standard,* June 2, 1909, 5.

10. *West Africa,* July 19, 1902.

11. NAI, CSO 7/1/2. Legislative Council Debates, March 14, 1891.

12. J.F.A Ajayi, *Christian Missions,* 77.

13. *Lagos Weekly Record,* August 29, 1891.

14. J.F.A Ajayi and M. Crowther, eds., *History of West Africa,* Vol. 2 (London: Longman, 1974), 452.

15. *Lagos Standard,* October 12, 1904.

16. PRO, CO 149/6. Legislative Council Debates, September 24, 1901.

17. Jean and John L. Comaroff, "The Colonization of Consciousness in South Africa," *Economy and Society* 18, 3 (1989): 289.

18. See J. F. A. Ajayi, *Christian Missionaries in Nigeria and Ayandele, The Missionary Impact on Modern Nigeria;* Lamin O. Sanneh, *West African Christianity: The Religious Impact* (London: C. Hurst, 1983); E. A. Ayandele, *'Holy Johnson,' Pioneer of African Nationalism, 1836–1917* (London: Cass, 1970); Elizabeth Isichei, *A History of Christianity in Africa: from Antiquity to the Present* (Grand Rapids, Mich.: W. B. Eerdmans, 1995).

19. Jean Comaroff and John Comaroff, *Of Revelation and Revolution,* Volume 1: *Christianity, Colonialism and Consciousness in South Africa* (Chicago: University of Chicago Press, 1991), 10–11.

20. Jean Comaroff and John Comaroff, *Of Revelation and Revolution,* Volume 2: *The Dialectics of Modernity on a South African Frontier,* 369.

21. Martin Chanock, *Law, Custom and Social Order. The Colonial Experience in Malawi and Zambia* (Cambridge: Cambridge University Press, 1985), 128.

22. Comaroff, *Of Revelation and Revolution, Volume 2,* 369 and 373. Emphasis added.

23. Caroline Brown, "Testing the Boundaries of Marginality: Twentieth-Century Slavery and Emancipation Struggles in Nkanu, Northern Igboland, 1920–29," *Journal of African History 37* (1996): 66.

24. See for example, T. F. Buxton, *The African Slave Trade and its Remedy* (London: Dawsons of Pall Mall, 1968 [1840]), 282, 511.

25. Don Ohadike, "The Decline of Slavery among the Igbo People," in Suzanne Miers and Richard Roberts, eds., *The End of Slavery in Africa* (Madison: University of Wisconsin Press, 1988), 444.

26. Cited in Ohadike, "The Decline of Slavery among the Igbo People."

27. *Church Missionary Intelligencer,* 1887, 501

28. NAI, Oyo Prof. 1/1207. Conflict between Christian and Pagan Customs: Memorandum from the Senior Resident to the Secretary, Southern Provinces, April 16, 1925.

29. PRO CO 149/ 5. Administrative Report by C. Hornby-Porter, Resident of Epe and Ileke.

30. *Nigerian Chronicle,* April 5, 1912; *Ijebu Weekly News,* May 13, 1912.

31. James Coleman, *Nigeria: Background to Nationalism* (Berkeley: University of California Press, 1958), 96–97.

32. Lamin Sanneh, *Abolitionists Abroad: American Blacks and the Making of Modern West Africa* (Cambridge, Mass.: Harvard University Press, 1999), 181.

33. *The Manchester Guardian,* February 2, 1898.

34. *The Lagos Standard,* August 17, 1910, 5.

35. Ohadike, "The Decline of Slavery among the Igbo People," 449.

36. *The Lagos Standard,* March 9, 1898.

37. *The Nigerian Chronicle,* September 13, 1910, 4.

38. E. D. Morel's concern for the damage he thought European colonialism was doing to Africans and their culture led him to his work as a journalist for the newspaper *West Africa* and later to found his own paper, the *West African Mail.* He also founded the Congo Reform Association. His life and works are extensively discussed in Adam Hochschild, *King Leopold's Ghost* (New York: Mariner Books, 1999).

39. Eric Eustace Williams, *Capitalism and Slavery* (New York: Capricorn Books, 1966 [1944]).

40. Sanneh, *Abolitionists Abroad,* 246.

41. *The Antislavery Examiner* 6, 1838.

42. Sanneh, *Abolitionists Abroad,* 246.

43. Some of these journals include *In Leisure Times,* published by the Church Missionary Society; *The Nigerian Baptist,* published by the Baptist mission; *The Nigerian Methodist,* published by The Wesleyans; and the *Catholic Herald,* published by the Catholic mission.

44. Sanneh, *Abolitionists Abroad,* 9–11.

45. PRO CO 588/1. Slave Dealing Proclamation.

46. NAI, CSO C157/ 1905. Notes on Cases of Slave Dealing.

47. Miers and Roberts, eds., *The End of Slavery in Africa,* 12–13.

48. Hugh Clifford, *Address of His Excellency the Governor of Nigeria, Sir Hugh Clifford to the School Children of Lagos in Empire Day, 24 May 1920* (Lagos: Government Printer, 1920). Original emphasis.

49. *The Lagos Times,* June 14, 1982.

50. PRO, CO 583/ 143/8. Practice of Pawning of Children in Yoruba Provinces 1926.

51. *The Lagos Times,* May 12, 1900.

52. CMS. CA2/L2. Secretaries to Missionaries in Yorubaland, February 17, 1857.

53. *The Lagos Times,* May 12, 1900. Echoing similar views, the *Lagos Observer,* on June 18, 1901, deplored the "tendency of many persons enjoying the rights and liberties of British subjects to possess slaves."

54. E. J. Alagoa and Ateri M. Okorobia, "Pawnship in Nembe, Niger Delta" in *Pawnship in Africa: Debt Bondage in Historical Perspective,* Toyin Falola and Paul E. Lovejoy, eds. (Boulder: Westview Press, 1994), 78.

55. Johnson, *History of the Yorubas,* 126–30.

56. See Falola, "Pawnship in Colonial Southwestern Nigeria," and Judith Byfield, "Pawns and Politics: The Pawnship Debate in Western Nigeria," in *Pawnship in Africa,* Falola and Lovejoy, eds. This was also evident from my own archival research. See for instance, PRO CO 583/143/8, Practice of Pawning of Children in Yoruba Provinces, 1926.

57. Johnson, *History of the Yorubas,* 128.

58. Byfield, "Pawns and Politics," 194.

59. Toyin Falola, "Slavery and Pawnship in the Yoruba Economy of the Nineteenth Century," *Slavery and Abolition,* 15, 2 (1994): 240.

60. NAI. CSO 26/06827 Vol. 1.

61. Recent studies on pawnship in West Africa show that pawns were, in fact, denied most of their personal liberties and social rights. Because of the degradation associated with the loss of status, people often regarded pawnship as worse than slavery and strove to avoid it. See Uyilawa Usuanlele, "Pawnship in Edo Society: From

Benin Kingdom to Benin Province under Colonial Rule," in *Pawnship in Africa,* Falola and Lovejoy, eds., 107.

62. For a more incisive study of the House system in the Niger Delta, see K. O. Dike, *Trade and Politics in the Niger Delta* (Oxford: Clarendon Press, 1956).

63. Tekena N. Tamuno, *The Evolution of the Nigerian State: The Southern Phase, 1898–1914* (London: Longman, 1972), 26.

64. *Nigerian Times,* August 11, 1910.

65. PRO, CO/520/121. House Rule Ordinance.

66. Walter Ibekwe Ofonagoro, "An Aspect of British Colonial Policy in Southern Nigeria: The Problems of Forced Labour and Slavery, 1895–1928," in *Studies in Southern Nigerian History,* Boniface I. Obichere, ed. (London: Frank Cass, 1982), 238.

67. NAI, Cd. 4907 1909.

68. Tamuno, *The Evolution of the Nigerian State,* 329 and 331.

69. Falola, "Pawnship in Colonial Southwestern Nigeria," 254.

70. NAI, BD 5/3, 6. Miscellaneous complaints, Benin Province, 1920.

71. References to the rights of "Englishmen" in this context did not necessarily mean all British citizens. In this period, British women had considerably fewer rights and liberties than men. They had no voting rights until 1928 and only limited rights to property.

72. Mary Kingsley, traveler and amateur ethnographer in West Africa in the 1890s, was an early advocate in the potential of Africans as "a distinct race, unsuited to European civilization." Similar sentiments found a growing audience at the turn of the century, and in 1901 the British African Society was founded to further the ideas of "Kingsleyinsm." See John Flint, "Mary Kingsley: A Reassessment," *Journal of African History* 4 (1963): 99–104.

73. Sanneh, *Abolitionists Abroad,* 10.

74. NAI CSO 5/8/4, "Instructions dated 13 January 1888, Clause 31." Emphasis added.

Chapter Three:
Stronger than the Maxim Gun:
Law, Rights, and Justice

1. John Comaroff and Jean Comaroff, *Of Revelation and Revolution*, Volume 1: *The Dialectics of Modernity on a South African Frontier* (Chicago: University of Chicago Press, 1997), 404.

2. NAI, CSO 5/8/4. Instructions dated 13 January 1888. Emphasis added.

3. *Daily Service,* February 2, 1943, 2.

4. The Maxim machine gun symbolized European military advantage that made colonial conquest possible in many parts of Africa and other parts of the colonized world. Many nineteenth-century European imperialists recognized and acknowledged the importance of the Maxim gun to their campaign in Africa. As the nineteenth-century anti-imperialist writer and poet Hilaire Belloc put it in his 1898 poem "The Modern Traveller," "When all is done/we have got/the Maxim Gun/and they have not!"

5. As in colonial laws affecting marriage that placed monogamous marriage on a higher pedestal than other forms of marriage.

6. Kristin Mann and Richard Roberts, eds. *Law in Colonial Africa* (Portsmouth: Heinemann, 1991); Martin Chanock, *Law, Custom, and Social Order: The Colonial Experience in Malawi and Zambia* (New York: Cambridge University Press, 1985); Sally Falk Moore, *Social Facts and Fabrications: "Customary" Law on Kilimanjaro, 1880–1980* (New York: Cambridge University Press, 1986); Margaret Jean Hay and Marcia Wright, *African Women and the Law: Historical Perspectives* (Boston: Boston University, 1982).

7. Mann and Roberts, "Law in Colonial Africa," in *Law in Colonial Africa,* Mann and Roberts, eds., 3.

8. NAI, CSO 543/233. Supreme Court Ordinance No. 4 of 1876.

9. PRO, CO/ 583/173/10. Petition of H. Macaulay against expulsion of Eshugbaye Eleko and CO 583/ 150/8, Appeal to Privy Council by Eshugbaye Eleko.

10. O. Chukwura, *Privy Council Judgements in Appeals from West Africa 1841–1073* (Lagos, 1979) 673.

11. Chanock, "Laws and Contexts," *Law in Context* 7, 2 (1989): 72.

12. J. F. A. Ajayi, "Judicial Approach to Customary Law in Southern Nigeria," Unpublished PhD thesis (University of London: 1958), 558.

13. T. O. Elias, "The Judicial Development of Customary Law in Nigeria," in T. O. Elias et al., eds. *African Indigenous Laws* (Enugu: Dimension, 1975), 169.

14. *Nigeria Law Report* (11, 1932), 43–50.

15. Bride wealth is the converse of dowry. Common in many African cultures, it involves the bridegroom's family paying substantial wealth in cash or goods for the privilege of marrying a young woman.

16. This customary practice was common to many African societies. In the patriarchal societies of the Zambian Copperbelt, a father's rights over children were secured by payment of *lobola* (bride wealth) to the wife's family. See Jane Parpart, "Where Is Your Mother? Gender, Urban Marriage, and Colonial Discourse on the Zambian Copperbelt,

1924–1945," *International Journal of African Historical Studies* 27, 2 (1994): 243.

17. *Nigeria Law Report* (11, 1932), 43–50.

18. *Lagos Standard,* March 15, 1933.

19. NAI, Ijebu Prof. 1. Circular letter from Secretary, Southern Provinces, February 17, 1938.

20. *The Lagos Standard,* July 27, 1910.

21. NAI, CSO 1/19/47. Governor Egerton to Colonial Office, February 24, 1912.

22. Collective Punishment Ordinance (No. 67, 1912), February 8, 1912.

23. NAI, CSO 26/3 28360. Intelligence Report on Ogidi and Abacha Villages.

24. Caroline Brown, "Testing the Boundaries of Marginality: Twentieth-Century Slavery and Emancipation Struggles in Nkanu, Northern Igboland, 1920–29," *Journal of African History* 37 (1996): 74.

25. NAI, War. Prof. 3/10 18/28: Collective Punishment on Evureni.

26. PRO, CO 657/14. Collective Punishment Ordinance.

27. The Unsettled District Ordinance (No. 15) of 1912, June 4, 1912.

28. PRO, CO 583/3. Acts of Southern Nigeria 1908–1920.

29. NAI, CSO 1/19/47. Governor Egerton to Colonial Office, February 24, 1912.

30. Section 3 and 4 of the Peace Preservation Ordinance (No. 14) of 1912.

31. PRO, CO 657/14, The Deposed Chiefs Removal Ordinance (No. 4) of 1925.

32. For a full treatment of this case, see O. Adewoye, *The Judicial System in Southern Nigeria 1854–1954: Law and Justice in a Dependency* (London: Longman, 1974), 261–63 and Margery Perham, *Native Administration in Nigeria* (London & New York: Oxford University Press, 1962), 264–70.

33. *West African Pilot,* February 16, 1939.

34. James S. Coleman, *Nigeria: Background to Nationalism* (Berkeley: University of California Press, 1972 [1958]), 284.

35. *West Africa,* November 8, 1930, 1590.

36. The term "native foreigners" was used to refer to Africans or peoples of African descent who were not indigenes of Nigeria.

37. Tekena N. Tamuno, *The Evolution of the Nigerian State: The Southern Phase, 1898–1914* (London: Longman, 1972), 159.

38. *Lagos Weekly Record,* October 20, 1916.

39. Joan Wheare, *The Nigerian Legislative Council* (London: Faber & Faber, 1950), 151–57.

40. Philip Zachernuk, *Colonial Subjects: An African Intelligentsia and Atlantic Ideas* (Charlottesville & London: University Press of Virginia, 2000), 32–33.

41. *Observer,* February 28, April 24, and September 25, 1884, cited in Fred Omu, *Press and Politics in Nigeria, 1880–1937* (London: Longman, 1978), 120.

42. *Lagos Weekly Record,* September 12, 1891.

43. Omu, *Press and Politics in Nigeria,* 132–33.

44. The famous declaration of *The Times* of London in 1858 became an article of faith for advocates of press freedom both in the metropole and the colony: "Liberty of thought and speech is the air which an Englishman breathes from his birth; he could not understand living in another atmosphere. Nor when you once allow this liberty can you restrict the range of its subjects."

45. PRO, CO 583/183/3. Proposals for the Review of the Native Authority Ordinance, 1932.

46. PRO, CO 583/183/3. Memorandum from Governor Donald Cameron to District Administrative Officers.

47. Quoted in the *Lagos Weekly Record,* April 25, 1903.

48. *Lagos Weekly Record,* April 25, 1903.

49. PRO, CO 586/17/301/39. Memorandum from Lugard to Harcourt, August 12, 1914.

50. *Lagos Standard,* May 21, 1902.

51. *London Morning Leader,* June 6, 1902, 8.

52. *The Lagos Standard,* November 17, 1909, 5.

53. *The Lagos Standard,* September 29, 1909, 5.

54. *The Lagos Standard,* September 29, 1909, 5. Emphasis added.

55. NAI, CSO 7/ 1/14. Legislative Council Debates, June 8, 1903.

56. W.C.E. Daniels, *The Common Law in West Africa* (London: Butterworths, 1964); A. N. Allott, *Essays in African Law* (London: Butterworths, 1960); and B. O. Nwabueze, *The Machinery of Justice in Nigeria* (London: Butterworths, 1963). Robert L. Kidder has made similar observations in the case of colonial India. See Robert L. Kidder, "Western Law in India: External Law and Local Responses," in *Social System and Legal Process*, Harry M. Johnson, ed. (San Francisco: Jossey-Bass, 1978), 159–62.

57. Omoniyi Adewoye, "Legal Practice in Ibadan, 1904–1960," *Journal of the Historical Society of Nigeria* 11, 1 and 2 (1982): 52.

58. Adewoye, *The Judicial System in Southern Nigeria,* 4. Other writers have made similar arguments. For example, A. E. W. Park, *The Sources of Nigerian Law* (London: Sweet & Maxwell, 1963), 24–36; Nwabueze, *The Machinery of Justice in Nigeria,* 17–19; and A. N Allott, *New Essays in African Law* (London: Butterworths, 1970), 48–65.

59. *The Lagos Weekly Record,* April 21, 1906.

60. NAI, Com. Col. 1 21381/1. Native Authority Rules.

61. Colonial officials defined "native law and custom" as "the collective acquiescence of a community to a habit of thought derived from long established precedent." What the Native Court enforced hardly fitted this definition. There was often no "collective acquiescence" of the community to these laws or even an established tradition of precedence.

62. Martin Chanock, *Law, Custom and Social Order: The Colonial Experience in Malawi and Zambia* (Cambridge: Cambridge University Press, 1985), 145–216.

63. NAI, Com. Col. 1 21381/1. Complaints against Native Authority Police.

64. PRO, CO 583/ 183/18. Use of Corporal Punishment in Southern Provinces during 1931 and CO 583/178/2, Punishment Inflicted upon Natives in Nigeria 1932.

65. *Lagos Weekly Record,* February 2, 1907.

66. NAI, CSO 5/8/2.

67. Adewoye, *The Judicial System in Southern Nigeria,* 150.

68. PRO, CO 583/183/18. Annual Flogging Returns from Nigeria.

69. PRO, CO 583/178/2. Arguments by Mr. Horraton, MP, at the parliamentary questions and answers session with the Honourable Undersecretary of State for Colonies, Lord Passfield.

70. *West Africa,* November 15, 1930, 1590.

71. PRO, CO 583/178/2. Punishment Inflicted upon Natives in Nigeria.

72. PRO, CO 657/20. Annual Administrative Report 1927.

73. PRO, CO 258/183/14. Native Court Matters Vol. 2 (1932).

74. PRO, CO 583/183/14. An Ordinance to Make Better Provision for the Administration of Justice in the Protectorate.

75. PRO CO 583/185/8. Comments by A. C. Prior, Attorney General, Legislative Council Debates, 11th session, 46.

76. Comaroff, *Of Revelation and Revolution, Volume 2,* 367.

Chapter Four:
Confronting State Trusteeship:
Land Rights Discourses

1. John L. and Jean Comaroff, *Of Revelation and Revolution*, Volume 2: *The Dialectics of Modernity on a South African Frontier* (Chicago: University of Chicago Press, 1997), 375.

2. Martin Chanock, "Paradigms, Policies and Property: A Review of

Customary Law of Land Tenure," in *Law in Colonial Africa,* Kristin Mann and Richard Roberts, eds. (Portsmouth: Heinemann, 1991), 62–63.

3. *The Lagos Standard,* August 14, 1912.

4. Charles Kingsley Meek, *Land Law and Custom in the Colonies* (London: Frank Cass, 1963 [1946]), 5.

5. Meek, *Land Law and Custom in the Colonies,* 5.

6. Rudolph W. James, "The Changing Role of Land in Southern Nigeria," *Odu: Journal of African Studies* 1, 2 (1956); Olawole Elias, *Nigerian Land Law and Custom* (London: Routledge & Kegan Paul, 1962); Kristin Mann, "Women, Landed Property and the Accumulation of Wealth in Early Colonial Lagos," *Signs* 16, 4 (Summer 1991).

7. "Treaty of Cession between the British Government and King Docemo in 1861," cited in 1942 *NLR,* 2, 8–9.

8. Olawole Elias, *The Nigerian Legal System* (London: Routledge & Kegan Paul, 1963), 324.

9. The colonial courts upheld this position in a number of cases, *Amodu Tijani v. Secretary, Southern Provinces,* 1921, *AC,* 2, 399; *Chief Omagbemi v. Chief Dore Numa,* 1923, *NLR,* 5, 19; *Chief Etim and others v. Chief Eke and others,* 1941, *NLR* 16, 43.

10. This customary practice was upheld by the courts in the case of *Chief Oshodi v. Dakolo,* 1930, *AC,* 667.

11. Olawale Elias, *The Nigerian Legal System,* 336.

12. Chanock, "Paradigms, Policies and Property," 63.

13. Crawford Macpherson, ed., *Property: Mainstream and Critical Positions* (Oxford: Blackwell, 1978).

14. Elias, *Nigerian Legal System,* 325.

15. Elias, *Nigerian Legal System,* 17–19.

16. Using a very legalistic definition of "ownership" Rudolph James posits that ownership exists where there are present the privilege of use, the privilege of outright disposability, and the privilege of destruction. He argues that before European incursion in the nineteenth century, these principles of ownership in relation to land only applied to the family as a group, not to the individual. These arguments, however, have been widely challenged. See James, "The Changing Role of Land in Southern Nigeria," 16.

17. *The Lagos Standard,* February 16, 1927.

18. *Egbaland Echo,* June 18, 1934.

19. PRO, CO 588/1. Public Lands Acquisition Proclamation No. 5 of 1903.

20. NAI, Ijebu Prof. 4/ J.1018. Petition from the people of Oke Agbo over farmlands.

21. Tekena Tamuno, *The Evolution of the Nigerian State: The Southern Phase, 1898–1914* (London: Longman, 1972), 310.

22. Comaroff, *Of Revelation and Revolution, Volume 2,* 373.

23. Meek, *Land Law and Custom in the Colonies,* 5.

24. As late as 1966, a conference on African customary law specifically rejected the notion that the individual rights exercised by Africans were much like the rights exercised in Europe. See Max Gluckman, *Ideas and Procedures in African Customary Law* (London: Oxford University Press, 1969), 56–57.

25. Tamuno, *The Evolution of the Nigerian State,* 313.

26. PRO CSO. 1/22/9, CO to Lugard dated November 12, 1912.

27. *The Lagos Weekly Record,* March 23, 1912.

28. Philip Igbafe, *Benin under British Administration, 1897–1938: The Impact of Colonial Rule on an African Kingdom* (Atlantic Highlands, N.J.: Humanities Press, 1978), 191–92.

29. *Tijani v. Secretary of Southern Nigeria,* 1921 *AC,* 309. Emphasis added.

30. For a more detailed analysis of this case, see Adewoye, *The Judicial System in Southern Nigeria,* 259–61.

31. 1921 AC, 2, 399, 407.

32. Challenging the government's arguments that the ownership of rubber plantations in Benin was customarily communal, an argument used to justify state trusteeship over land, the *Nigerian Chronicle* wrote in a November 1, 1921 editorial that communal land ownership was, in fact, a creation of the British government.

33. Igbafe, *Benin under British Administration,* 29.

34. James, "The Changing Role of Land in Southern Nigeria," 8.

35. Samuel Ojo, *The Origins of the Yoruba, Their Tribes, Language and Native Laws and Customs* (Lagos: Ife Olu Printing Works, 1957), 12.

36. The courts held that although the members of the family had equal rights in family property, they did not have equal shares on the partition of the property, nor did they share equally in the proceeds of the sale. See *Danmole v. Dowodu,* 1958, *Federal Supreme Court Cases,* 3, 46 and *Taiwo v. Lawani,* 1961, *All Nigeria Law Report,* 703.

37. 1909 *NLR* 1, 87.

38. Chanock, "Paradigms, Policies and Property," 73.

39. *Lagos Weekly Record,* September 8, 1894.

40. Herbert Macaulay was perhaps the most prominent Nigerian politician during this period and is widely referred to as the "Father of Nigerian Nationalism." He was a central figure in the early nationalist movement.

41. E. D. Morel Papers, P F/9. Morel to H. Strachnan, January 6, 1913.

42. E. D. Morel Papers, P F/9. Morel to Johnson, December 13, 1912.

43. Chanock, "Paradigms, Policies and Property," 73.

44. NAI, Ben. Prof. 309. Petition by the Benin Community Association to District Officer.

45. Ibid.

46. E. A. Ayandele, *The Ijebu of Yorubaland, 1850–1950: Politics, Economy, and Society* (Ibadan: Heinemann Educational Books, 1992), 46.

47. Similar developments occurred in colonial Tanzania, where a land tenure law was introduced in 1923 to regulate land ownership. See Issa Shivji, "Contradictory Perspectives on Rights and Justice in the Context of Land Tenure Reform in Tanzania," in *Beyond Rights Talk and Culture Talk: Comparative Essays on the Politics of Rights and Culture,* Mahmood Mamdani, ed. (New York: St. Martin's Press, 2000), 40.

48. *The Lagos Weekly Record,* July 6, 1912.

49. *Nigerian Chronicle,* November 8, 1912, 2.

50. James S. Coleman, *Nigeria: Background to Nationalism* (Berkeley: University of California Press, 1958), 181.

51. Raymond Leslie Buell, *The Native Problem in Africa* (New York: F. Cass, 1928) 770–71.

52. *The Lagos Standard,* October 2, 1912.

53. *The Lagos Standard,* September 18, 1912.

54. NAI, Com. Col. 1. General Complaints.

55. NAI, Com. Col. 1/197/Vol. III. Petition by the descendants of the Oloto Chieftaincy of Ebute Metta to the Governor dated July 15, 1941.

56. NAI, Com. Col. 1/ 197/ Vol. 9.

57. NAI, Com. Col. 1/197/ Vol. III. Petition by the Farmers Protection Society to the Governor, 11 February 1941.

58. Meek, *Land Law and Custom in the Colonies,* 6–8

59. Chanock, "Paradigms, Policies and Property," 80

60. Martin Chanock, *Law, Custom and Social Order: The Colonial Experience in Malawi and Zambia* (Cambridge: Cambridge University Press, 1985), 80; Mann and Roberts, eds., *Law in Colonial Africa,* 26.

61. Article 1, Land Use Act (originally Land Use Decree), Cap 202, No. 6 of 1978.

62. Section 5a and 6a, Land Use Act.

63. Section 14, 15 and 28(1) of the Land Use Act. Article 14 of the Act provided that the occupier [has] exclusive rights to the land against all persons other than the Governor.

64. *Report on the Land Use Panel* (Lagos: Federal Ministry of Information, 1977), 11.

65. C. B. A. Coker, *Family Property among the Yorubas* (London: Sweet and Maxwell, 1966).

66. G. I. Udom Azogu, "Women and Children—A Disempowered Group under Customary Law," in *Towards a Restatement of Nigerian Customary Law* (Lagos: Federal Ministry of Justice, 1991), 132.

67. Justice Beckley in *Sogeimo Davis v. Aldophous Davis,* 1947, *NLR,* 9, 80.

68. Other studies have suggested that women in Nigeria wielded more economic and political power in the precolonial period than they did later under colonial rule. See Nina Emma Mba, *Nigerian Women Mobilized: Women's Political Activity in Southern Nigeria, 1900–1965* (Berkeley: University of California, 1982) and Ifi Amadiume, *Male Daughters, Female Husbands: Gender and Sex in an African Society* (London & Atlantic Highlands, N.J.: Zed Books, 1978).

69. H. L. Ward Price, *Land Tenure in the Yoruba Provinces* (Lagos: Government Printer, 1939), 43. This practice was also common in other parts of Africa.

70. Martin Chanock, *Law, Custom and Social Order,* 145–216.

71. NAI, Ben. Prof. 203/439.

72. The letter did not have the mandatory attestation and signature of the letter writer required by law under the *Illiterate Protection Ordinance,* which was introduced by the colonial government in 1910 to protect illiterates from exploitative professional letter writers and to regulate the bourgeoning profession of letter writing.

73. NAI, Ben. Prof. 203/439.

74. The report was in response to the League's effort to place the question of women's political and economic rights on its agenda in 1935. In that year the League passed a resolution to extend the resolution on the Equal Rights Treaty signed at Montevideo in 1933 to the colonial world. Colonizing powers were subsequently invited to send to the Secretary-General, for consideration by the Assembly, a report on the status of women in their respective colonies.

Chapter Five:
Negotiating Inclusion:
Social Rights Discourses

1. "Exchange marriages" refer to the practice in which parents or families arrange to have their sons and daughters married, often done without the consent of the persons being married. This is seen as a way of strengthening ties between the families. Widow inheritance is an alternate term for levirate marriage.

2. John Comaroff and Jean Comaroff, *Of Revelation and*

Revolution, Volume 1: *Christianity, Colonialism, and Consciousness in South Africa* (Chicago: University of Chicago Press, 1991), 384.

3. Kristin Mann, *Marrying Well: Marriage, Status, and Social Change among the Educated Elite in Colonial Lagos* (New York: Cambridge University Press, 1985), 44; Arthur Phillips, *Marriage Laws in Africa* (London: Oxford University Press, 1971), 176–85 and Kristin Mann and Richard Roberts, eds., *Law in Colonial Africa* (Portsmouth, & London: Heinemann, 1991), 15.

4. Kristin Mann, *Marrying Well,* 114.

5. NAI, Com. Col. 1 3/9. Petition by O. B. Ekereke.

6. *Lagos Observer,* October 12, 1890.

7. This customary practice recognized the right of the widow to either elect to remarry within her late husband's family or not. See E. I. Nwogugu, *Family Law in Nigeria* (Ibadan: Heinemann Educational Books, 1990), 399.

8. F. O Okediji and O. O. Okediji, "Introduction," in *The Sociology of the Yoruba*, N. A. Fadipe, ed. (Ibadan: University of Ibadan Press, 1970) and P. C. Lloyd, "The Yoruba of Nigeria," in *Peoples of Africa,* J. Gibbs, ed. (New York: Holt, Rinehart & Winston, 1965).

9. *The Daily Service,* June 17, 1945.

10. E. A. Ayandele, *The Missionary Impact in Modern Nigeria 1842–1914: A Political and Social Analysis* (London: Longman, 1966), 337.

11. NAI, CSO 26/2 11930 111. Owerri Province, Annual Report for 1925.

12. Renne Elisha, " 'If Men Are Talking, They Blame It on Women': A Nigerian Woman's Comments on Divorce and Child Custody," *Feminist Issues* 10, 1 (1990): 37.

13. N. A. Fadipe, *The Sociology of the Yoruba* (Ibadan: University of Ibadan Press, 1970), 92.

14. NAI, Ben. Prof. 204/49, Petition by Nwanopka of Uteh-Okpu against the Obi of Uteh-Okpu for seizing her for a wife and requesting that she may be set at liberty, dated 11 September 1935.

15. NAI, Ben. Prof. 204/49.

16. 1932 *NLR,* 11, 47.

17. Philip Igbafe, *Benin under British Administration, 1897–1938: The Impact of Colonial Rule on an African Kingdom* (Atlantic Highlands, N. J.: Humanities Press, 1978), 241.

18. Omoniyi Adewoye, *The Judicial System in Southern Nigeria 1854–1954: Law and Justice in a Dependency* (London: Longman, 1974), 206.

19. Mann, *Marrying Well,* 113.

20. Cited in Judith Byfield, "Pawns and Politics: The Pawnship

Debate in Western Nigeria," in *Pawnship in Africa: Debt Bondage in Historical Perspective,* Toyin Falola and Paul E. Lovejoy, eds. (Boulder: Westview Press, 1994), 203.

21. Byfield, "Pawns and Politics," 203.

22. Mann, *Marrying Well;* Cheryl Johnson, "Class and Gender: A Consideration of Yoruba Women During the Colonial Period," in *Women and Class in Africa,* Claire Robertson and Iris Berger, eds. (New York: Africana Publishing Company, 1986), 237–54; Nina Emme Mba, *Nigerian Women Mobilized: Women Political Activity in Southern Nigeria, 1900–1965* (Berkeley: University of California, 1982).

23. Judith Byfield, "Women, Marriage, Divorce and the Emerging Colonial State in Abeokuta (Nigeria) 1892–1904," *Canadian Journal of African Studies* 30, 1, (1996): 45.

24. A. E. Afigbo, *The Warrant Chiefs: Indirect Rule in South Eastern Nigeria, 1891–1929* (New York: Humanities Press, 1972), 265.

25. Byfield, "Women, Marriage, Divorce and the Emerging Colonial State," 46.

26. Isaac Delano, *The Soul of Nigeria* (London: T. Werner Laurie, 1937), 142.

27. Byfield, "Pawns and Politics." 302.

28. *The Lagos Standard,* September 9, 1908.

29. Fadipe, *The Sociology of the Yoruba,* 43; Samuel Johnson, *The History of the Yorubas: From Earliest Times to the Beginning of the British Protectorate* (London: Routledge and Kegan Paul, 1973 [1921]).

30. Lorand J. Matory, *Sex and the Empire that Is No More: Gender and the Politics of Metaphor in Oyo Yoruba Religion* (Minneapolis: University of Minnesota Press, 1994), 11.

31. *Daily Times,* May 27, 1937.

32. *Daily Times,* May 27, 1937.

33. Igbafe, *Benin under British Administration,* 241.

34. Ibid.

35. NAI, CSO 3/ II/ 36592. Commission of Inquiry into the Native Court System.

36. NAI, Oyo Prof. 1/70. Memorandum from the Senior Resident, Oyo Province to District Officers on "Divorce and Adultery Cases in Native Courts," March 25, 1929.

37. Parpart, "Sexuality and Power on the Zambian Copperbelt," 115.

38. NAI, Com. Col. 1 3/9. Petition by O. B. Okereke to the Commissioner for Colony, 7 July 1939.

39. NAI, Ben Prof. 203/704. *Agbonghae of Ekpoma v. Ekhator of Irrua, Oba's Judicial Council holding in Benin,* 15 August 1933.

40. NAI, Com. Col. 1 3/9. Petition by O. B. Okereke to the Commissioner for Colony, 7 July 1939.

41. NAI, Com. Col. 1 3/9.

42. NA1 Com. Col. 1 3/28. General Complaints.

43. Ibid.

44. Mahmood Mamdani, ed., *Beyond Rights Talk and Culture Talk: Comparative Essays on the Politics of Rights and Culture* (New York: St. Martin's Press, 2000), 3.

45. In the Igbo societies east of the Niger River, this category of people of slave descent were called "osu" or "ohu." Several studies have looked at effects of the antislavery movement of these communities. See Don Ohadike, "The Decline of Slavery among the Igbo People," in *The End of Slavery in Africa*, Suzanne Miers and Richard Roberts, eds. (Madison: University of Wisconsin Press, 1988), 437–61 and Caroline Brown, "Testing the Boundaries of Marginality: Twentieth-century Slavery and Emancipation Struggles in Nkanu, Northern Igboland, 1920–29," *Journal of African History* 37, 1 (1996): 51–80.

46. NAI, Ben. Prof. 203/252. Petition by Nicholas Nwaukpele and others on behalf of the Idumu-Asaba Family Union to the Senior Resident of Benin Province, 3 March 1937.

47. Ibid.

48. Ibid.

49. Ibid.

50. NAI, Ben. Prof. 203/252/24. Reply by the Acting Resident Commissioner, Benin Province to the Petition by Nicholas Nwaukpele and others, 20 October 1937.

51. Ibid.

52. NAI, Ben. Prof. 203/253/252/24. Reply by N. C. Denton (Acting Resident Commissioner, Benin Province), 20 October 1937.

53. Ibid.

54. Ohadike, "The Decline of Slavery among the Igbo People," 454.

55. NAI, Ben. Prof. 203/252, Petition by Nicholas Nwaukpele and others.

56. NAI, Ben. Prof. 203/252. Petition by Paul Nwani and others to the Resident Commissioner, Benin Province on behalf of the Idumu-Asaba Family Union, 4 June 1945.

57. NAI, Ben. Prof. 203/252. Reply by the Umueze Issele Family Union, Lagos to the Petition by the Idumuashaba Family Union, 18 April 1944.

58. In several confidential memos, both the District Officer at Ogwasi-Uku and the Resident expressed their deep concern over the sorry plight of the Idumuashaba people. NAI, Ben. Prof.

203/252/55. Confidential memo from the Acting Resident Commissioner, Benin Province to the District Officer, Asaba Division, Ogwasi-Uku.

59. NAI, Ben. Prof. 203/252/55. Reply by L. L. Cantle, Acting Resident of Benin Province, to the Petition by the by Paul Nwani and others on behalf of the Idumu-Asaba Family Union, 23 June 1945.

60. The Atlantic Charter was a joint statement issued by Franklin D. Roosevelt and Winston Churchill in 1941, stating their mutual goals for the post-WWII world. This included respect for the right of all peoples to choose the form of government under which they will live.

61. NAI, CE/W3. *Report of the Commission Appointed to Enquire into the Fears of the Minorities and Means of Allaying Them* (London & Lagos: Government Printer, 1958), 97.

62. *Constitution of the Federal Republic of Nigeria 1963* (Lagos: Government Printer, 1964). See Chapter III, "Fundamental Human Rights."

63. *Constitution of the Federal Republic of Nigeria 1963,* Section 23.

64. This section of the constitution states: "Every person shall be entitled to respect for his private and family life, his home and his correspondence." However, there is no definition of what is meant by "family life" in the constitution for the purpose of this section.

65. Although the UDHR provided generally that "no one shall be subjected to arbitrary interference with his privacy and family" (Article 12), it did not affirm the right to "family life." What it affirmed was protection of the law from interference in the privacy of the family rather than an enforceable entitlement to family membership. D.I.O. Ewezukwa, "Nigeria: Constitutional Developments," in *Constitutions of the Countries of the World*, Albert P. Blaustein and Gisbert H. Flanz, eds. (Dobbs Ferry, N.Y.: Oceana Publications, 1986) 176.

66. *West African Pilot,* November 24, 1942, 2.

67. *Ondo Provincial Pioneer,* June 16, 1956, 2.

68. Lakshman Marasinghe, "Traditional Conceptions of Human Rights in Africa," in *Human Rights and Development in Africa,* Claude Welch Jr. and Ronald I. Meltzer, eds. (Albany: State University of New York Press, 1984), 34.

69. S. N. Chinwuba Obi, *Modern Family Law in Southern Nigeria* (London: Sweet & Maxwell, 1966), 38.

70. 1961 *All Nigerian Law Reports* 1, 400.

71. Marasinghe, "Traditional Conception of Human Rights in Africa," 35.

Chapter Six:
Citizens of the World's Republic:
Political and Civil Rights Discourses

1. "I am a citizen of the world; I am a citizen of the world."

2. *Lagos Weekly Record,* October 6, 1894.

3. *Report on the Amalgamation of Southern and Northern Nigeria, and Administration, 1912–1919* (London: H.M.S.O., 1920).

4. Quoted in Joan Wheare, *The Nigerian Legislative Council* (London: Faber & Faber, 1950), 31–32.

5. *Lagos Standard,* May 6, 1916.

6. *Lagos Weekly Record,* February 1, 1919.

7. Margery Perham, *Lugard: The Years of Authority 1898–1945* (London: Collins, 1960), 585–86.

8. Bandele Omoniyi, *In Defence of the Ethiopian Movement* (London: St. James, 1908), 30.

9. Hugh Clifford, *The German Colonies: A Plea for Native Races* (London: n.p., 1918), 64.

10. Fred Omu, *Press and Politics in Nigeria, 1880–1937* (London: Longman, 1978), 212.

11. *Lagos Standard,* August 14, 1916.

12. *Lagos Standard,* October 8, 1914.

13. *Lagos Pioneer,* April 30, 1915, cited in Akinjide Osuntokun, *Nigeria in the First World War* (Atlantic Highlands, N.J.: Humanities Press, 1979), 70.

14. *Lagos Weekly Record,* October 10, 1914.

15. *Times of Nigeria,* August 6, 1918.

16. *Lagos Standard,* August 1, 1917.

17. James S. Coleman, *Nigeria: Background to Nationalism* (Berkeley: University of California Press, 1958), 188.

18. *Lagos Standard,* August 7, 1918.

19. *Lagos Weekly Record,* October 7, 1916.

20. Philip S. Zachernuk, *Colonial Subjects: An African Intelligentsia and Atlantic Ideas* (Charlottesville & London: University Press of Virginia, 2000), 64.

21. Du Bois, "The Conservation of Races" (1897), in *The Seventh Son: The Thoughts and Writings of W. E. B. Du Bois,* Julius Lester, ed. (New York: Random House, 1971), 181.

22. *Lagos Weekly Record,* February 26, 1910.

23. *Lagos Weekly Record,* February 19, 1921.

24. W. E. B. Du Bois, *The World and Africa: An Inquiry into the Part which Africa Has Played in World History* (New York: International Publishers, 1965), 11–12.

25. The most prominent of the writings by Nnamdi Azikiwe include: *My Odyssey: An Autobiography* (London: Hurst, 1970); *Political Blueprint of Nigeria* (Lagos, African Book Company, 1945), *Zik: A Selection from the Speeches of Nnamdi Azikiwe* (London: Cambridge University Press, 1961).

26. *West African Pilot,* March 26, 1940, 2 (editorial titled "Jim Crow Hospitals").

27. *The Daily Service,* March 29, 1940, 2 (editorial titled "Race Superiority").

28. Nigerian Youth Movement, *NYM Charter, Constitution and Rules* (Lagos: Crown Press: 1938), 1.

29. Nigerian Youth Movement, *NYM Charter,* 2.

30. Cited in G. O. Olusanya, *The Second World War and Politics in Nigeria 1939–1953* (Lagos: University of Lagos and Evans Brothers Limited, 1973), 49.

31. *West African Pilot,* September 4, 1939.

32. *West African Pilot,* October 8, 1942, 2.

33. *West African Pilot,* January 19, 1940, 2.

34. *The Daily Service,* November 16, 1940.

35. *The Daily Service,* September 30, 1942.

36. Clause 3 of the Atlantic Charter.

37. For a general treatment of the Atlantic Charter, see Douglas Brinkley and David R. Facey-Crowther, eds., *The Atlantic Charter* (New York: St. Martin's Press, 1994).

38. Olusanya, *The Second World War and Politics in Nigeria,* 57.

39. *West African Pilot,* March 6, 1943, 2.

40. *West African Pilot,* November 5, 1941, 2.

41. *The Times,* November 11, 1942, 7.

42. *West Africa Review,* February (1946): 167–68.

43. Olusanya, *The Second World War and Politics in Nigeria,* 57.

44. *Daily Service,* March 3, 1945, 2.

45. *West African Pilot,* December 22, 1944, 2.

46. *New York Times,* October 27, 1942.

47. An "Atlantic Charter Committee" working under the auspices of the Phelps-Stokes Fund in New York issued a statement recommending that the eight points of the Atlantic Charter be applied to Africa "in keeping with the broad humanitarian and democratic principles enunciated in it." *West African Pilot,* March 6, 1943, 2.

48. *Daily Service,* September 25, 1944, 2.

49. *West African Pilot,* September 26, 1944, 2.

50. *Times* (London), November 21, 1942. The *Times* ran a series of articles on the Atlantic Charter and the future of the colonies in

November and December 1942. Also see *Manchester Chronicle,* August 18, 1941, and *West African Pilot,* November 13, 1941, 3.

51. The strong anti-imperialism of the Labour Party is common knowledge. In its early history, the slogan was doctrinaire "socialization and self-determination." The Labour Party's position on decolonization is well reflected in C. R. Atlee, *Labour Peace Aims* (London, n.p., 1934).

52. Nnamdi Azikiwe, *Political Blueprint of Nigeria* (Lagos: African Book Company, 1945), 72.

53. Azikiwe, *Political Blueprint for Nigeria*, 44–45.

54. Nnamdi Azikiwe also recommended drawing from the Magna Carta, Petition of Rights, and the Habeas Corpus Amendment Act of the United States. See Azikiwe, *Political Blueprint of Nigeria,* 40.

55. National Council of Nigeria and Cameroons (NCNC). *Freedom Charter* (Lagos: Sankey Press, 1948), 2.

56. Eyo Ita, *The Freedom Charter and Richard's Constitution in the Light of the Universal Declaration of Human Rights signed by the United Nations Assembly* (Calabar: WAPI Press, 1949), 14.

57. United Nations General Assembly Official Records, 3rd Session, Part 1, (1948), 934.

58. Ibid., 962.

59. However, at the World Conference on Human Rights held in Vienna in June 1993, 171 countries, including many African countries, reiterated the universality, indivisibility, and interdependence of human rights and reaffirmed their commitment to the UDHR.

60. Anthony Enahoro, *Fugitive Offender: The Story of a Political Prisoner* (London: Cassell, 1963), 77.

61. Doc A/777, *United Nations Yearbook, 1948*, (New York: UNO), 465.

62. Gaius Ezejiofor, *Protection of Human Rights under the Law* (London: Butterworths, 1964), 3.

63. Doc A/777, *United Nations Yearbook, 1948,* 465.

64. Article 2 of the Universal Declaration of Human Rights.

65. Comments by the Netherlands delegate to the Third Session of the United Nations General Assembly, United Nations General Assembly Official Records, 3rd Session, Part 1, Plenary Session (New York: UNO, 1948), 873.

66. Ibid., 962.

67. *West African Pilot,* January 17, 1949, 7.

68. Eyo Ita, *Freedom Charter,* 1.

69. Azikiwe, *Zik: A Selection from the Speeches of Nnamdi Azikiwe,* 109.

70. J. F. A. Ajayi, *Milestones in Nigerian History* (London: Longman, 1980), 36.

71. Obafemi Awolowo, *Thoughts on Nigerian Constitution* (Ibadan: Oxford University Press, 1968), 48.

72. NA1 B 12. *Record of Constitutional Conference 1953* (Lagos: Government Printer, 1965).

73. NA1 B10. *Record of Proceedings of the Nigerian Constitutional Conference held in London in July and August 1953.*

74. *Report of the Commission Appointed to Enquire into the Fears of the Minorities and Means of Allaying Them* (London & Lagos: Government Printer, 1958), 70–97. [Hereinafter *Minorities Commission Report*]

75. *Minorities Commission Report,* 97.

76. ibid, 97.

77. G. O. Olusanya, "Constitutional Developments in Nigeria," 542–43.

78. Akinola T. Aguda, "The Judiciary and the System of Laws," in *Nigeria Since Independence: The First 25 Years, Vol. 4,* T. Tamuno and J. A. Atanda, eds. (Ibadan: Heinemann Educational Books, 1989), 117.

79. Obafemi Awolowo, *The People's Republic* (Ibadan: Oxford University Press, 1968), 275.

80. Section 28[2] [d], *Constitution of the Federal Republic of Nigeria* 1963 (Lagos: Government Printer, 1964).

81. B. O. Nwabueze, *The Presidential Constitution of Nigeria* (London: C. Hurst, 1982), 458.

82. *West African Pilot,* February 15, 1953, 2.

83. Quoted in La Ray Denzer, "Gender and Decolonization: A Study of Three Women in West African Public Life," in *Peoples and Empires in African History,* J. F. Ade Ajayi and J. D. Y. Peel, eds. (London: Longman, 1992), 233.

84. Johnson-Odim and Mba, Nina Emme, *For Women and the Nation: Funmilayo Ransome-Kuti of Nigeria* (Champaign: University of Illinois Press, 1997), 111.

85. *Minorities Commission Report,* 70–97.

86. *Director of Public Prosecution (DPP) v. Chike Obi, 1961 All Nigeria Law Report (ALNR),* 1, 186.

87. Section 23 (2), *Constitution of Nigeria 1960* (Lagos: Government Printer, 1961).

88. *DPP v. Chike Obi, 1961 ANLR,* 1961, 186.

89. For a more detailed study of this crisis, see B. J. Dudly, *Instability and Political Order: Politics and Crisis in Nigeria* (Ibadan: Ibadan University Press, 1973).

90. Bonny Ibhawoh, *Human Rights Organisations in Nigeria: An Assessment of the Nigerian Human Rights NGO Community* (Copenhagen: Danish Centre for Human Rights, 2001), 16.

91. Abiola Ojo, *Constitutional Law and Military Rulership in Nigeria* (Ibadan: Evans Brothers Limited, 1987), 249.

Chapter Seven: The Paradox of Rights Talk

1. R. D. Pearce, "Governors, Nationalists, and Constitutions in Nigeria, 1935–51," *Journal of Imperial and Commonwealth History* 9, 3 (1981): 289.

2. John L. and Jean Comaroff, *Of Revelation and Revolution*, Volume 2: *The Dialectics of Modernity on a South African Frontier* (Chicago: University of Chicago Press, 1997), 396.

3. For example, Shula Marks, "History, the Nation and Empire: Sniping from the Periphery," *History Workshop Journal* 29 (1990): 115, and Ana Davin, "Imperialism and Womanhood," in *Tensions of Empire: Colonial Cultures in a Bourgeois World*, Frederick Cooper and Ann Stoler, eds. (Berkeley: University of California Press, 1997), 131–35.

Bibliography

Archival Sources

Colonial Office Records, Public Records Office, Kew.

E. D. Morel Papers, London School of Economics.

Herbert Macaulay Papers, University of Ibadan.

High Court Archives, Lagos.

Melville J. Hertsgovits Papers, Northwestern University Library.

Nigerian National Archives, Ibadan.

Newspapers and Periodicals

The Comet

Daily Service

Daily Times

Egbaland Echo

Ijebu Weekly Echo

Ijebu Weekly News

Lagos Observer

Lagos Standard

Lagos Weekly Record

New York Times

Nigerian Chronicle

Nigerian Echo

Nigerian Times

Ondo Provincial Pioneer

The Times

West Africa

West African Pilot

West African Times

Articles, Books, and Pamphlets

Adewoye, Omoniyi. "Legal Practice in Ibadan, 1904–1960." *Journal of the Historical Society of Nigeria* 11. 1, 2 (1982): 48–68.

————. *The Judicial System in Southern Nigeria 1854–1954: Law and Justice in a Dependency*. London: Longman, 1974.

Afigbo, A. E. *The Warrant Chiefs: Indirect Rule in South Eastern Nigeria, 1891–1929*. New York: Humanities Press, 1972.

Agiri, Babatunde. "Slavery in Yoruba Society in the 19th Century." In *The Ideology of Slavery in Africa*, Paul Lovejoy, ed. Sage: Beverly Hills, 1981.

Aguda, Akinola. "The Judiciary and the System of Laws." In *Nigeria Since Independence: The First 25 Years, Vol. 4*, T. Tamuno and J. A. Atanda, eds.

Aguda, T. Akinola. *The Judiciary in the Government of Nigeria*. Ibadan: New Horn Press, 1983.

Ajayi, Jacob Ade. *Christian Missions in Nigeria 1841–1891*. London: Longman, 1965.

————. *Milestones in Nigerian History*. London: Longman, 1980.

Akinyele, R. T. "States Creation in Nigeria: The Willink Report in Retrospect." *African Studies Review* 39, 2 (1996): 71–94.

Allott, A. N. *New Essays in African Law*. London: Butterworths, 1970.

————. *Essays in African Law*. London: Butterworths, 1960.

————. *Judicial and Legal Systems in Africa*. London: Butterworths, 1970.

Amadiume, Ifi. *Male Daughters, Female Husbands: Gender and Sex in an African Society*. London: Zed Books, 1987.

An-Na'im, Abdullahi Ahmed and Francis M. Deng, eds. *Human Rights in Africa: Cross-Cultural Perspectives*. Washington, D.C.: The Brookings Institution, 1990.

An-Na'im, Abdullahi Ahmed, ed. *Human Rights in Cross-Cultural Perspectives. A Quest for Consensus*. Philadelphia: University of Pennsylvania Press, 1992.

Anyebe, A. P. *Customary Law: The War Without Arms*. Enugu: New Dimension, 1995.

Ashforth, Adam. *The Politics of Official Discourse in Twentieth-Century South Africa*. Oxford: Clarendon Press, 1990.

Awolowo, Obafemi. *Path to Nigeria's Freedom*. London: Faber and Faber, 1956.

————. *The People's Republic*. Ibadan: Oxford University Press, 1968.

————. *Thoughts on Nigerian Constitution*. Ibadan: Oxford University Press, 1968.

Ayandele, E. A. *'Holy' Johnson, Pioneer of African Nationalism, 1836–1917*. London: Frank Cass, 1970.

————. *The Educated Elite in the Nigerian Society*. Ibadan: Ibadan University Press, 1974.

————. *The Missionary Impact on Modern Nigeria, 1842–1914: A Political and Social Analysis*. London: Longman, 1966.

Azikiwe, Nnamdi. *My Odyssey: An Autobiography*. London: Hurst, 1970.

————. *Political Blueprint of Nigeria*. Lagos: African Book Company, 1945.

————. *Zik: A Selection from the Speeches of Nnamdi Azikiwe*. London: Cambridge University Press, 1961.

Bassey, Magnus and Shitu Gambari. *Missionary Rivalry and Educational Expansion in Nigeria, 1885–1945*. New York: E. Mellen Press, 1999.

Bauer, Joanne R. and Daniel A. Bell, eds. *The East Asian Challenge for Human Rights*. Cambridge, UK & New York: Cambridge University Press, 1999.

Binder, Gujora. "Cultural Relativism and Cultural Imperialism in Human Rights." *Buffalo Human Rights Law Review* 5 (1999): 211–21.

Biobaku, Saburi O. *The Egba and their Neighbours*, 1842–1872. Oxford: Clarendon Press, 1957.

Brinkley, Douglas and David R. Facey-Crowther, eds. *The Atlantic Charter*. New York: St. Martin's Press, 1994.

Brown, Carolyn A. "Testing the Boundaries of Marginality: Twentieth-century Slavery and Emancipation Struggles in Nkanu, Northern Igboland, 1920–29." *Journal of African History* 37, 1 (1996): 51–80.

Buell, Raymond Leslie. *The Native Problem in Africa*. New York: F. Cass, 1928.

Byfield, Judith. "Pawns and Politics: The Pawnship Debate in Western Nigeria." In *Pawnship in Africa: Debt Bondage in Historical Perspective,* Toyin Falola and Paul E. Lovejoy, eds.

———. "Women, Marriage, Divorce and the Emerging Colonial State in Abeokuta (Nigeria) 1892–1904." *Canadian Journal of African Studies* 30, 1 (1996): 32–51.

Callaway, Helen. *Gender, Culture and Empire: European Women in Colonial Nigeria*. Urbana-Champaign: University of Illinois Press, 1987.

Carrier, J. G., ed. *Occidentalism: Images of the West*. Oxford: Clarendon Press, 1995.

Chanock, Martin. "Culture and Human Rights: Orientalising, Occidentalising and Authenticity." In *Beyond Rights Talk and Culture Talk*, Mahmood Mamdani, ed.

———. "Law and Contexts." *Law in Contexts* 7, 2 (1989): 68–85.

———. *Law, Custom and Social Order: The Colonial Experience in Malawi and Zambia*. Cambridge: Cambridge University Press, 1985.

———. "Paradigms, Policies and Property: A Review of Customary Law of Land Tenure." In *Law in Colonial Africa*, Kristin Mann and Richard Roberts, eds.

Chukura, Olisa. *Privy Council Digest: A Digest of Decisions of Her Majesty's Privy Council in Appeals from West Africa: 1841 to 1964*. Ibadan: Gillford, 1969.

Clarke, Peter B. *West Africans at War 1914–18, 1939–45: Colonial Propaganda and its Cultural Aftermath*. London: Ethnographica, 1986.

Coker, C.B.A. *Family Property among the Yorubas*. London: Sweet and Maxwell, 1966.

Coleman, James S. *Nigeria: Background to Nationalism*. Berkeley: University of California Press, 1958.

Comaroff, John L. and Jean Comaroff. *Of Revelation and Revolution*, Volume 1: *Christianity, Colonialism, and Consciousness in South Africa*. Chicago: University of Chicago Press, 1991.

———. *Of Revelation and Revolution*, Volume 2: *The Dialectics of Modernity on a South African Frontier*. Chicago: University of Chicago Press, 1997.

Conklin, Alice. *A Mission to Civilize: The Republican Idea of Empire in France and West Africa 1895—1930*. Stanford: Stanford University Press, 1997.

———. "Colonialism and Human Rights, A Contradiction in Terms? The Case of France and West Africa, 1895–1914." In *The American Historical Review* 103, 2 (1998): 419–42.

Cooper, Frederick and Ann Stoler, eds. *Tensions of Empire: Colonial Cultures in a Bourgeois World*. Berkeley: University of California Press, 1997.

Crenshaw, Kimberle "Were the Critics Right about Rights? Reassessing the American Debate about Rights in the Post-Reform Era." In *Beyond Rights Talk and Culture Talk: Comparative Essays on the Politics of Rights and Culture*, Mahmood Mamdani, ed. New York: St Martin's Press, 2000

Crowder, Michael. *The Story of Nigeria*. London: Faber and Faber, 1962.

Daniels, W. C. E. *The Common Law in West Africa*. London: Butterworths, 1964.

Davin, Ana. "Imperialism and Womanhood." In *Tensions of Empire: Colonial Cultures in a Bourgeois World*, Frederick Cooper and Ann Stoler, eds.

Delano, Isaac. *The Soul of Nigeria*. London: T. Werner Laurie, 1937.

Denzer, La Ray. "Gender and Decolonization: A Study of Three Women in West African Public Life." In *Peoples and Empires in African History*, J. F Ade Ajayi and J. D. Y. Peel, eds. London: Longman, 1992.

Dike, K. O. *Trade and Politics in the Niger Delta*. Oxford: Clarendon Press 1956.

Donnelly, Jack. "Cultural Relativism and Universal Human Rights." *Human Rights Quarterly* 6, 4 (1984): 400–19.

———. "Human Rights and Human Dignity: An Analytic Critique of Non-Western Human Rights Conceptions." *American Political Science Review* 76, 2 (1982): 303–16.

———. *Universal Human Rights in Theory and Practice*. Ithaca: Cornell University Press, 1989.

Dudley, B. J. *Instability and Political Order: Politics and Crisis in Nigeria*. Ibadan: Ibadan University Press, 1973.

Dworkin, Ronald. *Taking Rights Seriously*. Cambridge, Mass.: Harvard University Press, 1978.

Egbe Omo Oduduwa, *Constitution of the Egbe Omo Oduduwa*. Ijebu Ode: n.p., 1948.

Ejidike, Martin Okey. "Human Rights in the Cultural Traditions and Social Practice of the Igbo of South Western Nigeria." *Journal of African Law* 43 (1999): 71–98.

Elias, Olawale. *The Nigerian Legal System*. London: Routledge, 1963.

———. *Nigerian Land Law and Custom*. London: Routledge & Kegan Paul, 1962.

El-Obaid Ahmed El-Obaid, Kwadwo Appiagyei-Atua, "Human Rights in Africa—A New Perspective in Linking the Past to the Present." *McGill Law Journal* 41 (1996): 819–54.

Enahoro, Anthony. *Fugitive Offender: The Story of a Political Prisoner*. London: Cassell, 1963.

Esedebe, Olisanwuche. *Pan-Africanism: The Idea and Movement 1776–1963*. Washington, D.C.: Howard University Press, 1982.

Ewezukwa, D. I. O. "Nigeria: Constitutional Developments." In *Constitutions of the Countries of the World*. Albert P. Blaustein and Gisbert H. Flanz, eds. Dobbs Ferry, N.Y.: Oceana Publications, 1986.

Eze, Osita. *Human Rights in Africa: Some Selected Problems*. Lagos: Macmillan 1984.

―――. "Is the Protection of Human Rights and Democracy Strange to African Traditions?" In *Human Rights and Democracy in Africa*, Tunji Abayomi, ed. Lagos: Human Rights Africa, 1993.

―――. Ezejiofor, Gaius. *Protection of Human Rights under the Law*. London: Butterworths, 1964.

Fadipe, N. A. (Francis Olu. Okediji and Oladejo O. Okediji, eds.) *The Sociology of the Yoruba*. Ibadan: University of Ibadan Press, 1970.

Falola, Toyin. "Pawnship in Colonial Southwestern Nigeria." In *Pawnship in Africa,* Falola and Lovejoy, eds.

―――. "Slavery and Pawnship in the Yoruba Economy of the Nineteenth Century." *Slavery and Abolition* 15, 2, (1994): 221–45.

―――. and Paul E. Lovejoy, eds. *Pawnship in Africa: Debt Bondage in Historical Perspective*. Boulder: Westview Press, 1994.

Flint, John. "Mary Kingsley: A Reassessment." *Journal of African History* 4 (1963): 99–104.

Foucault, Michel. *Discipline and Punish: The Birth of the Prison*. New York: Pantheon Books, 1977.

Geary, William N. M. *Nigeria Under British Rule 1927*. London: Frank Cass, 1965.

Gibbs, J., ed. *Peoples of Africa*. New York: Holt, Rinehart & Winston, 1965.

Gluckman, Max. *Ideas and Procedures in African Customary Law*. London: Oxford University Press, 1969.

Hay, Margaret Jean and Marcia Wright, eds. *African Women and the Law: Historical Perspectives*. Boston: Boston University, 1982.

Hinchman, Lewis P. "The Origins of Human Rights: A Hegelian Perspective." *Western Political Quarterly* 37 (1984): 7–31.

Howard, Rhoda. "Evaluating Human Rights in Africa: Some Problems of Implicit Comparisons." *Human Rights Quarterly* 6, 4 (1984): 160–79.

―――. "Group versus Individual Dignity in the African Debate on Human Rights." In *Human Rights in Africa: Cross-Cultural Perspectives*, Abdullahi Ahmed An-Naim and and Francis M. Deng, eds.

————. *Human Rights in Commonwealth Africa*. Totowa, N.J.: Rowman & Littlefield, 1986.

————. "Is There an African Concept of Human Rights?" In *Foreign Policy and Human Rights: Issues and Responses*, R. J. Vincent, ed. Cambridge: Cambridge University Press, 1986.

————. "The Full Belly Thesis: Should Economic Rights Take Priority over Civil and Political Rights? Evidence from Sub-Saharan Africa." *Human Rights Quarterly* 5, 4 (1983): 467–90.

Hufton, Olwen, ed. *Historical Change and Human Rights: The Oxford Amnesty Lectures 1994*. New York: Basic Books, 1995.

Hayden, Patrick. *The Philosophy of Human Rights*. St. Paul, Minn.: Paragon House, 2001.

Ibhawoh, Bonny. "Between Culture and Constitution: Evaluating the Cultural Legitimacy of Human Rights in the African State." *Human Rights Quarterly* 22, 2 (2000): 838–60.

————. "Human Rights and Cultural Relativism: Reconsidering the Africanist Discourse." *Netherlands Quarterly of Human Rights* 19, 1 (2001): 34–62.

————. "Stronger than the Maxim Gun: Law, Human Rights and British Colonial Hegemony in Nigeria." *Africa—Journal of the International African Institute* 72, 1 (2002): 55–83.

————. "The Promise of Constitutionalism and the Challenge of Militarism: Constraints and possibilities of the Human Rights Movement in Nigeria." *Democracy and Development* 3, 2 (2003): 16–36.

————. *Between Culture and Constitution: The Cultural Legitimacy of Human Rights in Nigeria*. Copenhagen: The Danish Centre for Human Rights, 1999.

————. *Human Rights Organisations in Nigeria: An Assessment of the Nigerian Human Rights NGO Community*. Copenhagen: The Danish Centre for Human Rights—Evaluation and Reviews of Partnership Programmes Series, 2001.

Igbafe, Philip. *Benin under British Administration, 1897–1938: The Impact of Colonial Rule on an African Kingdom*. Atlantic Highlands, N.J.: Humanities Press, 1978.

Ignatieff, Michael. *Human Rights as Politics and Idolatry*. Princeton, N.J.: Princeton University Press, 2001.

Ikime, Obaro, ed. *Groundwork of Nigerian History*. Ibadan: Heinemann Educational Books for Historical Society of Nigeria, 1980.

————. *Merchant Prince of the Niger Delta: The Rise and Fall of Nana Olomu, Last Governor of the Benin River*. London: Heinemann, 1977.

————. Isichei, Elizabeth. *A History of Christianity in Africa: From Antiquity to the Present*. Grand Rapids, Mich.: W. B. Eerdmans, 1995.

Ita, Eyo. *The Freedom Charter and Richard's Constitution in the Light of the Universal Declaration of Human Rights signed by the United Nations Assembly*. Calabar: WAPI Press, 1949.

James, Rudolph W. "The Changing Role of Land in Southern Nigeria." *Odu: Journal of African Studies* 1, 2 (1956): 16–37.

Johnson, Cheryl. "Class and Gender: A Consideration of Yoruba Women during the Colonial Period." In *Women and Class in Africa,* Claire Robertson and Iris Berger, eds. New York: Africana Publishing Company, 1986.

Johnson, Harry M., ed. *Social System and Legal Process*. San Francisco: Jossey-Bass, 1978.

Johnson, Samuel. *The History of the Yorubas: From the Earliest Times to the Beginning of the British Protectorate*, O. Johnson, ed. London: Routledge, 1971.

Karibi-Whyte, A. G. *The Relevance of the Judiciary in the Polity: A Historical Perspective*. Lagos: Nigerian Institute of Advanced Legal Studies (NIALS), 1987.

Killingray, David and Richard Rathbone, eds. *Africa and the Second World War*. New York: St. Martin's Press, 1986.

Li, Xiaorong. " 'Asian Values' and the Universality of Human Rights." In *The Philosophy of Human Rights*, Patrick Hayden, ed.

Lloyd, P. C. "The Yoruba of Nigeria." In *Peoples of Africa*, J. Gibbs, ed. New York: Holt, Rinehart & Winston 1965.

Lovejoy, Paul E. *Transformations in Slavery: A History of Slavery in Africa*. Cambridge: Cambridge University Press, 1983.

Macdonald, Margaret. "Natural Rights." In *Theories of Rights,* Jeremy Waldron, ed. London: Oxford University Press, 1984.

Mamdani, Mahmood. *Citizen and Subject: Contemporary Africa and the Legacy of Late Colonialism*. Princeton, N.J.: Princeton University Press, 1996.

Mamdani, Mahmood, ed. *Beyond Rights Talk and Culture Talk: Comparative Essays on the Politics of Rights and Culture*, New York: St. Martin's Press, 2000.

Mann, Kristin. *Marrying Well: Marriage, Status and Social Change among the Educated Elite in Colonial Lagos.* New York: Cambridge University Press, 1985.

Mann, Kristin and Richard Roberts, eds. *Law in Colonial Africa.* Portsmouth: Heinemann, 1991.

Marasinghe, Lakshman. "Traditional Conceptions of Human Rights in Africa." In *Human Rights and Development in Africa,* Claude Welch Jr. and Ronald I. Meltzer, eds.

Matory, Lorand J. *Sex and the Empire That Is No More: Gender and the Politics of Metaphor in Oyo Yoruba Religion.* Minneapolis: University of Minnesota Press, 1994.

Matthews, James K. "World War I and the Rise of African Nationalism: Nigerian Veterans as Catalysts of Change." *Journal of Modern African Studies* 20, 3 (1982): 493–502.

Mba, Nina Emme. *Nigerian Women Mobilized: Women's Political Activity in Southern Nigeria, 1900–1965.* Berkeley: University of California, 1982.

M'Baye, Keba. "Organisation de L'Unite Africaine." In *Les Dimensions International de Droits de L'Homme.* Paris: UNESCO, 1987.

Meek, Charles Kingsley. *Land Law and Custom in the Colonies.* London: Frank Cass, 1963.

Menon, Nivedita. "State, Community and the Debate on the Uniform Civil Code in India." In *Beyond Rights Talk and Culture Talk,* Mahmood Mamdani, ed.

Miers, Suzanne and Kopytoff, Igor. *Slavery in Africa: Historical and Anthropological Perspectives.* Madison: University of Wisconsin Press, 1977.

Miers, Suzanne and Richard Roberts, eds. *The End of Slavery in Africa.* Madison: University of Wisconsin Press, 1988.

Moore, Sally Falk. *Law as Process. An Anthropological Approach.* London: Routledge and Kegan Paul, 1978.

———. *Social Facts and Fabrications: "Customary" Law on Kilimanjaro, 1880–1980.* New York, Cambridge University Press, 1986.

Mutua, Makau. *Human Rights: A Political and Cultural Critique.* Philadelphia: University of Pennsylvania Press. 2002.

———. "The Banjul Charter and the African Cultural Fingerprint: An Evaluation of the Language of Rights and Duties." *Virginia Journal of International Law* 35, 2 (1995): 339–80.

———. "The Ideology of Human Rights." *Virginia Journal of International Law* 36 (1996): 114–30.

National Council of Nigeria and Cameroons (NCNC). *Freedom Charter*. Lagos; Sankey Press, 1948.

Nhlapo, Thandabanto. "The African Customary Law of Marriage and the Rights Conundrum." In *Beyond Rights Talk and Culture Talk*, Mahmood Mamdani, ed.

Nwabueze, B. O. *A Constitutional History of Nigeria*. Essex & New York: Longman, 1982.

———. *Judicialism in Commonwealth Africa: The Role of the Courts in Government*. London: Hurst, 1977.

———. *The Machinery of Justice in Nigeria*. London: Butterworths, 1963.

———. *The Presidential Constitution of Nigeria*. London: C. Hurst, 1982.

Nwogugu, E. I. *Family Law in Nigeria*. Ibadan: Heinemann Educational Books, 1990.

Obi, S. N. Chinwuba. *Modern Family Law in Southern Nigeria*. London: Sweet & Maxwell, 1966.

Obichere, Boniface I., ed. *Studies in Southern Nigerian History*. London: Frank Cass, 1982.

Ofonagoro, Walter Ibekwe. "An Aspect of British Colonial Policy in Southern Nigeria: The Problems of Forced Labour and Slavery, 1895–1928." In *Studies in Southern Nigerian History*, Boniface I. Obichere, ed.

Ohadike, Don. "The Decline of Slavery among the Igbo People." In *The End of Slavery in Africa*, Suzanne Miers and Richard Roberts, eds.

Ojo, Samuel. *The Origins of the Yoruba, Their Tribes, Language and Native Laws and Customs*. Lagos: Ife Olu Printing Works, 1957.

Okediji, F. O. and O. O. Okediji. "Introduction." In *The Sociology of the Yoruba*, N. A. Fadipe, ed.

Omoniyi, Bandele. *In Defence of the Ethiopian Movement*. London: St. James, 1908.

Omu, Fred. *Press and Politics in Nigeria, 1880–1937*. London: Longman, 1978.

Oseghae, Eghosa. "Human Rights and Ethnic Conflict Management: The Case of Nigeria." *Journal of Peace Research* 33, 2 (1996): 171–88.

———. Crippled Giant: Nigeria Since Independence. Indiana: Indiana University Press, 1988.

Osuntokun, Akinjide. *Nigeria in the First World War.* Atlantic Highlands, N.J.: Humanities Press, 1979.

Parpart, Jane and Kathleen A. Staudt, eds. *Women and the State in Africa*. Boulder, Colorado: Lynne Rienner Publishers, 1989.

———. "Sexuality and Power on the Zambian Copperbelt 1926–1964." In *Patriarchy and Class: African Women in the Home and the Workforce*, Jane Parpart and Sharon Stichter, eds. Boulder: Westview Press, 1988.

———. "Where is your Mother? Gender, Urban Marriage, and Colonial Discourse on the Zambian Copperbelt, 1924–1945." *International Journal of African Historical Studies* 27, 2 (1994): 241–71.

Patterson, Orlando. "Freedom, Slavery, and the Modern Construction of Rights." In *Historical Change and Human Rights,* Olwen Hufton, ed.

Pearce, R. D. "Governors, Nationalists, and Constitutions in Nigeria, 1935-51." *Journal of Imperial and Commonwealth History* 9, 3 (1981): 287–310.

Perham, Margery. *Lugard: The Years of Authority 1898–1945*. London: Collins, 1960 (585–86).

———. *Native Administration in Nigeria*. London, New York: Oxford University Press, 1962.

Renteln, A. D. "A Cross-Cultural Approach to Validating International Human Rights." In *Human Rights: Theory and Measurement*, David Cingranelli, ed. New York: St. Martin's Press 1988.

Robertson, Claire and Iris Berger. *Women and Class in Africa*. New York: Africana Publishing Company, 1986.

Said, Edward. *Orientalism*. London: Routledge & Kegan Paul, 1978.

Sanneh, Lamin O. *Abolitionists Abroad: American Blacks and the Making of Modern West Africa*. Cambridge, Mass.: Harvard University Press, 1999.

Shivji, Issa. "Contradictory Perspectives on Rights and Justice in the Context of Land Tenure Reform in Tanzania." In *Beyond Rights Talk and Culture Talk: Comparative Essays on the Politics of Rights and Culture,* Mahmood Mamdani, ed. New York: St. Martin's Press, 2000.

————. *The Concept of Human Rights in Africa.* London: Council for the Development of Economic and Social Research in Africa-Codesria, 1989.

Tamuno, Tekena N. *The Evolution of the Nigerian State: The Southern Phase, 1898–1914.* London: Longman, 1972.

————. and J. A. Atanda, eds. *Nigeria Since Independence: The First 25 Years*, Volume IV. Ibadan: Heinemann Educational Books, 1989.

Udom Azogu, G. I. "Women and Children: A Disempowered Group under Customary Law." In *Towards a Restatement of Nigerian Customary Law*. Lagos: Federal Ministry of Justice, 1991.

Usuanlele, Uyilawa. "Pawnship in Edo Society: From Benin Kingdom to Benin Province under Colonial Rule." In *Pawnship in Africa*, Falola and Lovejoy, eds.

Vincent, R. J., ed. *Foreign Policy and Human Rights: Issues and Responses*. Cambridge: Cambridge University Press, 1986.

Wai, Dunstan M. "Human Rights in Sub-Saharan Africa." In *Human Rights: Cultural and Ideological Perspectives*, A. Pollis and P. Schwab, eds. New York: Praeger, 1979.

Welch, Claude E. Jr. & Ronald I. Meltzer, eds. *Human Rights and Development in Africa*. Albany: State University of New York Press, 1984.

Williams, Eric Eustace. *Capitalism and Slavery*. New York: Capricorn Books, 1966.

Zachernuk, Philip S. *Colonial Subjects: An African Intelligentsia and Atlantic Ideas*. Charlottesville & London: University Press of Virginia, 2000.

Index

Made in the USA
Middletown, DE
01 October 2023

39892600R00136